ORDER AND DISORDER
INTERNATIONAL

Global Interdisciplinary Studies Series

Series Editor: Sai Felicia Krishna-Hensel
Interdisciplinary Global Studies Research Initiative,
Center for Business and Economic Development,
Auburn Montgomery, USA

The Global Interdisciplinary Studies Series reflects a recognition that globalization is leading to fundamental changes in the world order, creating new imperatives and requiring new ways of understanding the international system. It is increasingly clear that the next century will be characterized by issues that transcend national and cultural boundaries, shaped by competitive forces and features of economic globalization yet to be fully evaluated and understood. Comparative and comprehensive in concept, this series explores the relationship between transnational and regional issues through the lens of widely applicable interdisciplinary methodologies and analytic models. The series consists of innovative monographs and collections of essays representing the best of contemporary research, designed to transcend disciplinary boundaries in seeking to better understand a globalizing world.

Also in the series

The New Security Environment
The Impact on Russia, Central and Eastern Europe
Edited by Roger E. Kanet
ISBN 978-0-7546-4330-2

Sovereignty and the Global Community
The Quest for Order in the International System
Edited by Howard M. Hensel
ISBN 978-0-7546-4199-5

International Order in a Globalizing World
Edited by Yannis A. Stivachtis
ISBN 978-0-7546-4930-4

Legacies and Change in Polar Sciences
Edited by Jessica M. Shadian and Monica Tennberg
ISBN 978-0-7546-7399-6

Order and Disorder in the International System

Edited by
SAI FELICIA KRISHNA-HENSEL
Auburn Montgomery, USA

LONDON AND NEW YORK

First published 2010 by Ashgate Publishing

2 Park Square, Milton Park, Abingdon, Oxfordshire OX14 4RN
52 Vanderbilt Avenue, New York, NY 10017

Routledge is an imprint of the Taylor & Francis Group, an informa business

First issued in paperback 2020

British Library Cataloguing in Publication Data
Order and disorder in the international system. -- (Global
   interdisciplinary studies series)
   1. International relations--History--21st century.
   2. World politics--21st century.
   I. Series II. Krishna-Hensel, Sai Felicia.
   327'.09051-dc22

Library of Congress Cataloging-in-Publication Data
Krishna-Hensel, Sai Felicia.
   Order and disorder in the international system / by Sai Felicia Krishna-Hensel.
      p. cm. -- (Global interdisciplinary studies series)
   Includes index.
   ISBN 978-1-4094-0505-4 (alk. paper) -- ISBN 978-1-4094-0506-1 1. International rela-
tions. 2. International relations--History--21st century. I. Title.
   JZ1308.K75 2010
   327.1--dc22

                                                                    2010029877

ISBN 13: 978-1-4094-0505-4 (hbk)
ISBN 13: 978-0-367-60551-3 (pbk)

Contents

List of Figures and Tables

Figures

Tables

List of Contributors

Murat Çemrek, Associate Professor, Selcuk University, Turkey

Tian Jia-Dong, Associate Professor, Westfield State College, USA

Pawel Frankowski, Assistant Professor, Maria Curie-Sklodowska University, Poland

Francesco Giumelli, Senior Lecturer, Metropolitan University Prague, Czech Republic

Sai Felicia Krishna-Hensel, President and Program Chair CISS/ISA; Director, Interdisciplinary Global Studies Initiative, Auburn Montgomery, USA

Tanya Narozhna, Assistant Professor, University of Winnipeg, Canada

Erdem Özlük, Selcuk University, Turkey

Natalia Piskunova, Moscow State Institute of International Relations, Russia

Glen Segell, Director, London Security Policy Study, United Kingdom

Irma Slomczynska, Assistant Professor, Maria Curie-Sklodowska University, Poland

Foreword

The study of international relations is a challenging endeavour. Nevertheless, scholars attempt it by putting together divergent perspectives to achieve an objective world view to help policy planners to undertake fruitful initiatives at regional and global levels. An admirable attempt has been made in this book to study the complexities in international relations away from a traditional national perspective. Scholars from around the world have studied trends in the globalized world – both evolutionary and revolutionary – be they in the field of communications or financial transactions, educational standards or scientific developments, attempt by force or terror to set right perceived historical grievances. They have studied fault lines of religions, ethnicity and poverty cutting across national boundaries. Countries like India and China pose particular challenges to a political study, because they are developing fast while still manifesting traditional social and regional distortions among their huge populations.

The regional alliances and free trade areas have given rise to hopes for a post-national and post-Westphalia system of world governance, guided by issues of human rights, transparency, and good political conduct. At the same time, piracy in coastal areas or sea lanes, cross-border terrorism and internal insurgencies require determined and firm action by states, often blurring the boundaries of good conduct by states.

If this volume helps in a better understanding of the issues in today's world, the labour of so many scholars would be rewarded. We can then hope to leave a world free from rancour and grief for succeeding generations.

Shri Shashank
(Fmr) Foreign Secretary
Government of India

This volume is dedicated to my daughter Nayantara
who is of the new world

Introduction

The Westphalian system is characterized by the nation-state as the primary actor in the global arena. The contemporary period, however, has witnessed the increasing importance of non-state actors, and even individuals, as key players in international relations. In short, the range of actors and their ability to influence the distribution of power and, in the largest sense, the global order, has changed in response to historical imperatives that include, among other factors, ideologies, economic and trade structures, and technological developments. This volume examines the complex international system of the twenty-first century from a variety of perspectives. Incorporating both critical theoretical perspectives, as well as case studies, the chapters focus on broad trends, as well as micro-realities of a complex international system. The process of transformation and change of the international system has been an ongoing cumulative process. Many forces, including conflict, technological innovation, and communication have contributed to the creation of a trans-national world with political, economic, and social implications for all societies. Trans-nationalism functions both as an integrative factor and one which exposes the existing and the newly emerging divisions between societies and cultures and between nations and states. The chapters in this volume demonstrate that re-thinking fundamental assumptions, as well as theoretical and methodological premises is central to understanding the dynamics of interdependence.

In Chapter 1 Sai Felicia Krishna-Hensel examines the distinctive character of the interconnected world of the twenty-first century. The analysis explores the influence of technology on the international system in the modern age, leading up to the unique challenges of the contemporary world. Historically, advances in transportation, scientific breakthroughs, and their military applications have profoundly influenced the ability of states to project power and have had an impact on political structures and configurations. There appears to be little consensus on how these changes influence the debates on power, deterrence, diplomacy, and other instruments of international relations. Traditionally, scholars of the international system have focused on the possession of knowledge and weapons that provided a military advantage in the interpretation of power configurations. The twenty-first century world has a different technological emphasis, that of communications and its supportive satellite and internet infrastructure that forms the basis of the information revolution. The new technologies have succeeded in creating an alternative universe presenting a governance challenge to traditional institutions, laws, and concepts of territoriality. The global diffusion of technology and industrial production is propelling the forces for internationalizing of the state in the sense that it is internationalizing the policy process in areas such as arms control and internet governance.

In Chapter 2, Irma Slomczynska examines the role of force in shaping the world order, taking issue with the argument that the establishment of democratic rules would be tantamount to eliminating the use of force within the international system. The author argues that the idea that democracies do not wage war is a simplistic interpretation of the democratic policy framework and overly reliant on democratic peace theory. While generally democracies may be less inclined to wage wars against other democracies, when a democracy is confronted with an undemocratic system, a different rationale towards force exists. In such instances, the application of force by democratic states might sometimes be unavoidable. In analyzing the application of force by democratic states or systems in contemporary international relations four issues are important: the reasons for use of force, the capabilities and abilities which states have at their disposal, the methods of application of force, and the aims to be achieved through the application of force.

The increase in the number of actors in the post-Westphalian international order underlies Francesco Giumelli's analysis of the targeted sanctions of the European Union in his exploration of the actors and tools of the changing international system. The introduction of new actors contributes to disorder as they pose new threats and challenges. The response has in many cases served to underscore the emerging threats and led to the formulation of new methods of dealing with the problem. Taking the sanctioning policy of the European Union to elaborate on his thesis, Giumelli examines targeted sanctions in a number of case studies. Prefacing his analysis with the legal aspects and mechanisms of sanctioning policy, he notes the influence of the European Union's measures on the sanctioning policies of the United Nations. The primacy of targeted sanctions in the European Union policy reflects a preoccupation with achieving maximum results from restrictive measures. The empirical evidence cited in support of the thesis establishes the growing importance of the EU in crisis management contributing to its overall role in the global community.

Global leadership in the contemporary international order is the focus of Tian Jia-Dong's argument that international order depends on effective global leadership through 'connective authority'. This chapter reflects on the diplomatic history of the United States in the twentieth century and asserts that neither realism nor idealism has been helpful in terms of providing theoretical guidance in constructing the identity of global leadership. History shows that the pursuit of national interest and/or culture value hurt the United States in its role as a global leader when it attempted to construct and maintain a peaceful international order. It has been the power of social reach, the connective power dynamics which produced connective authority that provided the genuine power to the US for it to pursue the identity of global leadership.

Paweł Frankowski concentrates his thoughts on global ideas as opposed to regional reality. An evaluation of uncertainty and disorder, which are the key characteristics of the current state of international environment, leads him to the conclusion that it is difficult to make the case that a single international order exists. Indeed, there are many competing orders in the world and they represent different visions of the world order. The key emphasis is on cooperation in an increasingly multilateral world rather than on the pursuit to create the one world order, based on a common vision. The chapter examines whether growing interdependence and complexity are an elemental challenge to the established world order.

Natalia Piskunova analyses state failure and its influence on the configuration of security. This chapter explores both theoretical and practical implications of state failure and examines how domestic political instability in underdeveloped regions reflects the declining capacities of the state as an institution of legitimization. The preliminary hypothesis is that the contemporary security configuration presents challenges to governance in underdeveloped regions. The result is often poor governance that serves to generate sustained internal conflict within the states of the region. This provokes a spiral of internal violence which may pose an existential threat to the states in the region. This perspective underlies Piskunova's analysis of Somalia as a 'failed state' resulting from poor governance, and leads her to conclude that the time has come for a realistic assessment of patterns of governance in the underdeveloped world.

Glen Segell focuses on micro-realities of the Post-Westphalia order in his case study of NATO's first mission to Africa – Darfur. He contends that the complex international system of the twenty-first century has seen an increase in bilateral inter-regionalism and trans-regionalism. This is seen as an element of globalization where regional organizations act outside of their originally defined parameters. This chapter examines NATO's answer to a call for assistance from the Africa Union in their AMIS mission in the Darfur region of Sudan in April 2005, providing airlift and training until the end of the AMIS mission in December 2007. This was the first time that NATO undertook a mission on the African continent. NATO justified the mission on humanitarian grounds. No existing treaties were invoked nor was a member state's security under direct threat. This was unprecedented in NATO's history. The Darfur mission set an example for further missions to assist the Africa Union in Somalia and in general in such matters as training. This mission served to raise important questions on NATO's role as a global actor and provided an opportunity for understanding regional alliances, regionalism, and the development of trans-regionalism in a globalizing world.

Even as suicide terrorism has become a major defining feature of contemporary political violence, the links between suicide terrorism and the existing global order remain largely unexplored. Tanya Narozhna approaches the issue from a critical theoretical perspective, affirming that suicide terrorism is a way of expressing non-Western collective views on the nature and legitimacy of current power relations, distinct meanings of justice, and opposing values held by those in the shadow of the current world order. Critical theoretical perspective requires calling into question the existing institutional and social power relations and examine whether and how they are changing. Therefore, the rise of suicide terrorism may be seen an indicator of pressures within the existing world order to re-assess the institutional and power relational status quo.

In Chapter 9 Erdem Özlük and Murat Çemrek argue that the post-1990 era was essentially shaped around the popular narratives of postmodernism, globalization, 'end of history', 'post-Cold War discourse', and the critiques of their counterparts. All of these are focused on the question of sovereignty paving the path towards the transformation of these narratives into a new narrative by itself. Sovereignty was the result of the Westphalian order at the time that it was the epicenter of international politics. They argue that the end of the Cold War and the adoption of the Maastricht Treaty resulted in the death of sovereignty in its birthplace, Europe. This modern period may be described as the era of info-medievalism and/or cyber-feudalism, and as the return of a new Middle Ages following the consolidation of the EU which ended the long intermediary phase that followed the Peace of Westphalia. With the return of the new Middle Ages, territorial borders and citizenship as the political identity started to erode the meaning of the nation-state crystallized in sovereignty. Focusing the discussion on pre-Westphalian dynamics rather than sovereignty as a reference point in explaining international relations presents a new perspective on the international order. Although neither feudalism nor theocracy of the Middle Ages have survived, the manner in which sovereignty was structured, suggests that it can be utilized as an instrument of analysis to suggest the revival of the new Middle Ages of the post-1990s. This is a provocative argument which does provide an interesting perspective on the global order.

Each of the chapters represents an original approach towards understanding the structure, actors, and policy initiatives that distinguish the changing international system. The authors bring new energy to the discussions of order and disorder in a globalizing world, and an awareness that there is much that remains intriguing in the quest for understanding. This book would not have been possible without the patience and enthusiasm of the contributors. I would like to thank Kirstin Howgate and the Ashgate Publishing team for their invaluable support and encouragement of this project. We hope that this volume will contribute to the understanding of a complex global order.

Chapter 1

Technology, Change, and the International System

Sai Felicia Krishna-Hensel

Introduction

The extraordinary contemporary developments in science and engineering have led to a renewed interest in the discussion of the influence of technological change on the international system. While structural changes in the international system are influenced by many factors, the role of technology in effecting changes in power configurations among nations has been widely discussed by scholars seeking answers to the question of order and disorder. Most of the discourse has centerd on the contribution of industrial progress and military strength towards a ranking in the order of states. The evolution of power configurations, the role of international actors, and the development of new policy initiatives in response to changing technology has been at the center of our efforts to understand the modern world. This chapter proposes to focus on the contributions of scientific and industrial developments to the expansion and decline of states and to the resultant changes in the structure of the international system, as well as the impetus for developing alternate instruments of policy. The analysis will consider the impact of technology during three phases: an overview of the expanding world of the scientific age of the sixteenth and seventeenth centuries and the emergence of the great industrial powers; the balance of power and nuclear deterrence world of the twentieth century; and the borderless world of the twenty-first century information and communications revolution. The brief overview of developments during the age of expansion and the nuclear age sets the context for a more extensive discussion of the unique issues involved in comprehending the global order of the twenty-first century. The first period witnessed the emergence of the nation-state as the primary actor in the international system (Wolf 1962). Great power status was achieved through industrial strength and the resulting economic advantage. This translated into military applications of industrial technology ushering in the option of expansion and conflict. The transition from the expanding world to a borderless world was bridged by the introduction of atomic energy and nuclear weapons which, emphasized deterrence and diplomacy. A fragile state of equilibrium based on a balance of power marked the twentieth-century milieu. The extraordinary challenge posed by the information revolution and other communications technologies to the borderless international system of the twenty-first century is explored in the final section of this analysis. The issue is whether the new technologies are leading to fundamental alterations in the structure and functions of the international or more aptly global system. Of particular interest is the challenge posed to traditional power structures by the asymmetric threats and the newly emergent actors empowered by the new technologies. The analysis is placed within the context of earlier discussions regarding the factors responsible for the rise of the West, including the technologies contributing to the industrial revolution, as well as the differing emphasis placed on the importance of technological innovation as a determinant of change in the international system. The traditional views of territorial possessions as indices of power and territorial expansion as the principal course through which states acquired prosperity and security is re-examined in light of the contemporary technologies. The current focus has shifted to information possession and control of communication as indices of global power. An important perspective relates to the view that there is no controlling authority in the international system which is seen as operating in an environment of anarchy (absence of formal governmental authority). This perspective has been attributed to confusion between concepts of stability and control (Bull 1977).

Periods of order and disorder in the international system can be examined in the context of broad changes in structure, as well as in terms of particular interactions between states. Order has characterized international relations when there has been equilibrium in the system based on an acceptance of the status-quo and the position of the component states within the often hierarchical arrangement. 'An international system is in a state of equilibrium if the more powerful states in the system are satisfied with the existing territorial, political, and economic arrangements' (Gilpin 1994: 11). Underlying this perspective is the suggestion that equilibrium is sometimes reflective of resignation when the goal of asserting superiority is unattainable and a state will settle for the status-quo as the least objectionable choice (Wolfers 1962). This would indicate a measure of realism in international relations. Changes within and between states caused often by socio-religious factors or technological developments has led to disequilibrium and concurrent disorder. The assumption that the basic goal of international relations has fundamentally remained the same through the ages is a significant component of the discussion of change in the international system. Many scholars see the international system in terms of an ongoing struggle for wealth and power among its constituents operating in a state of anarchy.

The transformation of the international system has been characterized by differing rates of change. Gradual change has typified some periods of history, while dramatic and rapid change has characterized others. The industrial revolution, the nuclear revolution, and the contemporary information revolution have often been viewed as benchmarks in studying the changing nature of power and relations between states. The ongoing discussion concerning whether technological innovation leads to revolutionary change or evolutionary change suggests that radical change has been induced by conflict in some instances and by technological innovation at other points in time (Skolnikoff 1993). Scholars are divided on the emphasis that should be placed on technological progress as an independent variable in the study of relations between states and as a factor in analyzing power configurations in the international system. While technology increases the options available to policymakers in their pursuit of the goals of the state, it simultaneously leads to complications in the decision-making process. Quite clearly, the material environment has a significant influence on transformation, although the social conditions and prevalent ideologies cannot be ignored in the analysis of change.

If the discussion were to center around gradual change versus dramatic change, it is possible to find historical points of reference that explain dramatic change, while gradual change would take into consideration the evolution of social values and political interests. The dramatic sequences would include technological breakthroughs, political revolutions, and other conflict-based scenarios. In these instances, the period of adjustment is compressed resulting in the perception of rapid or dramatic change. Instability also plays a role in such perceptions. Major political changes in the international system can be identified and understood more easily than progressive, gradual change. Both gradual evolutionary change (process-based change) and dramatic change (event-based change) have their proponents. This is reflected in the dichotomy between a deterministic approach and a predictive interpretation of change. Though it is tempting to explain change in universal terms, it is obvious that the conditions of the past are in many ways substantively different from those that prevail in the modern world. The ongoing discussion of change as a gradual process or as an event based phenomenon, obscures the reality that systemic adjustments are often driven by actors responding to the variables driving change.

The Expanding World

Transportation Technology, the Industrial Revolution, and the Great Powers

The rise of the West and the expanding reach of nations that had discovered modern sea power have been attributed to developments in transportation technology during the sixteenth and seventeenth centuries. A number of scholars emphasized the significance of navigational advances during the formation of the modern European states system (Mahan 1897). The engineering and scientific breakthroughs of this time transformed the nature of sea power. The dawning of a scientific age founded on scientific methodology, research, and theory went hand in hand with technological developments that impacted on commerce and warfare. Inventions such as the 'capital ship', gunpowder, and the artillery fortress, were credited with having altered the nature of warfare during this period leading to a rearrangement in the power structure of the international system. With the development of steamships and ancillary technologies that opened up new trade routes, the locus of power had dramatically shifted from land to the high seas. The advances in transportation profoundly influenced the ability of states to project power by facilitating movement of materials, military forces, and armaments. Brodie recognized that control over new inventions offered tactical advantages. He was convinced of the critical role of engineering, especially undersea technology, in the shifting balance of maritime and national power and viewed the extension of the battlefield below the surface of the sea as an important shift with strategic implications. Maritime technology and naval aviation were seen as a transformative influence on the projection of power in the modern age. The proponents of sea power, enthralled by the impact and application of modern inventions in altering the status-quo were not alone in recognizing the significant role of scientific advances (Brodie 1969).

The land routes and highways of earlier periods were no longer seen as the primary conduits of commerce or as channels for the projection of military power. The development of sea power had introduced a new highway that benefited countries with a shoreline. This perceived disadvantage to hitherto land-based communications routes was not universally accepted. Mackinder discussed the historical dominance of land routes and their modern transformation, arguing that railroads and improvements in communication had removed any disadvantages of being landlocked (Mackinder 1962). The disagreements on the relative significance between land and sea power did not alter the fundamental agreement that technology and innovation served to stretch the boundaries of human behavior beyond the limitations of the environment.

The industrial revolution has been recognized as a transformative influence on the predominantly agrarian economies of the time through the development of railroads, chemical industries, telegraph, electricity, and the internal combustion engine. The great industrial nations were sharply differentiated from states that lagged in industrial progress by an increase in total productivity that was achieved through the mechanization of agriculture and manufacturing production. Possession and control over raw materials were considered necessary and important elements of national power and contributed to the perception of strength. Power and industrial advantage served to highlight the widening gap between small states and the great powers. These changes impacted on the national political process and figured prominently in the discussion of great power status in the international system.

The focus on the interconnections between industrial growth and military strength has prominently featured in interpretations of the foreign policy positions underlying the balance of power in the international system (Taylor 2004). The conduct of modern warfare required that the nations that prevailed would be those that had a lead in industrial production. National capabilities, including industrial production, were measured against a historical framework that suggested a close association between power in production, power in the state, and power in international relations (Cox 1981). It was a logical step forward to assert that industrial strength, based on the presence of a highly-skilled workforce with a superior ability to process an abundance of raw materials, was a contributor to the projection of military power. Military power was more mobile than it had ever been and could be projected at great distances. Relations between states, alliances, and other interactions were driven by perceptions of relative power and status based on technological superiority. Decreasing industrial growth was correlated to a decline in military strength and a loss of political power (Morgenthau 1967). Powers that achieved world dominance during the industrial revolution, such as Britain, experienced a corresponding decline in the modern period. The continual pursuit of scientific and technological progress as a pre-requisite of power has been influential (Brodie 1973). A related contention suggests that innovation is fundamental to maintaining superiority since it has a tendency towards diffusion, enabling nations to challenge the dominance of established powers in the international system (Gilpin 1994). Gilpin noted as an example that while the United States continues to be the dominant and most influential state in the system, its ability to manage the system as it did in the past is diminishing. It is increasingly unable to maintain the existing territorial divisions and arrangements, its traditional domains of influence, and enforce the rules that govern the global economy. 'The redistribution of economic and military power in the system to the disadvantage of the United States has meant that costs to the United States of governing the system have increased relative to the economic capacity of the United States to support the international status-quo' (Gilpin 1994: 232).

An alternative viewpoint presented by Lewis Mumford is critical of the utilitarian perspective underlying the analysis of technology in society. This perspective attributes the emphasis on technology to the utilitarian bias that dominated the scientific community in the nineteenth century and seeks to place technological development within the framework of other cultural and social influences. Discussing Leonardo da Vinci and his forays into the scientific future, Mumford observed, 'Leonardo himself committed to paper even more remarkable forebodings of the world than science and mechanization would eventually bring into existence' (Mumford 1967: 291). As we consider the impact of information technology on the study and conduct of international relations in the contemporary world, it is interesting to note Mumford's prescient thoughts.

Military Technology and Warfare

As we have noted above, the relationship between scientific invention and warfare has been extensively studied in an effort to understand the origins of power and status in the international system. Over the centuries, efficiency and ingenuity in the development of weapons led to accelerated change. The notion that the balance of power between feuding parties and states had been altered by engineering innovations in bridge design, fire-tipped siege engines, chemical warfare, and gunpowder was widely explored. New designs and superior of engines of war impacted the existing urban and fortification designs, rendering them obsolete and leading to new patterns of conflict. By the twentieth century, the innovations that influenced the outcomes of World Wars I and II included chemical warfare and radar technology. Modern warfare was distinguished by an unprecedented level of mechanization characterized by the invention of sophisticated weapons and 'inventions in mechanization and mobility' (Wright 1944). It was widely accepted that for the first time in human history wars had been decisively impacted by the presence of weapons that had been inconceivable a few years earlier. The weapons represented a synthesis of advanced research from science-wave mechanics, electromagnetic theory, physical chemistry, cybernetics (Breckner 1964).

While the military application of technology underlies much of the discussion of modern warfare, the acknowledgement that the economic benefits of the new technologies translated into an advantage in preparing for conflict is central to this perspective. It is, therefore, not entirely clear whether the economic and military advantages conferred by technological superiority can be analytically separated in discussing great power status in the international system. The international order was determined by states that had the advantage in materials, facilities, and knowledge for the production of advanced weaponry over those which were lacking. States with advanced technologies dominated the system using their advantage to influence the policies of weaker members and to create dependency relationships. The technological imperative figures prominently in explaining the presence of an arms dynamic that is independent of an arms race. States are impelled by scientific and technological advances to keep current and are encouraged in this by an institutionalized military-industrial complex (Buzan 1987).

The strength of industrial nations lay not only in possessing resources and production facilities, but also in the ability to maintain and develop a sustainable knowledge base. Hence, the training of scientists and engineers and the support of research became an important component of political power. Innovation served to broaden the options available to policy makers and at the same time inserted greater complexity in the decision making process. This will be more apparent when we examine the changes wrought by the nuclear revolution and the information revolution.

The Nuclear World and the Balance of Power

The nuclear age ushered in a broad consensus that it was essential to construct a new international order founded on the common interest of all states to preclude irreversible destruction. The social and political implications of atomic energy profoundly impacted the argument on the international order. There was an uneasy feeling that, in the absence of a common understanding, neither fear nor recognition that the use of modern weapons has the potential to destroy civilization would prove to be an inhibiting factor in modern conflict. The foreboding that peace was increasingly unattainable in such an environment fuelled the concern that a pre-emptive strike could be a tempting strategy in calculus of war. The tradition of citing historical experience to demonstrate that states had a predisposition for conflict is quite well established in the analysis of the international order (Hamilton

1941). This line of thought undermines the converse belief that scientific progress would lead to fundamental change in the behavior of states.

A leading outcome of the nuclear impasse was the bi-polar world composed of two distinct constellations of states (Fox 1949). A sort of equilibrium was to be expected in this configuration, although it was subject to periods of crisis and proxy conflict from time to time. The nuclear revolution led to a significant investment in managed conflict and revived the need to examine other instruments of power. The paradox of nuclear weapons was the conferral of national status and power, with the simultaneous reduction in the option of rational employment. The value of a nuclear arsenal was essentially as a deterrent that enabled states to continue to maintain their conventional capacities. Prior to the nuclear age deterrence between nations did not have the conceptual significance that it acquired in relation to the premise of unacceptable retaliation. Based on the idea that a nuclear exchange, or a conventional conflict that could escalate into a nuclear exchange, would be unthinkable, the possession of nuclear weapons was seen as a deterrent to conflict involving the new technologies. The progress from simple destructive potential to swiftness of delivery prompted new strategic thinking that took into account the number of nuclear warheads and missiles, their survivability, range, accuracy, guidance systems, command and control systems, and other technological developments. Nuclear deterrence and strategy continued to evolve with new breakthroughs as policy makers attempted to determine vulnerabilities in a nuclear shield which would invite a pre-emptive attack. A state of affairs expressed as a balance of power based on possession of nuclear weapons and simultaneous efforts to establish global collective security increasingly came to characterize international relations. A more realistic assessment of the limits of war was introduced into superpower relations (Wolfers 1962).

The controversy surrounding the possession of nuclear arms has underscored the fundamental disagreement on deterrence as a contributor to stability. Deterrence was dependent on maintaining a technological advantage by continually keeping up with scientific advances (Mahan 1897). MAD (Mutually Assured Destruction) is what keeps deterrence relevant as a strategic concept. The knowledge that both parties have the same destructive potential is essential to the balance of power that deterrence represents. If technological development enables one side to develop faster more accurately deliverable weapons, there is an incentive for one side to use the weapons to execute a 'limited strike'. The basis for an effective deterrent is open communication and open knowledge so that both parties acquire parity. Deterrence is also dependent on the rational actor theory, that use will be discouraged by an assessment of the damage to ones own people. Deterrence would have no place in the calculations of leaders who have a messianic and radical world view.

The air strikes on Hiroshima and Nagasaki had provided a sobering demonstration of the effects and implications of the use of nuclear weapons. Since victory was no longer seen as an option in a nuclear confrontation and the consequence of escalation could include the potential of engulfing and destroying neutral and uninvolved states, the nuclear powers had to contemplate conventional warfare with built-in safeguards to prevent escalation. This realization demonstrated the limits of technology and introduced a new set of concerns regarding weapons development and their use. The emphasis on controlling force overtook all other objectives and it provided the opportunity for a re-thinking of the proper use of military advantage. Reversing the traditional propensity to apply force to achieve superiority and military advantage, the nuclear age presented an alternative policy choice to use a multiplicity of instruments other than atomic weapons to achieve the same goals of great power status through ensuring equilibrium. Status was achieved not by action, but precisely through inaction, not by use, rather by non-use of stockpiles, by possession rather than discharge of weapons. The result was the initiation of new protocols, the revival of diplomacy, the concept of non-proliferation, and arms control agreements. The post-nuclear environment saw a fundamental alteration of policy imperatives. The realization that the control of nuclear proliferation was beyond the capacity of a single nation led to reliance on cooperation and policy initiatives that emanated from international organizations and institutions. Mandelbaum (1981: vii) opined that 'technology and politics have combined to create what has been called a nuclear weapons "regime": a system of international obligations (formal accords, tacit commitments, and informal understandings), and doctrines (when, where, why, how, and which nuclear weapons ought to be used) that together govern the role of nuclear weapons in war, peace, and diplomacy'. The nature of the new scientific advances was accompanied by the belief that 'advancing technology makes war more horrible and presumably increases the desire for peace' and 'each major advance in the technology of war has found its prophet ready to proclaim that war is no longer possible' (Waltz 1965: 235).

The nuclear revolution highlighted the necessity for radical change in political thinking since traditional warfare that balanced political goals with proportionality of destruction was challenged by the new technologies. The expansion of nuclear proliferation introduced a new urgency for diplomatic solutions to conflict and elevated negotiation to a central role in international relations. An important effect of nuclear weapons on politics was the exploration of disarmament as a solution to the impasse presented by nuclear warfare. Driven by the virtually unusable nature of this technology in war, the pursuit of cooperative disarmament required states to consider removing the sources of insecurity that could lead to conflict. The advocates of disarmament took a historical approach towards cultural, strategic, and institutional restraints and projected that a managed balance-of-power system was essential to the conduct of international relations in a post-nuclear world. The frameworks representing this approach tended to exclude the non-nuclear powers and often those states which have acquired weaponry outside the accepted protocols. The responsibility to formulate conditions for this objective was given to the UN disarmament commission, a body composed of all UN members. The commission met infrequently, but it did serve to articulate world opinion on the issue. As an international instrument, its function was limited since the most significant disarmament initiatives would have to come from the two main powers that possessed large stockpiles of weapons – the Soviet Union and the United States. The idea of unilateral disarmament was urged on by numerous peace movements and extensively discussed in various forums. The proponents of nuclear disarmament had no investment in deterrence as a strategic policy. Tension-reducing and confidence-building agreements, such as 'non-aggression' pacts, 'no first use' pledges and other measures, have been proposed and honoured up to this point. A number of arms control measures accompanied the attempt to reduce, control, and hopefully eliminate nuclear weapons. The SALT (Strategic Arms Limitation Talks), SALT I (1969–72) and SALT II (1979) – were undertaken in an effort to reach agreement on the quantity and quality of weapons stockpiles, and the increasingly sophisticated delivery systems. They provided useful precedents for the control and limitation of major weapons systems. Other efforts to limit the use of nuclear weapons included the Seabed Treaty (1971) which was designed to ban nuclear weapons from the seabed and the Outer Space Treaty (1967) which sought to prevent the militarization of outer space. Innumerable meetings, conferences, and draft treaties have characterized the conduct of international relations in the nuclear age. As scientific breakthroughs have led to greater sophistication in size, destructive potential, and delivery of nuclear warheads, there has been a greater incentive to maintain an open dialogue between the major nuclear powers.

Nuclear non-proliferation efforts have not been spectacularly successful in halting the spread of nuclear technology. Indeed, an operational underground network of technical assistance and political encouragement has enabled several nations to develop and acquire nuclear warheads. The principal signatories to the NPT (Non-proliferation Treaty) have predictably been most of the major nuclear powers, with a few notable exceptions primarily among the emergent nuclear states. The major powers do not, however, possess the ability to convince states to desist from acquiring the nuclear weapons. It is doubtful whether they will be able to prevent non-state actors from acquiring and using these weapons. The underlying problem is the calculus involved in using atomic weapons. Many non-state actors are not invested in survival as the ultimate goal of conflict. They are more likely to subscribe to the vision of mutual destruction in the pursuit of a higher, other-worldly reward.

The acquisition and possession of advanced weapons has emerged as a symbol of prestige and an indicator of a nation's place in the hierarchy of international power. This is particularly characteristic of the aspirations of newly emergent states and underscores their pursuit of power and status. The sought-after technologies include nuclear weapons, fighter planes, missiles, AWACS, stealth technology, and drones (unmanned aircraft), and other symbols of scientific progress. The emergent nuclear powers, unconstrained by the concept of non-proliferation, have added an element of uncertainty to the existing balance that has characterized relations between the two major nuclear powers. It is unclear whether the new entrants to the nuclear circle are inclined to subscribe to the code of conduct that has defined the behavior of the superpowers or whether their political goals allow for large scale devastation. The acquisition and use of nuclear arsenals by non-state actors and groups represents the uncontrollable and unknown danger posed by nuclear proliferation. The fundamental concern is fear that the newcomers do not subscribe to the accepted rules by which the traditional actors of the international system operate (Van Creveld 1989).

The development of nuclear technologies provided an opportunity for states to engage in a measure of cooperation on the peaceful use of atomic energy. The inherently unequal relationship between the donor nations and the recipient states established another measure of superpower status in the international system. This anticipated the knowledge-based dominance of states in an increasingly competitive world and went a long way towards suggesting the importance of the connection between technology and world politics.

The Borderless World

The Communications and Information Revolution

The scientific advances in chemical, biological, nuclear, and communications areas during the twentieth and twenty-first centuries have transformed the traditional dynamic of the international order. The emergence of a globalized, interconnected world, advanced by the new information technologies, has led scholars to expand their understanding of a complex, interdependent, and often borderless world. The changes in the political environment, the emergence of the individual and the small group, and the increased prominence of non-state actors within the international arena have focused renewed interest on the transformative effects of technology on international relations. Technological progress underlies both cooperation and conflict between states – a reality that is particularly relevant to understanding the interdependent world shaped by information technology.

The twenty-first century is increasingly being defined by communications technology and its satellite and network infrastructure. The emergent role of communications technology and its speed, availability, and wide distribution has long been seen as transformative of societies and statecraft by analysts of the international system. This perspective anticipated transnational challenges, suggesting that the real revolution in statecraft would be the evolution of non-military instruments and processes (Sprout 1962). The central role played by global information networks in conduct of international relations was extensively analyzed in Howard H. Frederick's 1993 book, *Global Communications and International Relations.*

The information revolution has led to a fundamental reassessment of many of the assumptions underlying the study of the international system. Contemporary technological development has altered the accepted ways of thinking about the nature of war, national boundaries, and the principal actors in the international system. The effect of communications technology and the information revolution is global in scope and significance, and has extensively changed the economic, social, and political landscape. The dynamics of the information revolution insert a new motive force in international relations, the economy, and trade, as well as in aspects of personal life. Governments are faced with unprecedented challenges emanating from emerging technologies that represent a large measure of uncertainty and risk. The technologies that are expected to have the most transformative impact on the nature of governance and decision making are computers and electronic communications, as well as chemical and biotechnological developments that enable individual non-state actors to brandish a level of power that was hitherto confined to the collective control of the state.

The political implications of communications technology center on the study of power in a transnational environment. The communications revolution has resulted in new economic networks, new threat assessments, and new institutional structures. Today, as a result of the information revolution, power has shifted in the direction of information possession and information control. Individuals have been empowered by access to information, while states and institutions exert power by controlling and blocking access to the networks. Exerting control over information is complicated by the structure of networks. The internet is a decentralized system of interconnected nodes that operate in a complex network.

The internet of today has far outstripped its original form established during its initial stage of development as a cooperative, military-funded, public–private partnership. Its underlying technologies have been widely dispersed through global diffusion and its global networks have resulted in the creation of a global community. As the conduit for rapid information flows, the global networks have no precedent in the history of technology. Information technology is being increasingly viewed as a basic resource of mankind, ranking with energy and wealth. The World Wide Web, which functions as a vast digital library, offers billion pages of free and easily accessible information to a wide range of users including terrorist organizations. Large databases containing immeasurable details of interest regarding potential targets are available globally to subversive elements. It is generally known that members of terrorist groups are encouraged to use all available open public sources to gather information undetected and with anonymity. It is easy to access detailed information about nuclear power plants, public buildings, airports, and ports, transportation networks, and even about measures to counter threats. The internet provides intelligence on critical economic nodes, proffering the opportunity to examine structural weaknesses in systems and to predict the cascading failure throughout related networks. Weapons, such as bombs, are assembled with information available openly and the internet is used as a communications channel for coordination and planning. Networking enables subversive groups to operate as decentralized, independent units and helps to dispense with the need for a central command and control configuration. Network-based communications have the advantage of reducing transmission time, concealing identity, and being relatively difficult to identify. The internet has led to the erosion of hierarchical structures in many organizations, but especially among transnational groups whose activities have a global reach.

The new technologies are seen as fundamentally altering the accepted boundaries of time and space, and present challenges for political theorists used to dealing in physicality (Wolin 1960). Many analysts observe that the new technology is enabling people to conquer time. Real time transmissions of events require instant responses which are not structured into the decision-making process that has traditionally characterized the international system. Financial transactions, for example, can occur almost instantaneously. The global economy is based on financial data transmissions that disregard national borders and that result in empowering hitherto remote economies placing them in the same playing field as the economic powerhouses. The network facilitates the flow of information, including disinformation, at a rate which makes it difficult to absorb, organize, and react to in a measured manner. The response is required to materialize at a speed which is not structured into the existing decision-making process.

Thus, communications networks have succeeded in shifting people's spatial orientations based on traditional economic, social, and political boundaries. This has resulted in a dual trend of the reconfiguration of accepted identities and of the simultaneous reinforcement of traditional identities. The portrayal of the new environment as one of distant proximities, in which demographic and social distances have been compressed by the dynamics of technology, is central to Rosenau's insightful analysis of the fundamental changes that differentiate the information age from previous periods. It goes a long way towards making the case for a new conceptual and terminological framework for international relations in the information age (Rosenau 2003).

There is a substantial consensus that these technologies have succeeded in creating an alternative universe presenting a governance challenge to traditional institutions, laws, and concepts of territoriality. The need for a new conceptual vocabulary to describe the environment in which innovative integrated technologies, communications networks, and information utilities operate has been recognized and addressed, to some extent. Cyberspace is the most commonly used term for describing the new realm whose functioning is as significant as an economic or political system. The term enables the visualization of the electronic databases and flows of information, the source and consumers of that information. The virtual world crosses disciplinary boundaries, presenting a challenge for analysts. Geographically, it crosses and blurs physical boundaries and, from a sociological perspective, the communities of cyberspace cross societal and cultural boundaries. Politically, the governance of the virtual world presents a unique challenge for national and international institutions. The power of networks is diffused beyond the sovereign states' capacity to exert complete control. The result has been that policing the internet has varied from self-regulation to government censorship.

Cyberspace can be thought of as a new (virtual) planet separated from and simultaneously existing within the known geographical world. It is defined by its lack of an identifiable spatial presence, as well as its seemingly borderless nature and its fluid and constantly changing (virtual) communities. Mapping cyberspace, identifying its communities, and comprehending its vulnerabilities is a step towards determining the level of governance that is needed. Complementing the private and public regulatory initiatives that have characterized the evolution of the internet is the evolution of the debate on governance. The dialogue has alternated between advocates of an open network that is largely self-regulated and supporters of state intervention in the interests of security. An overview of the current and nascent regulatory and governance challenges provides a preview of the dilemmas facing states and regulators. While it is analytically possible to distinguish between social and economic crimes, subversive political activities, and national security threats, the fundamental need for control and monitoring of internet exchanges is a common concern. This is where the debate between freedoms and protections come into play.

The global diffusion of technology and industrial production is propelling the forces for internationalizing of the state in the sense that it is internationalizing the policy process in such areas as arms control, internet governance, and global environmental policy. Skolnikoff suggests that technological change underlies decentralization of power and maintains that it would be difficult for absolute power to continue to be exercised in the new technology-driven political environment. He notes that 'there is today a large and expanding sector of national and international activities not under the direct control of governments, nor accountable to them, that impinges on the authority of governments and constrains to varying degrees their freedom of action or ability to order events. This is arguably the most significant aspect of evolution in international affairs that has accompanied technological change' (Skolnikoff 1993: 224–5). He is convinced that the new technological environment will place limits on national action. In *The International Imperatives of Technology* (1972), he articulates his position definitively, suggesting that the degree of international regulation and control over the internal affairs of nation-states would be in excess of anything that has ever existed. Interdependence impels cooperation in a global economy. Such analysis highlights the increasing realization that states no longer possess exclusive access to destructive technologies. With the proliferation of knowledge through the internet and the growing presence of non-state actors, biological, chemical, and nuclear technology is within the reach of a larger constituency in a global world. The discussion of disorder centers on creating disequilibrium in the international system through traditional war and conflict, as well as asymmetric war. Technology has given an advantage of sorts to the forces of asymmetric warfare and provided them with the means for communication and the knowledge for manufacturing weapons. In the contemporary world, the possibility of NBC (nuclear, biological, and chemical) being first used by non-state actors is particularly alarming.

The information revolution has created digital capital that is empowering groups and individuals in ways that often challenge the dominant power of the nation-state. Those nation-states with the greatest freedom of information and the technology for its transmission have political and economic influence. It is interesting to note that attempts to control access and censure free information on a large scale have been counterproductive. The technology that enables the free flow is resistant to restrictions. China has discovered that, notwithstanding its rising status as a world power, its attempts to maintain a totalitarian environment with respect to information is proving to be a liability in terms of international perceptions and with regard to economic investment and trade relations.

We have been conditioned to believe that financial capital contained in physical assets with monetary value is a most valuable resource. In the twenty-first century, the most valuable capital is progressively non-physical and weightless. Much of traditional finance and money is now manifest as digital capital. Financial transactions, bank accounts, shares, bonds, and similar financial instruments have been transformed into data exchanges independent of physical documents and ledgers. The gravity-bound capital of previous centuries – land and physical wealth – has acquired a virtual character. Digital capital is increasingly a major new domain of power and property based on new paradigms and scope. Notwithstanding its creative and ephemeral character, digital capital continues to require enhanced risk assessment and remains subject to concerns of privacy, regulation, and legal oversight. Management of digital capital is increasingly accomplished through cloud computing. Cloud architecture is reliant on cooperative systems. The increasing placement of financial, medical, legal, and logistic, information to the cloud makes the implications of disruption extremely severe. The collapse of financial systems, the disruption of manufacturing, and the breakdown of essential utilities are alarming scenarios to contemplate. Cybernetic systems consist of culturally informed interrelationships between human beings and proliferating technologies. These inter-relationships include the attempts to fuse technological segments with human and additional biological organisms, with human society, and cultural environments. Characterized by complexity and greater risk, this novel sphere of twenty-first century technology is crucial to the operation of a global world.

The traditional battlefields of land, sea and air are being superseded by cyberspace and its networks which are vulnerable to continual security intrusions. This acknowledgement that cyberspace is an arena that is crucial to US defence strategy is conveyed in the government's 2010 Quadrennial Defense Review: '… cyberspace – a global domain within the information environment that encompasses the independent networks of information technology infrastructures, including the Internet and telecommunications networks. Although it is a man-made domain, cyberspace is now as relevant a domain for DoD activities as the naturally occurring domains of land, sea, air, and space.' The review elaborates further, pointing out that since information networks are essential for intelligence, as well as, command and control, they are targets of attack and require constant security and vigilance. The interdependence between the military and commercial infrastructure is inherent in the configuration of the networks. Reflecting the increasing need to have a comprehensive approach towards security from cyber threats, the QDR recommends developing up-to-the-minute cyber skills, cooperative partnerships with states and agencies, and centralizing cyberspace operations through USCYBERCOM – a specific command set up for this purpose. In developing its own strategy to counter cyber threats, the US is also recognizing that cooperation with foreign agencies and governments is central for success (Quadrennial Defense Review 2010).

Cyber technologies have succeeded in altering the scope and meaning of invasion through cyber threats, which are a blend of cyber crime and cyber war and which are often undifferentiated in terms of the kind of destruction caused, as well as the required level of defence. The cyber threat is the idea that organizations or individuals may be spying on, tampering with, or preparing to inflict damage on electronic networks. Sometimes, there may be a 'blended threat', in which terrorists attack computer systems that operate water supplies, traffic signals, air-traffic control, power grids, financial markets, or healthcare systems. These intrusions have several goals; some are classified as simple cyber crimes involving identity theft and essentially representing a modern form of burglary and highway robbery. Cyber warfare is an attempt to infiltrate secure economic systems and infrastructure grids to paralyze the economy and effectively neutralize societies. These assaults are designed to destroy the electronic systems underlying financial transactions, including banking; disrupting transportation networks such as air traffic, inducing massive power failures such as blackouts and definitely aiming to disable defence and national security infrastructures. Defending against such threats has been a preoccupation for quite some time, but it is a realm where the threats are continually evolving and require a constant response. This engineering-based knowledge war is still developing. The source is not always unambiguously identifiable. The data-flooding attack against Estonia in 2006 emanated from millions of computers in different locations. These botnet or mercenary computers were used to obscure the real identity of the attacker, who remained shadowy, although the speculation focused on Russia. Google's recent revelation of widespread spying originating from China is the latest incident drawing attention to a problem that is projected to increase. China's young population of internet users increases the odds that some, if not many, of them will join the hacker culture. In most cases it is impossible to separate the amateur intrusion from government-planned attack.

The difficulty in formulating an adequate response against an unknown adversary is central to cyber defence. Virtual invasions are a cost-effective strategy to project power and dominance and dispense with the need to invest in military organization, hardware, and personnel. Cyber attacks may emanate from states, non-state actors, and/ or a combination of forces. Cyber attacks originating from a suspected nation-state present a real threat. The sophistication is reflected in extremely focused targeting of defence engineering data. The security of electronic information systems continues to be viewed with complacency in the absence of dramatic and attributable cyber invasion. Electronic-commerce systems are already in a constant war against online fraud, requiring high investment in risk management. The most desirable solution would be international efforts to secure data networks, under the assumption that as states become more integrated into the global structure of interrelationships, financial and otherwise, it will be essential to develop cooperative international protocols to secure the networks.

It is only a matter of time before cyber warfare becomes more frequent and may be launched by any number of other states and organizations to culminate in a devastating impact. As we have noted, preventing and launching cyber attacks has become a continual and ever more complex challenge for traditional militaries. Cooperation between private sector experts and military professionals has become central to the efforts to meet this challenge. While identifying the source of attack is intimidating, there has been a measure of success in tracing the origin of the attack. The information revolution faces a fundamental predicament since the networks are a potent force for building a global society across territorial boundaries. Balancing the benefits of this technology against its vulnerabilities is a central concern of governance.

Conclusion

In conclusion, advances in technology, and especially the information revolution, have led to renewed interest in discussion focusing on the sources of stability and order in the contemporary global environment and on the nature of the international system. The interpretation of power configurations in the international system has often relied on measurements of military technology and scientific knowledge. Military superiority, which is an outgrowth of technological progress, contributed to political status and economic power. An important and widely held view was that scientific breakthroughs in themselves were not as significant as their military applications in determining the changes in political structure. Further, scientific knowledge was defined by a combination of features, such as its 'cumulative' character, 'accelerative' tendency, its 'irreversibility', and its ability to 'diffuse' (Sprout 1962). Scientific knowledge, unlike invention, was a process that required the presence of a tradition of research, individual initiatives, and state sponsorship. Thus, the progress of scientific innovation was manifested in the establishment and security of nation-states, European expansion, European contraction, bipolarity in the international system, and the emergence of new configurations. Technology came to be seen as a consistently transformative influence on how we think and what we do.

Scientific advances and industrial progress continue to be integral to the discourse on power and status in international relations. It is equally evident that advanced military technology with its enormous potential for destruction creates an environment for exploring diplomatic and other alternatives to war. In a world that finds itself technologically limited to conventional conflict, peace becomes a critical objective. Finally, the expansion of nuclear, biological, and chemical weapons has introduced the prospect that nation-states may compete in the global arena with a new set of systemic actors for the role of principal players in international affairs. The diffusive potential of technology has demonstrated the ease with which individuals and non-state actors can have access to sophisticated weapons and introduces an element of uncertainty into the strategic calculus. Retaliation degrades as an option in an environment where the adversary cannot be identified and actors may have no determinate and recognizable location.

Many analysts see conflict and competition rendered obsolete by integrative economic forces. In the past, economists thought that only goods could be traded across borders, while most services could not be imported and therefore were not subject to the same pressures from international competition. Technology has undermined this assumption and the movement of services from the West to the developing world has shifted the power equation. The transformation of the geo-political environment is driven by change that operates in a virtual world that poses tremendous challenges for governance. These challenges exceed the capacity of any one state or group of states and require cooperative institutions, policies, and enforcement mechanisms. This has led some analysts to envisage a multi-governance structure based on multiple identities and loyalties held by the population (Drucker 1989). The debate on the new world order has coalesced primarily around two perspectives – one proclaiming the continued relevance of the nation-state and its institutions, and the other anticipating the eventual development of and strengthening of supra and transnational bodies which would supersede in some instances at least the authority of the individual state.

The argument for the continued relevance of the nation-state in setting policy rests on the observation that if technologies are the driving force behind the development of supra-national institutions, then the lack of access to these technologies by a large proportion of the global population continues to give the upper hand to national elites that control access to technology. This perspective reinforces the idea of the continuing supremacy of the state in the international order.

The proponents of a transformed world order draw our attention to the presence of another set of actors, individuals, NGOs, and terrorist groups, whose access to technology is not effectively controlled by the state and whose ability to communicate across borders can have far reaching consequences. It is the role of these elements that is central to the discussion surrounding the establishment of a global order reflecting multiple influences. It is possible to envision a world where possession of armed force and military superiority is being gradually replaced by smart power of information technology. It is apparent that every century, a wave of new technologies from mass-production, to modern chemicals, to aviation and atomic energy, emerges creating new economic opportunities and impacting industrial and military growth. Contemporary technologies led by the information and geospatial technologies, as well as biological genome discoveries that are the product of public funding and private enterprise, appear to be leading us into an ever more cooperative world.

Bibliography

Benjamin G. (ed.) (1982) 'The Communications Revolution in Politics'. *Proceedings of the Academy of Political Science*, 34 (4), 1–205.

Breckner, L.V. (1964) *The Scientific Age: The Impact of Science on Society.* New Haven, CT: Yale University Press.

Brodie, B. (1969) *Sea Power in the Machine Age.* New York: Greenwood.

Brodie, B. (1973) *From Crossbow to H-Bomb.* Bloomington, IN: Indiana University Press.

Bull, Hedley. (1977) *The Anarchical Society: A Study of Order in World Politics.* New York: Columbia University Press.

Buzan, B. (1987) *An Introduction to Strategic Studies: Military Technology and International Relations.* London: Macmillan.

Buzan, B. (1994) 'The Idea of International System: Theory Meets History'. *International Political Science Review* 15 (3), 231–55.

Cox, R.W. (1981) 'Social Forces, States and World Orders: Beyond International Relations Theory'. *Millennium: Journal of International Studies*, 10 (2), 126–55.

Drucker, P.F. (1989) *The New Realities: In Government and Politics, in Economics and Business, in Society and World View.* New York: Harper and Row.

Fox, William T.R. (1949) Atomic Energy and International Relations, in *Technology and International Relations*, edited by William Fielding Ogburn. Chicago: University of Chicago Press, 102–25.

Frederick, H.H. (1993) *Global Communication and International Relations.* Belmont, CA: Wadsworth.

Gilpin, R. (1994) *War and Change in World Politics.* Cambridge: Cambridge University Press.

Hamilton, A.J. (1941) *The Federalist.* New York: Modern Library.

Hoffman, S. (1978) *Primacy or World Order: American Foreign Policy since the Cold War.* New York: McGraw-Hill.

Krishna-Hensel, S.F. (2010) 'Technology and International Relations', in Denemark, R.A. (ed.) *The International Studies Encyclopedia.* vol. XI. Oxford: Wiley-Blackwell, 6947–59.

Mackinder, H. (1904) 'The Geographical Pivot of History'. *Geographical Journal*, 23 (April), 421–4.

Mackinder, H. (1962) *Democratic Ideals and Reality.* New York: Norton.

Mahan, A.T. (1897) *The Influence of Sea Power upon History, 1660–1783.* Boston: Little, Brown.

Mandelbaum, M. (1981) *The Nuclear Question: The United States and Nuclear Weapons 1946–1976.* Cambridge: Cambridge University Press.

Mandelbaum, M. (1983) *The Nuclear Revolution: International Politics Before and After Hiroshima.* Cambridge: Cambridge University Press.

McNeill, W.H. (1982) *The Pursuit of Power: Technology, Armed Force and Society Since AD 1000.* Chicago: University of Chicago Press.

Morgenthau, H.J. (1967) *Politics among Nations: The Struggle for Power and Peace*, 4th edn. New York: Knopf.

Mumford, L. (1967) *The Myth of the Machine*. New York: Harcourt, Brace and World.

Nef, J. (1968) *War and Human Progress*. New York: Norton.

Parker, G. (1996) *The Military Revolution: Military Innovation and the Rise of the West 1500–1800*. Cambridge: Cambridge University Press.

Peraton, M. (1984) *Diplomacy, War, and Technology since 1830*. Lawrence, KA: University Press of Kansas.

Rosenau, J.N. (2003) *Distant Proximities: Dynamics Beyond Globalization*. Princeton, NJ: Princeton University Press.

Skolnikoff, E.B. (1972) *The International Imperatives of Technology*. Berkeley, CA: Institute of International Studies, University of California.

Skolnikoff, E.B. (1993) *The Elusive Transformation: Science Technology, and the Evolution of International Politics*. Princeton, NJ: Princeton University Press.

Sprout, H. (1962) *Foundations of International Politics*. Princeton, NJ: Van Nostrand.

Taylor, M.Z. (2004) 'The Politics of Technological Change: International Relations vs Domestic Institutions'. *Millennium: Journal of International Studies*, 32 (3), 441–56.

Van Creveld, M. (1989) *Technology and War: From 2000 BC to the Present*. New York: Free Press.

Waltz, K.N. (1965) *Man, the State and War: A Theoretical Analysis*. New York: Columbia University Press.

Wendt, A. (1992) 'Anarchy is What States Make of It: The Social Construction of Power Politics'. *International Organization*, 46 (2), 391–425.

Wilhelm, D. (1990) *Global Communications and Political Power*. New Brunswick, NJ: Transaction.

Wilson, E.J. (1998) *Globalization, Information Technology, and Conflict in the Second and Third Worlds*. New York: Rockefeller Brothers.

Wolf, John B. (1962) *The Emergence of the Great Powers 1685–1715*. New York and Evanston: Harper and Row.

Wolfers, A. (1962) *Discord and Collaboration: Essays on International Politics*. Baltimore: The Johns Hopkins Press.

Wolin, S.F. (1960) *Politics and Vision: Continuity and Innovation in Western Political Thought*. Boston: Little, Brown.

Wright, Q. (1944) *A Study of War*, vol. 2. Chicago: University of Chicago Press.

Wright, Q. (1955) *The Study of International Relations*. New York: Appleton-Century-Crofts.

Chapter 2

Shaping the World Order by Force

Irma Slomczynska

The belief that 'democracies do not wage war' linked with 'democratic peace theory' has gained a lot of popularity after the Cold War (Russett 1996a, Russett 1996b, Owen 1996). However, some thought should be given to a far too simplistic statement that the establishment of democratic rules across the world would be tantamount to ceasing to use force in international relations. Analyzing this issue it should first be pointed out that generally 'democracies do not wage wars' with other democracies. Yet some prominent scholars (e.g., Layne 1996, Spiro 1996, Farber and Gowa 1996) underline that 'democratic peace theory' is irrelevant and should not be perceived as a scientific theory because any classification of wars between democracies depends mostly on the definition of democracy. If one decides to choose a broad definition describing democracy as a system of government in which political decision-making processes are based on open public debate and political decisions are implemented by the representatives of the nation elected in fair elections, then the number of wars between democracies is higher in comparison with the number of wars between democracies based on a narrow definition of democracy. Therefore, if the quality of democracy is taken into account, the number of wars between democracies tends to fall (White 2005). James Lee Ray is right in noticing that 'democracy is a continuous concept; states are democratic to lesser or greater degrees, and therefore it is impossible to sort states into two categories, democratic and non democratic' (Ray 1998: 32–3). Furthermore, he thinks that, proportionally, democratic states do not form a prominent group within existing states. Therefore, there is also a low probability of inter-state war between these democratic regimes, which at the same time proves the initial assumption that democracies do not wage wars. Maybe low probability is the only reason for that, apart from the fact that geographical distances between democracies sometimes made any war between them physically impossible (Ray 1998: 35).

Another problem is the definition of war. In the contemporary strategic environment, most armed conflicts are civil wars, not inter-state ones. Only a few inter-state wars have occurred between democratic states in post-WWII history, yet at the same time it does not necessarily mean that democracies have not used armed forces internationally. White (2005) notices that of 39 international wars which took place during the post-WWII period (until the year 2000), only six might have been labelled as wars between democracies. One can also come to the same conclusion using the Correlates of War data (Sarkees 2000). According to them, during the post-WWII period until the year 1997, there were 23 inter-state wars, yet it is nearly impossible to indicate how many of them were between democratic states. Moreover,

> to be classified as an inter-state war, at least two participants in sustained combat should qualify as members of the interstate system and there should be at least 1000 battle related fatalities among all of the system members involved. A state involved is regarded as a participant if it incurs a minimum of 100 fatalities *or* has 1000 armed personnel engaged in fighting. (Sarkees 2000)[1]

In that context one has to agree with Christian Reus-Smit who notices that '... there appears to be something unique and interesting about relations between democracies, but precisely what this is, and why it is, remains uncertain and unproven' (Reus-Smit 2005: 87). He has grave doubts about the meaning of democracy and strict criteria which allow us to draw the line between democracy and non-democracy, and to construct a 'pacific union' or 'coalition of democracies'. If we accept the fact that the quality of each particular democratic state differs, it will, therefore, be unjust to create special rights for a 'coalition of democracies' as far as use of armed force is concerned.

According to the global survey carried out by the Freedom House Organization at the beginning of 2008, among 193 states in the world, 47 per cent were free, and respected human rights and political freedoms and 31 per cent were partly free, having weak enforcement of the rule of law and basic human rights limitations. The authors of that survey also underlined that 'although democracy has scored impressive gains in recent times, we have also begun to experience a new drive to prevent the further spread of democracy and, where possible, roll back some of the achievements that have already been registered' (*The Worst of the Worst* 2008). Therefore, the analysis of the use of force internationally by democratic states should not be limited to the relations between democracies because it seems to be of marginal importance for contemporary world order. Instead, we should turn our attention to relations between democratic and undemocratic states to understand this phenomenon.

Because such terms as war, democracy and security are constantly under redefinition in the context of the contemporary strategic landscape, it is necessary to describe and put some order into the ways contemporary democracies use force in international relations. Yet, it seems the explanatory value of the 'democratic peace theory' is limited, since it could narrow the analysis to the relations between democratic states. To ponder the 'use of force' issue by democratic states or systems in contemporary international relations, four issues will be analyzed in this chapter (see Figure 2.1). Firstly, what aims should be achieved as a result of use of force.

---

1   COW Inter-State War Data, 1816-1997 (v3.0) [Online]. Available at: http://www.correlatesofwar.org/cow2%20data/WarData/InterState/Inter-State%20War%20Format%20(V%203-0).htm [accessed: 4 December 2009].

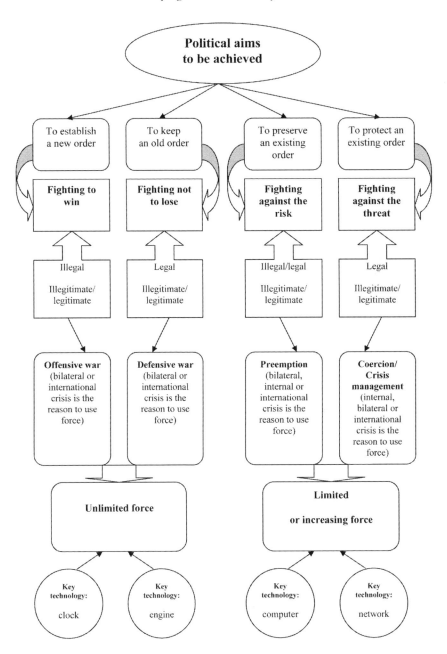

Figure 2.1 **Reasons, aims, methods and capabilities concerning the use of force in the contemporary international environment**

Secondly, reasons for use of force. Thirdly, methods of use of force. Fourthly, capabilities which states have at their disposal concerning the use of force.

What For? Aims to be Achieved as a Result of the Use of Force

As already mentioned, democratic states usually do not have recourse to use of force in relations between each other, yet norms and institutions which are the basis for peace between democratic states differ and should rather be perceived as complementary not identical ones (Farnham 2003: 398). The situation looks different when a democracy meets an undemocratic system, which, additionally, has an extremely different approach towards the use of force and an entirely opposite rationality. In such case, the use of force by democratic states might be sometimes unavoidable, which simultaneously contradicts the initial theory that 'democracies do not wage wars'. Yet Christian Reus-Smit (2005) is absolutely right to stress that all states should use armed forces internationally in order to maintain peace and stability within international society. He also notices that '… as international society has expanded the number of traditional interstate wars has declined' (Reus-Smit 2005: 72). More importantly, nowadays, we have an 'equalitarian regime', which means that all recognized states have the same rights, and there are strictly limited principles of using force internationally. Yet the material ability of states having power status differ from other states' capabilities. Therefore, earlier 'colonial hierarchy' was replaced by the 'equalitarian rule' (Reus-Smit 2005: 73).

Thus, there is a question as to whether liberal democracy is somehow exceptional in resorting to the use of force within the contemporary international environment. If we presume that the essence of liberal democracy emanates from the fact that it is established in order to check the power of the state over its citizens and provide the necessary legitimacy for its rulers (Baum 2008: 444), we have to accept, as a consequence, that liberal democracy is also exceptional as an international actor because it is obliged to act according to stricter rules, both national and international, compared to non- or partly-democratic states. Yet, in practice, the most important issue is perception. A democratic state has to perceive another one as a democracy in order to avoid war in crisis situations. Therefore, rather subjective criteria are the basis for evaluation. So it is possible that two democratic states can wage war, because one of them does not perceive the other as a democratic state (for example, undemocratic ideology or leaders are in power). We have also to bear in mind that the perception of the democratic state's essence has changed. States that have been historically perceived as democratic would not be recognized as democracies when using modern standards. Therefore, it is rather useless to refer historical examples when analyzing contemporary activities. Methods and capabilities of the states regarding the use of force within the international arena have dramatically changed. That is why contemporary democracy can use its power more sophisticatedly and effectively. Yet, it is much more difficult to start war in a legitimate way and finish it as the evident winner. Sometimes, war might be waged for several years not only by soldiers but also diplomats, financiers, humanitarian relief services, policemen, teachers and medical services. Usually, it is also really hard to assess if the end of a war or conflict can be regarded as victory or defeat. Nevertheless, it could be observed that if a democratic state is an element of the broader liberal international system, then it can be less war-prone because peaceful conflict resolution is the norm within. Its behaviour can be changed when faced with the non-liberal principles of a non-liberal system. Sometimes, it can be pushed to wage war with its opponents to defend its democratic and liberal status.

Moreover, the privatization of war, professionalization of armed forces and accessibility to non-lethal weapons may cause democratic states to be more war-prone, regardless of their liberal ideology because war affects their own citizens only indirectly. Sometimes, the executive branch takes a decision concerning the use of armed force abroad without any recourse to the citizens' will. For analyzing the issue of future major and minor wars, Väyrynen (2007) underlines that we are witnessing, nowadays, a huge decline in the number of inter-state wars. Yet, this is not equivalent to the complete depreciation of force as an instrument of international politics. He is also right in noticing that there are two basic features which distinguish the contemporary strategic environment from the past: the continuing resort to military intervention (usually in the form of multilateral action); and the rise of small-scale, local violence (including civil wars).

Yet, as Michael J. Williams (2008) aptly points out, risk and uncertainty are two main characteristics of the contemporary strategic landscape. And all modern states should take them into consideration when undertaking actions across the world. According to Williams, 'no longer is war about achieving a decisive end point … war is a way to reduce and manage the possible adverse consequences of a security risk such as Iraq and Afghanistan' (Williams 2008: 64). Moreover, he claims that war should be analyzed and perceived as a 'more cyclical process with no real end in sight'. Therefore, the contemporary war is, rather, a risk management activity based on the risk transfer. Yet, one has to bear in mind that 'contrary to assessment in terms of intentions and capabilities, risk is based upon probability and the magnitude of consequences. Risks are never real' (Williams 2008: 66). As mentioned above, all states are constrained by strict rules as far as the use of force in the international environment is concerned. And that is why they should resort to force only when there is a real threat to international peace and stability from a specific actor or actors having definite resources, assets and clear intentions. But the contemporary strategic landscape is so complex that states (democratic and non-democratic) face infinitely more perceptual risks compared to a finite number of measurable and definable threats. 'Since risks are only possible scenarios … they can exist to a far greater extent than threats. … Risk management is a never-ending process – it is about living with insecurity, not providing security through deterrence of the threat from an outside actor …' (Williams 2008: 66). Moreover, the risk cannot be defined because risk is a socially constructed subjective term.

So, every state or every decision-maker can perceive the same risk differently. Therefore, the 'coalition of the willing' is usually created to manage an abstract risk, rather than a defined military threat. It is hard to define that risk precisely as well as to determine when it has been reduced or eliminated (Williams 2008: 67–70).

Nowadays, almost all states and societies perceive themselves as threatened and try to manage or reduce risks by peaceful or military means. Despite the fact that during the post-Cold War period democratic states enjoyed a 'peace dividend' and wanted to believe that democracy eliminates war, systemic transitions towards democracy turned out to be very painful, in some cases. Although the level of military expenditures has drastically decreased for several years, it has become apparent that, even in peaceful times, democratic states still need to have recourse to force in order to preserve and protect their existing order. That is why democratic states have started to use force for humanitarian reasons, undertaking missions within larger multinational coalitions or organizations. Still international law in general and, particularly, the sovereignty principle, mark the limits of the use of force in the international environment. But those limits are interpreted more and more flexibly. Nicholas Kerton-Johnson, who analyzes US war decisions taken after 2001, notices three important changes as far as the use of force is concerned.

> First, the shift in language from earlier post-Cold War instances of the use of force; second, the growing dominance of the combined national interest/egoist morality justifications; and third, a growing disjunction between these justifications for the use of force and those drawing on the concept of 'international society', and a concomitant weakening of the U.S. commitment to the rules and norms of international society more generally. (Kerton-Johnson 2008: 1003)

Compared with earlier periods, the main difference concerning the resort stems from the fact that any use of force is, nowadays, connected with post-intervention aid, as well as the long-term reconstruction of the state. This, in turn, means that democratic states should view force through the lens of responsibility. Thus, the level of military expenditures of a particular state should be as important as development aid. Yet, decision-makers should not fall into a trap of 'over-securitization' because security risks can never be totally eliminated. Vivienne Jabri (2006) characterizes war as a technology of control. She poses questions concerning the real nature of war noting, at the same time, that in modern times all distinctions between war and criminality, war and peace, as well as war and security, seem to be irrelevant and non-existent. War, especially war on terror, became a global phenomenon, not only an inter-state one. In this regard, time and space are not important factors for analyzing war. Jabri claims that 'when security becomes the overwhelming imperative of the democratic state, its legitimization is achieved both through a discourse of 'balance' between security and liberty and in terms of the 'protection' of liberty' (Jabri 2006: 51). For her, violence and the recourse to force become integrated mechanisms of power and, therefore, are 'a mode of control, a technology of governmentality' (Jabri 2006: 54).

Moreover, the use of force in the contemporary international environment means, at the same time, that the intervener has an obligation to resolve the conflict, plus assist in and support the reconstruction of the state and society. This almost eliminates the will to defeat the enemy in a battle. That is why the use of force by democratic states is nowadays perceived through the 'just war' category. Yet, Marieke de Goede, referring to Jacques Derrida, notices that the violence itself is neither just nor unjust because only law can make it just or unjust. The other issue is that law can be produced in an undemocratic way because securitization of certain issues requires special entitlements for decision-makers, which can place them above the law in certain aspects (de Goede 2008: 179). Nevertheless, if the 'just war' principle is used, intervention should first of all have both an international and internal legitimacy, as well as a clear consent of the society/nation within which an intervention will be conducted. Therefore, the military advantage is not enough to use force efficiently.

Cécile Fabre (2008) points out three sets of principles concerning the 'just war': *jus ad bellum*, *jus in bello* and *just post bellum*. She notices that the dominant view on the 'just war' is that only a legitimate authority has the right to take any decision concerning the war. Yet, recently, many scholars have departed from that principle, because they claim an individual as point of reference in that regard. That is why states have some rights and privileges only when they guarantee basic rights to their own citizens. Therefore, the basic rights and freedoms of individuals should be respected regardless of the state's borders and war should be perceived 'as a mechanism for enforcing cosmopolitan moral norms, rather than a mechanism for resolving interstate disputes' (Fabre 2008: 963–4). Fabre states that 'the state's right to wage war is one which it has precisely in so far as it is better than individuals at protecting their fundamental human rights through the use of lethal force. If the state is unable or unwilling to wage war on behalf of its individual members, the right to do so reverts to the latter' (Fabre 2008: 972). She also underlines the premise that 'we generally do not need a state, or a state-like entity, to judge the permissibility of a particular act of force' (Fabre 2008: 975), which seems to be very controversial. The author analyzes the problem of a proper authorization for the use of force internationally, but she mistakenly mixes legality with legitimacy. Almost all arguments used by Cécile Fabre concern the rights of particular individuals, or a group consisting of individuals, to resort to war with their own national authorities. It gives the impression that there is no distinction between civil wars, internal conflicts and interstate wars.

The strategic environment is influenced not only by states but also by non-state actors described as 'dogs of war': private military companies, military industries, mafias, terrorists, organized criminals. For them, war and its attendant chaos are the only way to increase their political and financial profits; something they can never achieve in a stable or democratic society. Sometimes even NGOs push for engagement in peace operations stressing that there is a moral or special obligation for a state or coalition of states to intervene because of humanitarian reasons. Nevertheless, idealistic motivations are often backed by narrow, national interests of the intervener(s). Gelb and Rosenthal remark that morality, values, ethics or universal norms, which form the basis of human rights, are also basic reasons for armed actions in the international scene. Interestingly, ethic rhetoric is evoked more often by traditional realists than liberals and perceptions of universal values and particular interests of states become more and more identical (Gelb and Rosenthal 2003).

According to Thomas Ohlson (2008), who analyzed the issue of internal conflicts, people usually start violent conflicts because they have reasons (grievances and goals), resources (capabilities and opportunities), and resolve (no alternative to violence in order to achieve their goals). He thinks his arguments can also be applied to inter-state wars. James Lee Ray (1998), in turn, refers to the findings of Bueno de Mesquita and Siverson, who noticed that, regardless of the type of regime, all political leaders share the same wish – they like to stay in power as long as possible. Therefore, authors have observed some important regularities concerning democratic states: the tendency to wage war with different types of states with regularity; to win in wars they conduct; to have fewer casualties in the wars they start; to reach peaceful settlements of disputes; and surprisingly, the tendency of major-power democracies to be more constrained in going to war in comparison with less powerful ones (Ray 1998: 41). Therefore the fear of failure, not values or principles of international law is the main constraining factor for democratic states.

According to the *Global Progress Report* (2008) 'the world appears to be experiencing a period of democratic stagnation. For many nations, however, this is a time of ongoing democratic consolidation'. Yet, researchers are not able to predict to what extent firm and newly-established democratic states will resort to force to shape regional or global order. Nevertheless, most of them agree that peace is cheaper and guarantees stability of the world order in the long run. That is why Jabri (2006) exaggerates, claiming that

> what is significant about using war as analyzer of the present is that the technologies of control constituting the global matrix of war confer primacy on violence, of both direct and indirect kinds, targeted against the very corporeal presence of those framed as enemies and a threat to the existing order and the modes of control that the state is capable of implementing and mobilizing. (Jabri 2006: 60)

Why? Reasons behind the Use of Force

Democratic states have recourse to force in international relations in order to enhance their national security; limit all or only the most dangerous possible risks or threats to their security and international order; preserve their standards and way of life; or establish and then preserve a more stable global order. Yet, Western and non-Western perceptions of the legitimate use of force in international relations differ. Contemporary strategic cultures of democratic states stem from their historical experiences, yet it has shifted (Rengger and Kenedy-Pipe 2008). As Jeremy Black aptly points out, 'the porous and contested definition of war suggested by its current usage, as in war on drugs or war on terror, let alone war on poverty, further complicates understandings of force and legitimacy, and makes it difficult to define the military' (Black 2005: 139). Therefore, he suggests that in order to fully understand the contemporary approach of democratic states' legitimate use of force in international relations, one has to treat the nature of force as an independent variable. It is hard to agree with Black's approach towards that issue because the nature of force should always be perceived through the prism of political aims. States and sub-state actors resort to force to achieve political goals, not just to wage war. Therefore, the nature of force has to be perceived as a dependent variable.

Usually, democracies act together in a multilateral coalition and resort to force when there are no prospects for a peaceful resolution. As mentioned above, armed force is an especially important tool in relations with undemocratic or partly democratic states and societies. Nevertheless, sometimes even the most oppressive undemocratic states are tolerated. Not because of the principle of sovereignty, but on account of the fact that they do not threaten major powers, or do not destabilize regional or global order; therefore. they are not perceived as opponents. That is why undemocratic regimes are sometimes pushed to change their system and policy; sometimes they do not adhere. The most influential determinant in that regard is perception. Democratic states decide to form a coalition and use force only when decision-makers perceive threats as dangerous for international order, or great powers. Those who examine the use of force through the principle of responsibility stress that the international society, or part of it, has the moral obligation to act when basic human rights and freedoms are violated. Yet, even a cursory analysis of the international relations recent history shows that it is not enough to treat its own citizens badly, although it is 'nice' when a regime is oppressive to them, because it is much easier to legitimize the use of force and conduct the operation by foreign actors.

According to Howard M. Hensel (2008b), states should resort to force only when there is a certainty that it will result 'in greater good than harm'. Moreover, the international society will recognize the specific use of force in international relations is 'good' or 'just', yet eight criteria have to be fulfilled. First, there must be a legitimate goal underpinning any decision concerning the use of force – the attainment, restoration, preservation, and/or enhancement of true peace. Second, only legitimate authorities can justly authorize the use of armed forces as an instrument to resolve conflicts. Third, authorities must calculate their decision on right intentions. Fourth, there must be a just cause. Fifth, any recourse to force has to be a last resort, and the final decision must be taken after the exhaustion of all non-violent and peaceful alternatives. Sixth, the principle of proportionality concerning the cost associated with the decision to use force has to be applied. Seventh, there must be a reasonable prospect for military success. Eighth, belligerents must declare their intentions prior to initiating armed hostilities (Hensel 2008b: 5–6). Hensel also underlines that theocentric natural law proponents perceived *jus ad bellum* in the context of a cosmopolitan perspective emphasizing the common good of all mankind. According to supporters of that approach, there is a possibility of using force internationally but only to build a peace, the ultimate goal being 'the creation of an environment in which all human beings can fulfil themselves and flourish to the greatest degree possible' (Hensel 2008b: 11). Moreover, resort to force is justified by unjust behaviour of the other party, both states and individuals. Yet, the main problem is the common sense of rationality between opponents. If they share the same rationality, the probability of an open armed conflict and recourse to force can be smaller, because they perceive a crisis situation in the same way. In other cases, both sides can use armed force believing that they will eliminate evil. Dominic D.P. Johnson and Dominic Tierny (2006: 5) also notice that

> quite often, people end up evaluating outcomes on the basis of factors that are largely independent of the battlefield: their pre-existing beliefs, the symbolism of events, and manipulation by elites and the media. Understanding these sources of bias is vital because perceptions of victory can make or break the careers of leaders, shape relations between countries, and skew the historical lessons that guide future policymaking.

As far as the anthropocentric natural law approach is concerned, there are two basic paradigms – realism and liberalism. For Hobbesian realists, peace is the only legitimate goal of war, yet they defined peace as a state in international relations in which states struggle for power and realize their narrow interests, although they do not use armed forces in an open clash. Peace is never permanent, nor is the balance of power (Hensel 2008a: 40). To quote Howard M. Hensel (2008a: 40): '... realists are prepared to sanction the use of armed force to defend the state's national security, to protect and promote the national interests, to maintain or enhance the power of the state within the international arena, and to prevent any other power from establishing hegemony within the international community.' It seems that, according to that approach, the anticipatory self-defence cannot be excluded as a 'just war'. Moreover, realists recognize that undemocratic regimes exist within the international system, but, at the same time, it does not mean that democratic states should use their armed forces to intervene, as long as those regimes do not threaten their vital national interests. Yet, there are two justifications for 'right intervention'. First, in response to domestic instability within a particular state that is perceived by the intervener as critical for its national interests. Second, intervention is justified when there is a probability that domestic instability and violence can spread and result in regional instability, which in turn is vital for the dominant state or coalition national interest. A reasonable expectation of victory is also very important in unison with proportionality, regarded as a key rule, because the particular intervention cannot turn into a total war (Hensel 2008a: 42–3).

For supporters of liberal school, a better peace is the only legitimate purpose of war, but it must be always 'right intervention'. For them, wars are products of irrationality, ignorance, prejudice, passion, fear or corruption. States can use armed force only in order to defend other states that are victims of aggression or peoples, whose rights are constantly violated. Therefore, the international community has an obligation or responsibility to intervene in several circumstances, but it should be done in the name of the aggrieved. That is why pre-emptive self-defence, predicted upon unambiguity and imminence of the threat cannot be excluded. Moreover, states have to keep to the principle of proportionality, and there should not be any collective punishment after the war (Hensel 2008a: 50–53).

Any legal debate concerning the use of force by democratic states recently has focused on humanitarian intervention and the right to anticipatory self-defence. Main issues discussed are the legality and legitimacy of resorting to force in the international environment. According to Richard Falk, 'legality clarifies the core obligations relating to force, while legitimacy tries to identify and delimit a zone of exception that takes account of supposedly special circumstances' (Falk 2005: 35). That is why some interventions are illegal but legitimate (e.g., Kosovo war) and some are illegal and illegitimate (Falk 2005). For Nicholas Rengger (2005), legality of military intervention is intrinsically linked with both moral (philosophical) and formal (jurisprudential) determinants. He underlines that the contemporary 'just war' tradition is deeply rooted in the juristic approach. Moreover, the author suggests that all analysis of the 'just war' tradition should start from the 'right intention' principle, because both the rulers and soldiers have to obey it, thus avoiding immoral claims and actions – intimidation, illegitimate coercion or hatred – aimed at the enemy. Therefore, the 'right intention' principle should, in practice, consist in the incorporation of moral judgment 'into the realm of war' (Rengger 2005: 153). Analyzing the invasion of Iraq in 2003, Rengger rightly quotes Michael Walzer who wrote that 'a war fought before its time is not a just war' (Rengger 2005: 155).

Andrew Hurrell in turn underlines that 'legitimacy implies a willingness to comply with rules or to accept a political order even if this goes against specific interests at specific times' (Hurrell 2005: 16). He suggests that power is strongly linked with the issue of international order and legitimate use of force, yet sometimes instrumentality is the main reason to refer to legitimacy. It means that contemporary relations between law and morality and law and power in the context of use of force are highly complex and sometimes they just do not go hand in hand. For David Armstrong and Theo Farrell, legitimacy 'is a far more elusive concept than law' (Armstrong and Farrell 2005: 5). To achieve the legitimacy for use of force, it is not enough to refer to international written or customary law. In that regard, legitimacy should also take account of different sets of moral values or ideological elements. They think that 'the just war tradition provides a guide to thinking about moral action rather than a guide to moral action itself. This comes closer to the idea of morality, in this case the just war tradition, as a site rather than a source of legitimacy' (Armstrong and Farrell 2005: 11).

Hurrell (2005: 18–25) sets apart five dimensions of legitimacy. First, 'input legitimacy', referring to an accordance with generally accepted principles of the right process. Within the international environment, there are minimalist rules and procedures that are indispensable to avoid or limit conflicts, which in turn are characteristic of the international fragmented system. Sovereign states should, therefore, perceive their interests and any possibility to resort to force through these common rules and institutions. In contemporary international relations, the process to create norms and procedures is much more complex and pluralistic than it was before. That is why we have an integrated normative order based on equality within which even a superpower cannot act without broader consent. International legal constitutionalism is built around the UN Charter, which clearly delineates cases in which the coercive force can be perceived as legitimated. Moreover, international institutions should apply the same standards of legitimacy as liberal democratic states. Values such as participation, transparency, representation and accountability are important also within the international level. 'Legitimacy requires more than unanimity among the great powers .....'[2] Legitimacy needs domestic consent and domestic constitutionalism. If democratic legitimacy is important, the non-democratic regimes should not have any claims towards sovereignty. An example of that approach is the Responsibility to Protect formula. Second, Hurrell thinks that institutions or agreements are legitimate when their basic principles are justifiable on the basis of shared aims and values. Self-determination, human rights and democracy mark the contemporary understanding of the concept of using force within the international level. We are now witnessing the shift from legitimacy built around a state's consent towards legitimacy based on a shared conception of 'substantive justice'. That is why the use of force is, to a large extent, linked with moral values and justice. Third, legitimacy of the use of force has to be rooted in specialized knowledge and expertise experience as bodies involved in the decision-making processes. Decision-makers should have the necessary intelligence data to minimize the probability of taking an improper decision. Fourth, 'output legitimacy' understood as predicted effectiveness. Fifth, 'legitimacy is about providing persuasive reasons as to why a course of action, a rule, or a political order is right and appropriate'. Three elements are crucial in that regard: audience, institutions, and language.

Hurrell (2005: 26–30) underlines the normative and descriptive meaning of legitimacy, yet he also claims that legitimacy of the use of force in the international environment should be applied on a case by case basis because, in practice, every crisis situation differs from the other one. Therefore, the rules and procedures should meet requirements of a strategic environment, but at the same time, they

---

2   Quotation from Henry R. Nau (2005), quoted by Andrew Hurrell, 'Legitimacy and the use of force: can the circle be squared?' *Review of International Studies*, vol. 31, special issue, p. 19.

should be constantly reinterpreted. The main problem is, however, which body should perform that reinterpretation?

For Lawrence Freedman (2005), legitimacy of use of force stems from the fact that, nowadays, armed forces are being used to realize liberal values. Analyzing the contemporary strategic environment, Freedman notices that during the process of legitimization, states are eager to invoke the normative stream of human security and underline the need to protect weak and vulnerable individuals and groups. Therefore, he calls that type of warfare a liberal war. Yet, he stresses that 'the problem with the notion of liberal wars ... lies less with the ends than the means. Wars are inherently illiberal in their effects and their consequences' (Freedman 2005: 95). Therefore, a liberal war is waged in the name of basic values, not strategic imperatives, and it may be called 'a war of choice' in opposition to the classical wars, which were 'wars of necessity' or 'of survival'. One has to agree with Freedman, who rightly points out that 'there are therefore a number of opportunities to engage in liberal wars, but only a few are likely to be taken up' (Freedman 2005: 104). Moreover, any use of armed forces by democratic states in the international environment will result from the support of liberal values and principles. Therefore, soldiers will be deployed to protect civilians from those who prepare for, support or engage in civil destruction.

Nevertheless, Mueller (2005) is right to suggest that it is rather unlikely for democratic and developed states to establish and continuously support instruments that have the task of policing civil wars abroad as well as dealing with violent regimes. In his opinion, there are several reasons which determine that approach. First, the lack of interest. Second, the perception that, because almost all conflicts are perceived as so complex and deeply rooted in a particular society, any military intervention by outside forces may only worsen the conflict. Third, in operations not directly linked with national security interests, both casualties and collateral damages are not accepted. Humanitarian missions are perceived positively as long as loss of human life is rare. Fourth, there is a huge aversion as far as long-term policing is concerned. Fifth (in the democratic states only), final political gains matter: and, sometimes, even the achievement of a strategic success during a humanitarian operation may not turn into a spectacular political success within the domestic policy realm. Sixth, international policing is effective if the international community abandons the narrowly understood principle of sovereignty (Mueller 2005: 114–18).

Martha Finnemore (2005) notices that, apart from legality and legitimacy, multilateralism is also a vital source of international activism for democratic states. Many differences concerning the use of force in international relations stem from two basic issues: the nature of multilateralism as a rule of behaviour, which is generally perceived as more legitimate than other principles; and an artificial differentiation made between legitimacy and efficiency of force. Finnemore underlines that differences concerning the use of force are not new. They are prominent features of international relations and, nowadays, they just seem to be more apparent. She is right in noticing that there are at least four gaps in the use of force issue: transatlantic gap, intra-Europe, intra-US ones, and between the most powerful states – like the US, China, India, Russia and others.

The transatlantic gap stems from the American presumption of greater efficiency of armed forces as almost being the only appropriate tool to counter security threats, which in turn have been and are still perceived as more dangerous and imminent by Americans than by Europeans. The intra-Europe gap concerns issues like global responsibilities, power projection, and the role of multilateral undertakings, as well as the lack of indispensable capabilities for power projection. The intra-US gap has been dominated by partisan discourse about the use of force: the Republican Party and its supporters believed that even pre-emption could be carried out; while the Democratic Party and its supporters preferred diplomatic tools, being wary of military involvement. Finally, the most powerful states do not have a consensus for the use of force. They are afraid of possibly undermining the sovereignty principle by the enhancement of human rights (Finnemore 2005: 190–96).

According to Finnemore, there are two major factors which made multilateralism genuinely exceptional. First, major powers' restraint. Second, equality of all under the same rules. Yet one has to bear in mind that the major powers usually set these rules. Nevertheless, the main advantages of multilateral actions stem from the fact that behaviours of the most powerful become more predictable. Finnemore stresses that not all individual actions should be, in this regard, perceived as unilateral ones, because an essence of multilateralism is its delimitation of policy between individual states and communities of states. Particular states perceive the efficiency of force differently because they want to achieve different political goals, have different predictions about the intended and unintended results with the use of force and receive different level of legitimacy, which entails a lot of subjective elements. Finnemore aptly points out that 'force must be coupled with legitimacy for maximum effect. Legitimacy is important because it creates some degree of support for, or at least acquiescence to, those using force. Legitimate force attracts allies, contributions, and approval from outsiders and diminishes resistance in targets of force' (Finnemore 2005: 196–202).

How? Methods of Use of Force

Democratic states bound by written and customary international law are obliged to use force internationally as a last resort, lawfully with as much legitimacy as possible in a particular crisis situation. There is also a tendency to act multilaterally in order to make other states and organizations feel responsible for solving the crisis and use force more efficiently. That is why, nowadays, democratic states usually do not have recourse to armed forces to conduct an offensive or defensive war, but fight against security risks and threats. Therefore, strategic coercion, crisis management, pre-emption and prevention are basic methods of using force in the contemporary strategic environment. The main difference between these methods is the intensity of forced used. Strategic coercion as a purely diplomatic strategy is the least oppressive one, because it is based on the threat of using force or violence. Crisis management is perceived as a more complex political strategy, which entails diplomatic activities combined with the gradual use of specialized armed forces. Yet all decision-makers who decide to conduct a crisis management operation abroad should bear in mind that even after a successful military phase of operation, external humanitarian and development aid are indispensable to achieve prescribed political goals. Sometimes even a long-term 'just occupation' is the only way to solve the crisis. Pre-emption and prevention are in turn the most militaristic strategies used as an anticipatory defence to mitigate or eliminate a particular risk or threat for security. Both their legality and legitimacy are, nowadays, widely discussed.

According to Robert J. Art (2003: 5) '… coercive diplomacy is not meant to entail war, but instead employs military power short of war to bring about a change in a target's policies or in its political makeup'. Paul Gordon Lauren, Gordon A. Craig and Alexander L. George (2007: 200) think that coercion 'attempts to reverse actions that are occurring or have been undertaken by an adversary'. The opponent must behave in a way the coercer prefers, because the results of defiance will possibly be very harmful. Moreover, coercion should affect the opponent's motivation and will to change, start or stop some activities. Nevertheless, when the coercer must resort to armed force, coercive diplomacy has failed. If there is too much coercion in a crisis situation, there is also a possibility that after some period a newly established political solution will be rejected by one or several groups of indigenous people. Yet, lightweight coercion can be inefficient and none of the prescribed political aims will be achieved.

Lauren, Craig and George formulated five principles for successful coercion. First, the coercer must convey that it is more highly motivated to achieve its stated demands than the adversary is to oppose them. Second, the coercer's demand should aim at a particular opponent's behaviour. The coercer should not want too much, because then the whole coercive strategy can easily collapse. Third, threats posed by the coercer must be both credible and potent enough to make the opponent change its behaviour or be aware of an inevitable punishment if it will not change it. The coercer should have a capability and will to coerce the opponent, because the potential power to hurt the opponent is the most important measure in that strategy. Fourth, apart from coercive measures, the coercer can offer some positive incentives as well, and they should be used in a flexible manner. Fifth, the opponent should be given a fixed period of time to comply with the coercer's demand (Lauren, Craig and George 2007: 201–2). Moreover, the rationality of both the opponent and coercer matters, because a shared rationality can make the coercive policy successful.

Alexander L. George is right in noticing that 'coercive diplomacy is an attractive strategy insofar as it offers the possibility of achieving one's objectives economically, with little if any bloodshed, and with fewer political and psychological costs than warfare exacts and with less risk of conflict escalation' (George 2003: VII).

Nevertheless, it is sometimes difficult to succeed with a coercion strategy when there two or more coercers and multiple actors being coerced. When a coalition of states wants to apply this strategy, there is a high probability that there will be some divisions concerning the means to achieve their goals. In practice, it is really difficult to use coercion diplomacy for purely humanitarian reasons. Moreover, it should be fully taken into account that 'carrots' should not be offered before 'sticks'. There is always a problem with how to estimate a successful coercion. Usually, coercion diplomacy fails when it is perceived as a last resort after the military option or total inactivity. George underlines also that there is a possibility that an opponent will not comply with the demand for several reasons: it will take a demand as a bluff; it will take a demand very seriously and in turn decide on pre-emptive activities; it will take the demand as credible and imminent, but because of prestige or honour it prefers warfare; the opponent may conditionally comply with the demand in order to weaken the coercer's ability to use the threat of force. When coercive diplomacy fails, there is a hard choice between war and political retreat (George 2003: VIII–XII). In that context one has to bear in mind that

> ... coercive diplomacy ... is highly context-dependent. It does not take place in a vacuum, and thus must be tailored in an exacting way to fit the unique configuration of each situation and to take into account the particular behavioral characteristics of a specific adversary. ... Efforts to engage in coercive diplomacy therefore rest heavily upon skill at understanding the nature of the conflict, correctly assessing the adversary and empathizing with them, providing reassurances, adjusting to ever-changing circumstances, and relying more on diplomatic communication rather than military signals alone. (Lauren, Craig and George 2007: 218)

As mentioned, crisis management is a complex political strategy that entails diplomatic activities combined with the gradual use of selected armed forces. Lauren, Craig and George (2007: 222–4) notice that in a crisis situation, confrontations between adversaries can be managed and terminated if one side is willing to back away. When a crisis occurs, every side is forced to protect or advance its most strategic interests. At the same time these interests make opponents' behaviour more self-restraint to reduce the possibility of escalation. Decision-makers should develop the politico-military strategy that 'combined force and statecraft in a way appropriate to the situation at hand'. Diplomacy and force should be used in a wise manner, and both measures should focus on a political resolution for the crisis. Yet, it is far easier to resolve a crisis when opponents limit the objectives they pursue for the confrontation. Moreover, limiting the means to employ for achieving the goals can be influential regarding final success. All adversaries engaged in the crises must understand, create and adhere to operational principles that favour crisis management; and politicians must avoid war, at first.

As far as the crisis management is concerned, several basic rules have to be applied: to maintain top-level civilian control of military institutions and actions;

to create pauses in the tempo of military actions; to coordinate diplomatic and military actions; to avoid misperceptions – clear messages expressed in particular actions are indispensable; to avoid military actions that push the opponent to start pre-emption and large-scale warfare; to choose a mixed diplomatic-military strategy in order to negotiate not to wage war; to make visible for the opponent that selected diplomatic-military options are compatible with its fundamental interests (Lauren, Craig and George 2007: 224). Moreover, Roger Mac Ginty (2008) aptly points out that it is better to use indigenous people to undertake crisis management activities in the theatre of operation than conduct Western-style peace-making which can be contested by that population and counterproductive. It should be strongly underlined that in contemporary strategic environment crisis management missions have to be linked with post-operational management to succeed. To quote Mark Duffield (2007b: 45): 'War is no longer a Clausewitzian affair of state, it is a problem of underdevelopment and political breakdown and, as such, it requires development as well as security professionals to conjoin and work together in new ways'. That is why we are witnessing a shift towards post-conflict reconstruction which creates 'contingent sovereignty' established by NGOs, foreign administrations and aid agencies, although some military activities are usually points of departure for reconstruction phases. Therefore, real power projection and skilful crisis management is the ability to deliver aid so effectively as to stabilize the situation. Yet some coercive and politically directed programming is needed. So every successful crisis management operation should comprise of three phases: intervention, post-intervention and state reconstruction (Duffield 2007a: 29).

According to Gregory H. Fox (2008: 3–4),

> *Humanitarian occupation* is an effort to capture more precisely two salient characteristics of the missions. First, their purpose has been to end human rights abuses, reform governmental institutions and restore peaceful coexistence among groups that had recently been engaged in vicious armed conflict. In this sense, they are *humanitarian*. The missions are social engineering projects that take international standards of human rights and governance as their blueprints. … Second, the governing authority assumed by the international administrators is quite similar to the de facto authority of traditional belligerent occupiers. Both are outsiders to the territory they control, both assume ultimate legal authority and both are avowedly temporary. … *Humanitarian occupation*, then, may be defined as the assumption of governing authority over a state or a portion thereof, by an international actor for the express purpose of creating a liberal, democratic order.

So during the post-intervention phase 'humanitarian occupation' is conducted in order to preserve a state, to reinvigorate it and to make it efficient, enhancing the stability of the global or regional order in the same time.

Raymond Kuo (2008) aptly points out that researchers usually miss three key elements regarding post-war occupation or *jus post bellum* as he called it: a success requires not only military victory, but first of all it can be measured through the level of support from the local community; influence and control can be acquired by the occupier's administrative apparatus, which in some cases has a critical military purpose; an occupier's civil administration can realize projects, which can be regarded by the local community as dangerous for local interests. To quote Kuo (2008: 301): 'occupations impose a unilaterally mandated administrative system and proactively intrude upon an occupied population. It is itself in some respects a form of aggression, a violation of the inhabitants' rights to bring about a return to peace and fulfill legal and ethical duties.' That is why Kuo provides several basic rules concerning 'just occupation'. First, the occupied population retains sovereignty over their land. Second, every occupation implies asymmetric responsibilities for both the occupant and occupied. The occupant is responsible for the whole area and not only for its civilian and military personnel but also for indigenous population, its safety and well-being. Third, during an occupation, force and control can take political, economic and social dimensions (Kuo 2008: 311).

The most contested and discussed methods of use of force are pre-emptive and preventive interventions (Bobbitt 2002, Buchanan and Keohane 2004, Doyle 2008). Some researches argue that pre-emption and prevention are both illegal and illegitimate, because they violate the principle of sovereignty which is the basis of inter-state relations. Moreover, they are usually based on a false premise and subjective premonitions of decision-makers who are overwhelmed with a desire to eliminate existing or imagined security threats or risks. There is also another prominent group of academics who find preventive interventions as the particular and moral obligation of the international community to act in the name of the oppressed. Basic rights and freedoms of human beings are the point of reference in that approach. Therefore, this type of intervention is perceived as a legal and legitimate one.

Gregory A. Raymond and Charles W. Kegley Jr (2008) set two ways of the anticipatory defence. First, pre-emptive attacks in which military force is used in order to quell or mitigate an imminent strike by an opponent. Second, preventive attacks in which military force is applied to eliminate any possible strike, even if there is no premise to believe that aggression is imminent and the opponent has the operational ability to conduct a strike. Yet authors underline that

> ... determining when the first use of force is warranted can be difficult. The initiator must consider the certainty of the threat, the magnitude and severity of the harm that will be suffered in the absence of pre-emption, the probability that pre-emptive military action will succeed, the costs incurred, and the gravity of the consequences that may result from taking pre-emptive action. (Raymond and Kegley Jr 2008: 102)

Moreover, any pre-emptive use of force could have opposite results leading to the escalation of conflict and long-term instability. Sometimes a pre-emptive strike can be perceived as just and moral, yet the danger must be imminent and huge. However, there is a problem with how to forecast the danger appropriately. Preventive intervention is criticized for two main reasons. First, it is really hard to forecast, and that is why misperception is quite possible. Second, two basic principles, discrimination and proportionality, are nearly impossible to use during the preventive warfare. Sometimes the worst case scenario forms the basis for military action (Raymond and Kegley Jr 2008: 108).

Marieke de Goede (2008: 164–5) points out that '… the war on terror recognizes that the sheer uncertainty and randomness of terrorist attack renders conventional risk assessment techniques inadequate. … it subsequently moves to incorporate this uncertainty into policy-making as a basis for pre-emptive action.' Therefore, one must decide to undertake pre-emptive action based on inadequate knowledge about the situation and 'raw' intelligence data. The threat is perceived as more imminent and less precise when we compare pre-emption with prevention. She is right in noticing that if the uncertainty is a basis for military action, decision-makers take subjective elements like 'suspicion, premonition, foreboding, challenge, mistrust, fear, anxiety' into account to avoid the worst case scenario. The author, referring to Jacques Derrida, stresses that the violence itself is neither just nor unjust, because only law can make it just or unjust. The other issue is that law can be produced in an undemocratic way and, for example, the securitization of certain issues requires special entitlements for decision-makers, which can place them above the law in some aspects.

Michael Byers (2005) claims in turn that the right of self-defence has constantly been widening since 9/11. Yet many states opposed that trend, and they were reluctant as far as agreed international principles are concerned. International law has not been changed, but its core rules are subjectively reinterpreted. Therefore, there must be a wide consensus to change international law and the principle of self-defence. Even the most powerful states cannot do it unilaterally. As a result, great powers choose to function as a 'legal outcasts' violating the basic norm of international law in order to preserve their own security interests. One has to agree with Byers, who points out that the imminence of the threat is not a main criterion for pre-emption in the contemporary strategic environment because threats are instant and overwhelming, and there is no time for deliberation with almost no choice as far as means are concerned (Byers 2005: 61).

Yet, Rengger (2008: 952), after Doyle (2008), enumerates four standards of prevention, which should be taken into consideration during the discourse concerning the legitimate prevention: lethality, likelihood, legitimacy and legality. The lethality principle refers to the possibility of mass loss of life if the imminent threat is not eliminated. Analyzing the likelihood, the probability that a particular threat will occur should be fully considered. Legitimacy should be understood via traditional 'just war' criteria like principles of proportionality, necessity or deliberativeness of proposed action. The legality principle in turn should be used to answer two questions: whether legal or illegal actions constitute the threat. And, what kind of response (more or less legal) should be chosen? As far as 'just war' tradition is concerned, Rengger aptly points out, that it 'has no prohibition at all on many types of preventive action – up to and including political, legal and/ or economic sanctions – it prohibits only preventive force, assuming that force should always be the tool of last resort, not only because it is intrinsically bad (because it must require killing) but also because of its unpredictability' (Rengger 2008: 956). Rengger adds that prevention as an idea is not new, but what we are witnessing nowadays is an attempt to make it a legitimate rule of international relations. Helen M. Kinsella (2005) underlines that in the context of preventive or pre-emptive intervention the laws of war should be applicable, although some suggest that the laws of war protecting prisoners of war are not fully relevant during the war on terror and criminal law can be used instead. She is right in her claim that 'the distinction between combatants and civilians is invoked to order the difference between civilized and barbaric states' (Kinsella 2005: 182).

As mentioned earlier, there is also a prominent group of academics who find preventive interventions to be the particular and moral obligation of the international community to act in the name of the oppressed. They assume that states are not allowed to do everything within the state's borders, but they have the responsibility to protect their citizens from atrocity crimes as well as help others to do so. In a situation when a state is unable or unwilling to protect, then the international community has the obligation to undertake an appropriate action, including military measures (Evans 2008: 285). Yet there are three challenges to overcome in order to make the 'Responsibility to Protect' (R2P) principle truly 'operational'. First, the conceptual challenge concerning the scope and limits of the principle. It should not be perceived as 'a Trojan Horse for bad old imperial, colonial and militarists habits, but rather the best starting point the international community has … in preventing and responding to genocide and other mass atrocity crimes' (Evans 2008: 289). Second, the institutional challenge which concerns preparedness or the physical capability to undertake an action backed by the common, agreed and legitimate decision. The political preparedness constitutes the third challenge – how to build the common will which is indispensable to starting any effective action. Evans underlines that '… military action is not excluded when it is the only possible way to stop large-scale killing and other atrocity crimes … But it is an absolute travesty of the R2P principle to say that it is about military force and nothing else' (Evans 2008: 291). Moreover, he warns that it is a common misunderstanding that the R2P principle is just another name for humanitarian intervention; always means the use of military force; applies only to weak and friendless countries; covers all human protection issues; and that the operation in Iraq was an example of the application of the principle (Evans 2008: 291–6). Also, Alex J. Bellamy (2008: 624) thinks that '… R2P does not set out criteria for the use of force …'. It does not offer a new way to evade international law in order to conduct an intervention without a clear international mandate. Yet, to avoid the 'moral hazard', states should bind themselves with several principles.

First, any foreign intervention should start only when government's actions are hugely disproportionate. Second, external players should use any and all resources 'to persuade states to address the legitimate grievances of non-violent movements'. Third, the civil population should be carefully protected during the intervention and regime change. Fourth, the humanitarian relief should be delivered in such a way that minimizes possible benefits to the rebels (Bellamy 2008: 631). Bellamy aptly points out that foreign governments should promise to do what they are ready and able to deliver on.

What? Capabilities to Use of Force

Revolution in Military Affairs (RMA) deeply transformed states' military tactics and made military assets and capabilities adjust to a strategic environment which is complex, dynamically and unpredictably changeable, as well as comprised of different kinds of players – state, sub-state or private ones (Koivula and Helminen 2007). According to Lauren, Craig and George (2007: 113) RMA impacts a strategic environment because it is combined with the diplomatic revolution, which in turn is backed by the possibility of using 'advanced sensing and information-reporting computer technologies, and precision-guided munitions (PGMs)'. Therefore, states have acquired abilities to control and solve crisis situations, not only by destructive weapons but also non-lethal ones, which are of utmost strategic importance to democratic states 'obsessed' with two things – the efficiency of force, and the avoidance of casualties at any cost in the course of operation. The lack of success, as well as a lot of heavy casualties and damages, in the theatre of operation could easily undercut the conducted operation internal and external legitimacy. Yet, 'the power and capabilities of others, allies and adversaries … can place severe restrictions upon any state's freedom of action in the use of force by creating a fear of unacceptable consequences, and thereby make it refrain from doing something that it wants to do or do something that it otherwise would not choose to do' (Lauren, Craig and George 2007: 246).

Michael Howard (2009) asserts that the development of science and industry before and after two world wars resulted in an enormous increase in the destructive capabilities available to major powers. Having the modern weapons and means of transporting them, as well as almost endless human resources, power-states could use their armed forces to fulfil 'the classical objectives of warfare' – to defeat the enemy and win the war. Therefore, the mobilization of resources, both human and material ones, was needed in order to converse them into effective military strength. Nowadays, 'in order to confront one's adversary with the alternatives of annihilation or surrender it is no longer necessary to mobilize major forces and deploy them according to classical principles of strategy' (Howard 2009: 148), because states have at their disposal new weapons, like for example, cruise missiles with guidance systems capable of comparing landmarks with pre-recorded maps to guide them to targets, or jet fighters with radar-evading stealth technology, electronic jamming, 'smart bombs' guided by lasers, infrared signals or TV cameras. Work had been started on electromagnetic pulse weapons and space weapons. Therefore, space as a new dimension of warfare was added (Lauren, Craig and George 2007: 113). Along with these changes, the role of modern armed forces has shifted. Timothy Edmunds (2006: 1059) points out that as far as the nature of contemporary armed forces military roles is concerned, one can distinguish four basic trends. First, the defence of national territory is not a determining and core principle for organization and training of regular armed forces. Second, there is a tendency to abandon the conscription army and form professional forces – smaller, better equipped, skilled and flexible in order to be constantly ready for projection tasks, both war-fighting as well as crises management ones. Third, military roles ought to be redefined due to the emergence of new security challenges and threats, like, for example, terrorism, illegal migration or transnational crime. Fourth, contemporary armed forces become constantly more and more important for domestic purposes.

Apart from technical changes and advancements, many strategists stress an important shift as far as military tactics go. For Colin S. Gray (2005) strategic surprise is the main challenge to which states' tactics should adapt. It could be, as well, a useful tactic, when used properly. Therefore, he formulates seven arguments concerning it. First, the bureaucratic improvements within intelligence structures can be beneficial, but they will not have a decisive significance for the reduction of risks linked with strategic surprise. Second, the main challenge is a surprise effect, not a surprise as such. Third, there is room to avoid many unpleasant surprises, if political and military actions are carried out without much tension. Fourth, because any threat or the use of armed forces is a political act set in a particular geopolitical context; any strategic surprise should be analyzed through the lens of that context. Fifth, there is no reason to exaggerate the threats resulted from the strategic surprise, because long-standing strategic benefits are definitely more important. Sixth, 'the Army's transformation plan, privileging flexibility and agility, should minimize the danger of being caught on the wrong side of truly major decisions'. Seventh, the operational level of warfare is important, and its transformation should be done carefully, yet 'an enhanced adaptability for effectiveness in different political circumstances' is a matter of the utmost importance (Gray 2005: VI–VIII).

Frank G. Hoffman (2007) notes that, nowadays, an overwhelming military power is not enough to win, but at the same time it does not mean that military power is completely useless. The main challenge is to adjust military instruments to the new strategic environment. Fourth generation warfare (4GW), also known as the Complex, Irregular or Hybrid Warfare is more of a shift in a degree, combined with favourable social and political conditions, than the invention of a new crucial technology. 4GW is unique because it blurs the differences existing between combat and conflict, soldiers and civilians, as well as the physical and metaphysical. Hoffman warns that 'our opponents eagerly learn and adapt rapidly to more efficient modes of killing. We can no longer overlook our own vulnerabilities as societies or underestimate the imaginations of our antagonists.

In a world of 4GW or Hybrid Wars, the price for complacency and inept strategy only grows steeper'.

According to Antoine Bousquet (2008), chaoplexic warfare will influence the future of tactics. He assumes that the contemporary strategic environment is distinguished by chaos and complexity, which combined form chaoplexity. Therefore states having recourse to force should adjust their tactics to chaoplexity and remodel their militaries. Bousquet points out that we are now experiencing a network era in almost every sphere of human activity, including warfare. That is why a network-centric warfare, or chaoplexic warfare as he called it, marks limits for states' abilities as far as the military dimension is concerned. Using three criteria – a key technology, scientific concept and form of warfare – Bousquet distinguishes four regimes of the scientific way of warfare: mechanism, thermodynamics, cybernetics, and chaoplexity. A mechanism was a symbol of the first regime, which was based on a clock as a key technology whereas force, matter in motion, linearity, and geometry were basic scientific concepts. The close order, drill and rigid tactical deployments characterized the warfare. As far as the thermodynamic regime is concerned, an engine together with energy, entropy and probability were its essence. Therefore, the mass mobilization, motorization and industrialization were indispensable for warfare. Cybernetics – a third regime – was based on computers, command and control, as well as automation. The latest regime – chaoplexity – comprises information, non-linearity, positive feedback, self-organization and emergence. Bousquet thinks that 'from the perspective of chaoplexity, the most successful systems are those that retain flexibility and openness in the interaction and organization of their parts within environments which elude complete predictability' (Bousquet 2008: 924). Moreover, network-centric theorists underline that command and control components should be decentralized and individual units have to feel free to act on their own, which in turn should lead to self-synchronization. 'Swarm' is perceived as the special network of distributed intelligence, which allows troops for complex forms of collective behaviour using simple rules of interaction between individual members. Additionally, resilience, flexibility and the lack of dependence on any single individual are the main advantages of a 'swarm' organization. Highly specialized and adaptable components of forces should interact like the cells of a body. Bousquet suggests that 'rather than throwing themselves onto the enemy in "waves", forces will be able to converge on their target from all directions in offensive bursts, thereby maximizing the shock effect' (Bousquet 2008: 928). After an attack, troops should be easily dispersed thus avoiding enemy strikes as well as causalities and damages.

Apart from the fact that states can resort to sophisticated force and use the most advanced tactics, there is a grave problem concerning the blurred distinction between 'public' and 'private' force, which in turn impacts on modern warfare. According to Patricia Owens (2008), nowadays both state and sub-state actors can readily 'purchase "security" in the market for force'. Moreover, she claims that distinctions made between public and private violence are artificial. Therefore, we should set apart the violence that is made 'public' and that which is made 'private' (Owens 2008: 979). Contemporary democratic states, which still possess the monopoly on the use of a violence internationally, are sometimes faced with the security challenges posed by individuals or a group of rebels, who blur the line between the private and public military forces. Moreover, sub-state actors do not obey international law concerning war, and they focus their attention on political aims, which have to be achieved. Therefore, one should pose the question regarding with the existing dichotomy between the private and public forces at a state level. Is this distinction still valid? What about the political scrutiny of the states, which decide on the 'outsourcing'? Owens notes that modern states carry out modern wars, and this inevitably leads towards a merger of private and public, yet this is rather the process of de-staticization or commercialization of war than its 'privatization'. Nevertheless, she dismisses the fact that the process of commercialization/de-staticization refers to warfare, not war as such, because the latter should still be perceived as a domain of states.

Conclusion

Michael Howard is perfectly right in noticing that 'the use of violence, between states as between individuals, is seldom the most effective way of settling disputes. It is expensive in its methods and unpredictable in its outcome; and these elements of expense and unpredictability have both grown enormously over the last hundred years' (Howard 2009: 149). Yet, we cannot naively believe that states, even democratic ones, relinquish force as a tool of their foreign and security policy. Resort to force still is and will be a prominent part of international activity for states, but some important shifts are visible. Previously, states decided to have recourse to force in the international sphere in order to establish a new order or to keep an old order. That is why fighting to win and fighting not to lose were the main reasons to carry out an offensive or defensive war. Illegally or not, unilaterally, bilaterally or multilaterally, states waged war and were able and ready to use even unlimited force to achieve political aims. A clock and engine were symbols of that so-called 'classic' approach. In the contemporary strategic environment, clock and engine were replaced by the computer and network. States are still able to use force internationally but more restrictively and in a limited way. Inter-state wars are rare and states involve themselves in civil wars, counterinsurgencies or indefinite crises. Therefore, strategic coercion, crisis management and pre-emption/prevention are basic methods of using armed force. Nevertheless, written and customary international law, as well as the sovereignty principle, are still valid, and democratic states have to undertake activities with a legal mandate and legitimacy to act. In spite of that there are some states which redefine these legal norms in a flexible manner, blurring at the same time the difference between legality and legitimacy. Some strategists agree that this unequivocal trend is inevitable, because contemporary states have to fight against risks and threats, which usually are elusive. Almost all states that use force in the international arena invoke their particular responsibility regarding the preservation or protection of an existing order.

Bibliography

Armstrong, D. and Farrell, T. 2005. Force and Legitimacy in World Politics. Introduction. *Review of International Studies*, 31 (special issue), 3–13.

Art, R.J. 2003. Introduction, in *The United States and Coercive Diplomacy*, edited by R.J. Art and P.M. Cronin. Washington DC: United States Institute of Peace Press, 3–20.

Baum, T. 2008. A Quest for Inspiration in the Liberal Peace Paradigm: Back to Bentham? *European Journal of International Relations*, 14(3), 431–53.

Bellamy, A.J. 2008. The Responsibility to Protect and the Problem of Military Intervention. *International Affairs*, 84(4), 615–39.

Black, J. 2005. War and International Relations: A Military-Historical Perspective on Force and Legitimacy. *Review of International Studies*, 31 (special issue), 127–42.

Bobbitt, P. 2002. *The Shield of Achilles: War, Peace and the Course of History*. London: Allen Lane.

Bousquet, A. 2008. Chaoplexic Warfare or the Future of Military Organization. *International Affairs*, 84(5), 915–29.

Buchanan A. and Keohane, R. 2004. The Preventive Use of Force: A Cosmopolitan Institutional Proposal. *Ethics and International Affairs*, 18(1), 1–22.

Byers, M. 2005. Not yet Havoc: Geopolitical Change and the International Rules on Military Force. *Review of International Studies*, 31 (special issue), 51–70.

Doyle, M. 2008. *Striking First: Preemption and Prevention in International Conflict*, edited by S. Macedo. Princeton, NJ: Princeton University Press.

Duffield, M. 2007a. *Development, Security and Unending War. Governing the World of Peoples*. Cambridge: Polity Press.

Duffield, M. 2007b. *Global Governance and the New Wars. The Merging of Development and Security*. New York: Zed Books.

Edmunds, T. 2006. What are Armed Forces For? The Changing Nature of Military Roles in Europe. *International Affaires*, 82(6), 1059–75.

Evans, G. 2008. The Responsibility to Protect: An Idea Whose Time has Come … and Gone? *International Relations*, 22(3), 283–98.

Fabre, C. 2008. Cosmopolitanism, Just War Theory and Legitimate Authority. *International Affairs*, 84(5), 963–76.

Falk, R. 2005. Legality and Legitimacy: The Quest for Principled Flexibility and Restraint. *Review of International Studies*, 31 (special issue), 33–50.

Farber, H.S. and Gowa, J. 1996. Polities and Peace, in *Debating the Democratic Peace*, edited by M.E. Brown, S.M. Lynn-Jones and S.E. Miller. Cambridge: MIT Press, 239–62.

Farnham, B. 2003. The Theory of Democratic Peace and Threat Perception. *International Studies Quarterly*, 47(3), 395–415.

Finnemore, M. 2005. Fights About Rules: The Role of Efficacy and Power in Changing Multilateralism. *Review of International Studies*, 31 (special issue), 187–206.

Fox, G.H. 2008. *Humanitarian Occupation*. New York: Cambridge University Press.

Freedman, L. 2005. The Age of Liberal Wars. *Review of International Studies*, 31 (special issue), 93–107.

Freedom House Report. 2008. *The Worst of the Worst. The World's Most Repressive Societies 2008*. New York: Freedom House.

Gelb, L.H. and Rosenthal, J.A. 2003. The Rise of Ethics in Foreign Policy. *Foreign Affairs*, 82(3), 2–7.

George, A.L. 2003. Foreword, in *The United States and Coercive Diplomacy*, edited by R.J. Art and P.M. Cronin. Washington DC: United States Institute of Peace Press, VII–XIII.

Global Progress Report. 2008. *Current History*, 107(705), 3–12.

Goede de, M. 2008. The Politics of Preemption and the War on Terror in Europe. *European Journal of International Relations*, 14(1), 161–85.

Gray, C.S. 2005. *Transformation and Strategic Surprise*. Carlisle: Strategic Studies Institute.

Hensel, H.M. 2008a. Anthropocentric Natural Law and its Implications for International Relations and Armed Conflict, in *The Legitimate Use of Military Force. The Just War Tradition and the Customary Law of Armed Conflict*, edited by H.M. Hensel, Aldershot: Ashgate, 29–62.

Hensel, H.M. 2008b. Theocentric Natural Law and Just War Doctrine, in *The Legitimate Use of Military Force. The Just War Tradition and the Customary Law of Armed Conflict*, edited by H.M. Hensel, Aldershot: Ashgate, 5–27.

Hoffman, F.G. 2007. *4GW as a Model of Future Conflict*. [Online]. Available at: http://smallwarsjournal.com/blog/2007/07/4gw-as-a-model-of-future-confl/ [accessed: 3 November 2009].

Howard, M. 2009. Military Power and International Order. *International Affairs*, 85(1), 145–55.

Hurrell, A. 2005. Legitimacy and the Use of Force: Can the Circle be Squared? *Review of International Studies*, 31 (special issue), 15–32.

Jabri, V. 2006. War, Security and the Liberal State. *Security Dialogue*, 37(1), 47–64.

Johnson, D.D.P. and Tierny, D. 2006. *Failing to Win. Perceptions of Victory and Defeat in International Politics*. Cambridge, MA: Harvard University Press.

Kerton-Johnson, N. 2008. Justifying the Use of Force in a Post-9/11 World: Striving for Hierarchy in International Society. *International Affairs*, 84(5), 991–1007.

Kinsella, H.M. 2005. Discourses of Difference: Civilians, Combatants, and Compliance with the Laws Of War. *Review of International Studies*, 31 (special issue), 163–85.

Koivula, T. and Helminen, J. 2007. Armed Forces' Roles and Capabilities 2020: Reflections from the Suomenlinna Groupwork Sessions, in *Armed Forces for Tomorrow*, edited by T. Koivula and J. Helminen. Helsinki: Edita Prima Oy, 85–99.

Kuo, R. 2008. Occupation and the Just War. *International Relations*, 22(3), 299–321.

Lauren, P.G., Craig, G.A. and George, A.L. 2007. *Force and Statecraft. Diplomatic Challenges of Our Time*. New York: Oxford University Press.

Layne, C. 1996. Kant or Cant: The Myth of the Democratic Peace, in *Debating the Democratic Peace*, edited by M.E. Brown, S.M. Lynn-Jones and S.E. Miller. Cambridge: MIT Press, 157–201.

Mac Ginty, R. 2008. Indigenous Peace-Making Versus the Liberal Peace. *Cooperation and Conflict*, 43(2), 139–63.

Mueller, J. 2005. Force, Legitimacy, Success, and Iraq. *Review of International Studies*, 31 (special issue), 109–25.

Ohlson, T. 2008. Understanding Causes of War and Peace. *European Journal of International Relations*, 14(1), 133–60.

Owen, J.M. 1996. How Liberalism Produces Democratic Peace, in *Debating the Democratic Peace*, edited by M.E. Brown, S.M. Lynn-Jones and S.E. Miller. Cambridge: MIT Press, 116–54.

Owens, P. 2008. Distinctions, Distinctions: 'Public' and 'Private' Force? *International Affairs*, 84(5), 977–90.

Ray, J.L. 1998. Does Democracy Cause Peace? *Annual Review of Political Science*, 1, 27–46.

Raymond, G.A. and Kegley Jr, C.W. 2008. Preemption and Preventive War, in *The Legitimate Use of Military Force. The Just War Tradition and the Customary Law of Armed Conflict*, edited by H.M. Hensel, Aldershot: Ashgate, 99–115.

Rengger, N. 2005. The Judgment of War: On the Idea of Legitimate Force in World Politics. *Review of International Studies*, 31 (special issue), 143–61.

Rengger, N. 2008. The Greatest Treason? On the Subtle Temptations of Preventive War. *International Affairs*, 84(5), 949–61.

Rengger, N. and Kenedy-Pipe, C. 2008. The State of War. *International Affairs*, 84(5), 891–901.

Reus-Smit, C. 2005. Liberal Hierarchy and the Licence to Use Force. *Review of International Studies*, 31 (special issue), 71–92.

Russett, B. 1996a. The Fact of Democratic Peace, in *Debating the Democratic Peace*, edited by M.E. Brown, S.M. Lynn-Jones and S.E. Miller. Cambridge: MIT Press, 58–81.

Russett, B. 1996b. Why Democratic Peace? in *Debating the Democratic Peace*, edited by M.E. Brown, S.M. Lynn-Jones and S.E. Miller. Cambridge: MIT Press, 82–115.

Sarkees, M.R. 2000. The Correlates of War Data on War: An Update to 1997. *Conflict Management and Peace Science*, 18(1), 123–44.

Spiro, D.E. 1996. The Insignificance of the Liberal Peace, in *Debating the Democratic Peace*, edited by M.E. Brown, S.M. Lynn-Jones and S.E. Miller. Cambridge: MIT Press, 202–38.

Väyrynen, R. 2007. The Future of Major and Minor Wars, in *Armed Forces for Tomorrow*, edited by T. Koivula and J. Helminen. Helsinki: Edita Prima Oy, 7–15.

White, M. 2005. *Democracies Do Not Make War on One Another ... or Do They?* [Online]. Available at: http://users.erols.com/mwhite28/demowar.htm [accessed: 23 October 2009].

Williams, M.J. 2008. (In)Security Studies, Reflexive Modernization and the Risk Society. *Cooperation and Conflict*, 43(1), 57–79.

Chapter 3

Actors and Tools in the Post-Westphalian World: The Targeted Sanctions of the European Union[1]

Francesco Giumelli

Introduction

The international system is inhabited by a growing number of actors, and this seems to be the distinguishing character of this post-Westphalian twenty-first century. Since 1648 the treaty of Westphalia and the principle of *cuius regio, eius religio* created the conditions for an international system in which nation-states were the most important actors. The collapse of the Soviet Union inaugurated an order where individuals and non-state entities could become actors and not only mere spectators of international events. Hence, contemporary threats and challenges that undermine global peace and stability do originate also from these newly arrived actors, and the evolution of foreign policy tools seems to confirm this qualitative change of the system. For instance, the evidence of the existence of a post-Westphalian order can be found in the changing practices of international sanctions. Embargoes were common tools adopted in foreign policy and the act of interrupting trade was often used against cities or states to support invasions or to force them into obedience. Nevertheless, this practice came recently to an end as individuals and non-state entities replaced nation-states on the pedestal of targets,[2] marking a radical change in international relations that was possible only under the new conditions created by the new world order.

This chapter aims at presenting the sanctioning policy of the European Union (EU) after the Cold War in order to unveil the functioning mechanisms of the post-Westphalian system. Indeed, the practice of targeted sanctions is a sure determinant of the balance of order and disorder in the international system. On the one hand, targeted sanctions maximize their impact on the responsible for wrongdoings and contribute to placate the causes for disorder. On the other hand, targeted sanctions contrast with the golden rule of border inviolability that holds the system together.

---

1   A previous version of this chapter was presented at the Ninth CISS Millennium Conference in Potsdam, Germany, on June 2009.

2   Conventionally, the actor who imposes sanctions is referred as 'sender', while the one who receives them is referred as 'target'.

Thus, their practice can create the conditions for a redistribution of power that is likely to increase the trend towards disorder rather than order.

The discourse and the practice of targeted sanctioning are mainly determined by human rights and legalistic concerns that pertain mainly to individual rights and responsibilities. In the past, sanctioning Hitler, Pol Pot or Stalin could have taken place only through waging a war against the countries they ruled, but today the international community has at its disposal a new tool that can yield a formidable power if properly used. The EU has widely adopted targeted measures to deal with a variety of contexts including the fight against international terrorism and the proliferation of nuclear weapons, but also to manage crises and to promote human rights. The more than 20 cases of EU sanctions analyzed in this chapter help to reveal eventual interaction dynamics among actors of this post-Westphalian system.

This chapter is divided in four parts. The first section focuses on the evolution of sanctions practices from comprehensive to targeted. The second part presents the sanctioning policy of the EU by describing its legal aspects and its mechanisms. The third part describes EU restrictive measures according to types, frequency and context of adoption. Finally, the last part summarizes the problem of the chapter and advances a few recommendations on how to improve the sanctioning policy of the EU.

The Evolution of Sanctions: From Comprehensive to Smart

For centuries, the immutability of the international system provided a common ground to understand and analyze international sanctions so that both the siege against Masada in 73 AD and the UN's comprehensive embargo on Iraq in the 1990s could have been analyzed in a similar way. However, the practice of sanctions has changed radically in the past decade with the emergence of 'smart sanctions' to a point where the UN embargo on South Africa of the 1970s is not comparable with the UN sanctions on Iran in 2009 (Cortright and Lopez 2002). Indeed, sanctions were aimed at harming entire states, whereas today the main targets are individuals and non-state entities. This shift was caused by the poor performance of sanctions, by their high humanitarian costs, and by a normative change occurred in the international system.

The effectiveness of sanctions measured by their capacity to change the behaviour of targets was heavily under question in the 1980s and early 1990s. Since the publication of Galtung's work on Rhodesia (1967), there seems to be a wide consensus in arguing that sanctions were not decisive in coercing targeted governments to comply with the demands of senders. This belief was only partly questioned by David Baldwin (1985), who maintained that sanctioning would be an effective tool under the proper circumstances, and by a study published by the International Economic Institute (Hufbauer, Schott and Elliott 1990 and 2007), which sustained that the success's rate for sanctions, above 30 per cent, was much higher than previously thought. However, it was acknowledged that sanctions impose costs on senders as well as on targets, therefore the utility of sanctions was diminished by the principle that the higher is the burden on targets, the more expensive would be for senders to impose certain measures. This proportionality would, *de facto*, annul the marginal value of sanctions compared to the adoption of other foreign policy tools (Wagner 1988).

Not only was the scepticism over the utility of sanctions very strong, but also their imposition had tremendous humanitarian consequences that reduced further their effectiveness. Sanctions practices needed to be changed because they were linked to humanitarian disasters in the early 1990s, above all in Iraq and Haiti (Walker 1995, Mueller and Mueller 1999, Cortright and Lopez 2002). In a 1995 report released by the Red Cross, Peter Walker wrote that sanctions against Iraq, Haiti and Serbia-Montenegro 'have paid only minimal political dividends at a very high price in human terms' (Walker 1995). Sanctions proved to be more harmful to civilians than to the political elites that they often intended to punish, as could be observed in the Iraqi case after a widely reported study accused UN sanctions for the deaths of 500,000 children (Ali and Iqbal 2000, Alnasrawi 2001). The externalities of sanctions have been largely studied and there is little doubt concerning the humanitarian damage that they cause (Clawson 1993, Weiss, Cortright and Lopez 1997, Mueller and Mueller 1999, Naylor 2001). 'Although many people favour economic sanctions as more humane than military force, the preference for nonforcible (economic, diplomatic or cultural) over forcible (military) sanctions often has little to do with humanitarian values. Rather, it is due to the low domestic political cost combined with the low risk of lost credibility in case of failure' (Weiss, Cortright and Lopez 1997: 15). Sanctions were supposed to stop rogue states from violating human rights, but, in fact, they were criticized as being worse than the disease that they wanted to cure (Mueller and Mueller 1999).

The shift from comprehensive to targeted sanctions became possible with the normative change that characterized the international system in the 1990s. First, governments became responsible for their actions abroad in the 'New World Order', as declared by the Economic and Social Council of the United Nations (1997). Accordingly, the signatory states of the International Covenant on Economic, Social and Cultural Rights (1966) were to be held responsible for human rights violations provoked by sanctions in other states (United Nations 1997). The second normative change regards the growing relevance of international responsibility for individuals. This principle was established with the creation of the *ad hoc* Tribunals for the atrocities committed in the Former Yugoslavia and in Rwanda, where individuals were prosecuted for crimes against humanity. Another crucial step was the establishment of the International Criminal Court (ICC), which reinforced the norm that individuals become responsible personally before the international community for their actions, and they are excused neither for their actions as government officials nor by the position that they hold. In other words, individuals and non-state entities entered the international stage.

The evolution from comprehensive to targeted sanctions – restrictive measures that target individuals and entities instead of entire states – shifted the attention from 'how much does a state suffer' to 'who suffers' (Cortright and Lopez 1995, Morgan and Schwebach 1996: 25–52, Kirshner 1997: 32–64). In other words, a microfoundation approach is preferred to a macro one (Morgan and Schwebach 1996: 252).

> A microfoundations approach looks not at economic sanctions in general, but at the differences between various forms of economic statecraft. Instead of considering how those sanctions hurt the target state, this approach emphasizes how groups within the target are affected differentially, and how these consequences change with the form of statecraft chosen. (Kirshner 1997: 33)

The need to make sanctions more effective while reducing their unintended consequences was satisfied with the contemporary possibility of influencing the domestic mechanisms of targeted societies. Individuals and non-state entities became the targets of international sanctions that exerted an influence by restricting their travels, freezing their assets, limiting their access to certain resources or services, and preventing their possibility to buy weapons. The novelty of the matter found the international community unprepared to design and implement such specific measures, therefore the Swiss, the German and the Swedish governments launched three initiatives to cooperate on the improvement of the effectiveness of sanctions in order to make them 'smarter'. The first conference on how to make targeted financial sanctions more effective was held in 1998 and 1999 in Interlaken, Switzerland, and 'The result of the Interlaken process significantly advanced the collective understanding of the promise and feasibility of targeted financial sanctions' (Wallensteen and Staibano 2005: 16). To maximize the utility of the two sessions of the conference, the Swiss government launched a cooperation with the Watson Institute for International Studies at Brown University to develop a manual for practitioner – *Targeted Financial Sanctions* – that was submitted to the Security Council in 2001.[3] Subsequently, a manual with a variety of proposals to improve the effectiveness of financial targeted sanctions was published in 2006 (Biersteker and Eckert 2006) and an updated version is forthcoming.

Interlaken paved the way for other similar events, which took place in Bonn-Berlin and in Stockholm. The former aimed at improving the effectiveness of sanctions tailored against individuals or specific groups and the results of the conference have been published in *Design and Implementation of Arms Embargoes and Travel and Aviation Related Sanctions: Results of the 'Bonn-Berlin Process'*.[4] Finally, the Swedish government funded the Stockholm Process, a large international

---

3   The results of the Interlaken Process are available at: http://www.smartsanctions.ch [accessed: 16 November 2009].

4   The results of the Stockholm Process are available at: http://www.smartsanctions. de [accessed: 16 November 2009].

conference in which the activity was divided in three groups that provided their recommendations about the implementation process of sanctions, about the challenges posed by the legislation of nation states, and about the possibilities for targets to evade sanctions. The results of the meeting were published in *Making Targeted sanctions Effective: Guidelines for the Implementation of UN Policy Options*.[5]

Targeted sanctions are different from comprehensive ones insofar as they aim at imposing coercive pressures on specific individuals and entities through restricting selected products or activities, while minimizing the unintended economic and social consequences for vulnerable populations and innocent bystanders (Cortright and Lopez 2002: 2). The EU built its sanctioning policy mainly within this framework.

The Sanctioning Policy of the EU

The importance of the European Union in the international system is growing and part of the explanation is certainly due to the fact that it has not only frequently used sanctions in the past years, but it has also made crucial decisions in this field that have also influenced the sanctioning policy of the United Nations.

The European Union can impose sanctions by receiving UN Security Council resolutions, by enforcing art. 96 of the Cotonou Agreement (Partnership Agreement 2000) and by autonomous decisions taken under the CFSP umbrella. This article limits the scope of its analysis only to the latter type given their political nature. Since the early 1980s, the EU has decided in favour of autonomous adoption, namely without receiving the input from the UN, of restrictive measures on more than 40 occasions (Kreutz 2005, Jones 2007: 96–135). In reality, the sanctioning practices of the EU could go back in time, as some have traced them to the Treaty of Rome and others to the signing of the 'London Report' in 1981 (Kreutz 2005: 9). The creation of the second pillar in 1992 is taken here as the starting point of the EU sanctioning policy.

International restrictive measures are foreign policy decisions and, therefore, any recourse to this tool has to be approved unanimously by the Council as established by art. 15 of the Treaty Establishing the European Union (TEU). The list of sanctions types that can be imposed by the EU is long,[6] but the most

---

5   The results of the Stockholm Process are available at: http://www.smartsanctions. se [accessed: 16 November 2009].

6   Diplomatic sanctions (expulsion of diplomats, severing of diplomatic ties, suspension of official visits); suspension of cooperation with a third country; boycotts of sport or cultural events; trade sanctions (general or specific trade sanctions, arms embargoes); financial sanctions (freezing of funds or economic resources, prohibition on financial transactions, restrictions on export credits or investment); flight bans; and restrictions on admission.

common ones are financial restrictions, commodity and service boycotts, arms embargoes and travel bans.

The Treaty assigns different roles to different bodies according to the type of measure. Whereas trade and financial sanctions have to be implemented by the EU according to art. 60 (financial restrictions), 301 (economic restrictions), and sometimes 308,[7] of the Treaty establishing the European Community, visa bans and arms embargoes have to be implemented by the adoption of national legislation of state members. In other words, the former are dealt with by the EU, while the latter by member states. Arms embargoes are an exceptional case to art. 301 because of a provision on national security that has been part of the Treaties since 1957.[8] In case of financial or economic restriction, the Commission has to elaborate a Regulation that has to be approved by the Council. If the target is a state, then the Council can pass the Regulation with a qualified majority, but if the target is an individual or an entity, then the Council must approve the Regulation with a unanimous vote and consult with the European Parliament before the vote.[9]

The governance of sanctions that encompasses monitoring, implementation and evaluation of their effectiveness is handled by a plurality of actors in the EU, but there is little coordination that could contribute to the creation of institutional memory.

The policy-making process is quite convoluted and could be considered a case of cross-pillar policy (Stetter 2004). The President or a member of the Council, assisted by the Council Secretariat or by the Commission, can make a proposal regarding the imposition of restrictive measures. The proposal is received by the geographical groups assigned to deal with the target and analyzed also by the Foreign Relations Counsellors Working Group (RELEX) and the Political and Security Committee (PSC). Subsequently, it is the COREPER II that has the responsibility of drafting a common position to be submitted to the Council for the final approval.

The sanctioning policy has received growing attention in recent years, so that three documents were approved by the Council with the aim of improving the mechanisms for deciding to adopt this policy tool and how to implement it. On 8 December 2003, the Council approved the 'Guidelines on Implementation and Evaluation of Restrictive Measures (Sanctions) in the Framework of the EU Common Foreign and Security Policy'. This document, which was updated on December 2005, contains definitions and principles on how to design restrictive measures, important information in regards to the different types of restrictions

---

7   This article was prepared before the entry into force of the Lisbon Treaty, now the articles are 75, 215 and 352. Furthermore, the Council can now pass a Commission regulation imposing sanctions on individuals and non-state entities with qualified majority voting.

8   Art. 57 before, now art. 296 of the TEU.

9   See the Commission's web page on Sanctions available at http://ec.europa.eu/external_relations/cfsp/sanctions/index_en.htm [accessed: 16 November 2009].

that can be imposed and on how to measure their effectiveness (Council of the European Union 2005).

The main principles that inspire the adoption of sanctions are presented in the second relevant key document of the EU restrictive measures' policy. The document, which is named as 'Basic Principles on the Use of Restrictive Measures (Sanctions)', was approved by the Council in June 2004 and it states that the EU should impose sanctions in accordance with the UN, but also autonomously whenever 'necessary ... to fight terrorism and the proliferation of weapons of mass destruction and as a restrictive measure to uphold respect for human rights, democracy, the rule of law and good governance' (Council of the European Union 2004: 2). In any case, the document called for the use of targeted sanctions with the twofold aim of minimizing the unintended consequences of comprehensive measures on civilians and maximizing the impact on those responsible for misconducts.

Finally, the third document is a living text on the implementation of restrictive measures that was passed initially in December 2004. The last version of 'The EU Best Practices for the Effective Implementation of Restrictive Measures' was approved in April 2008 and it contains the relevant information on how to identify the correct designated individuals or entities, and on the administrative modalities for freezing assets and banning products, including the procedure on how to grant exceptions and exemptions to the measures (Council of the European Union 2008).

Indeed, since the EU is a regional actor, its restrictive measures policy is bound by the provisions of international treaties and additional EU legislations. For instance, EU trade bans are imposed in accordance with GATT and WTO provisions, while travel bans are not enforced in case listed individuals have to attend intergovernmental meetings that are held in member states as part of their duties as government officials (Council of the European Union 2005: 6). The sanctioning policy of the EU also considers those international obligations with regard to the individual rights of those who may incur in the consequences of the imposition of sanctions, so the EU is at the forefront of including guarantees and exceptions on these bases as well.

Exemptions are usually considered when restrictive measures are adopted considering the humanitarian needs and international obligations of targeted persons (Council of the European Union 2005: 9). For instance, if a targeted individual is in need for medical assistance in the EU, then the Council can grant an exception and allow a targeted persons' entry in the EU (in the case of a travel ban) as has happened when Germany allowed the entry of Zakirjon Almatov, the Uzbek interior minister into its borders (Uzbekistan Surprised by EU Move to Extend Sanction 2006). Another exception was the granting of visas to banned Transnistrian officials in order to attend meetings in Europe, notably at the OSCE headquarters in Vienna, during the conflict negotiation process with Moldova.

Each exception has to be assessed on a case-by-case basis and the competent authorities are requested to do so in accordance with the overall spirit of the restrictive measure. The guidelines underline that if 'there are grounds to grant an exemption from one restrictive measure (e.g. financial restrictions) this does not by default justify granting an exemption from another measure (e.g. restrictions on admission) which affects the person or entity concerned' (Council of the European Union 2005: 9).

The 'Best Practices' specifies another instance when exemptions can be granted, namely the legal obligation of targeted individuals or entities to satisfy creditors. Under request either by the target or by interested parties, the competent authorities can provide access to frozen funds, but there must be a legal obligation that links the creditor with the targeted individual or entity, an evaluation of the existence of any risk of circumvention (e.g. if creditors' links with the designated person or entity are such as to raise suspicions), and a verification that the request was not presented in multiple countries (Council of the European Union 2008: 22).

Despite the fact that both exemptions and exceptions limited evident violations of rights, many European citizens felt they had been abused as their assets were frozen or their travels prohibited arbitrarily, thus challenging these decisions in the EU courts. Initially, since the Court of First Instance tended to deny all the requests by claiming its lack of competence or authority, the EU did not intensify the effort to modify and establish clear procedures to uphold human rights such as the ones related to due process and effective remedy. However, this trend has changed and the Courts have posed fundamental challenges to the contemporary practice of targeted sanctions.

The most well-known case is the Kadi and Al Barakaat decision of the Court of Justice that was delivered in September 2008. Yassin Abdullah Kadi from Saudi Arabia and the Al Barakaat foundation, located in Sweden, were included in the UN counter-terrorist lists and, therefore, their financial assets were frozen. Kadi and Al Barakaat appealed against the EU regulation that implemented the Resolution of the Security Council by claiming their right to property and right to defence. After the case was rejected by the Court of First Instance on the base of the inappropriateness since the court was not empowered to question matters of *jus cogens* (i.e. UN Security Council Resolutions), the Court of Justice upheld the appeal and annulled the regulation that froze the assets of the applicant on the basis of patent violation of the rights of the defence and the right to be heard, including the right to have access to the motivation of the listing. Thus, the European Court of Justice (ECJ) decided that the assets of Kadi and Al Barakaat were to be unfrozen within three months had the Council not acted to solve the procedural irregularities (Kadi and Al Barakaat vs Council 2008). As of today, the names of Kadi and Al Barakaat are still on the list and they have brought their case before the Court of First Instance (ECFI) again, but the crucial aspect of this case law is that the ECJ established the principle that even the resolutions of the Security Council can be reviewed by European courts in case they contrast with Community law.

A further case of delisting occurred in January 2009, when the Council delisted the People's Mojahedin Organization of Iran (PMOI). This case was slightly different from the previous one as the PMOI appealed because the right to information was violated, but also because the national courts of the proposing state decided to remove PMOI from the terrorists' list. A first ruling of the ECFI annulled the decision of the Council that failed to inform PMOI about the reasons motivating its listing, but the organization remained targeted because the Council was given the opportunity to remedy. Following a decision of the UK government to de-list PMOI, the Council based the motivation to deny delisting on the decision of a French prosecutor to open an investigation against PMOI (PMOI vs. Council 2008). Nevertheless, when the French government failed to provide the classified information to the ECFI, the Council decided to remove the Iranian organization from the list (Runner 2008).

Another delisting Court case involves Jose Maria Sison, founder of the Communist Party of the Philippines (CPP) and its armed wing the New People's Army (NPA), who is also a Dutch citizen. The CPP and NPA were included in the list in 2001, and Sison first appealed against the freezing of his funds in the forms of savings and social benefits in 2005, although in this case the ECFI did not annul the council regulation. Subsequently, Sison appealed against the decision of the European Union to base the listing on previous rulings of Dutch courts that condemned Sison for crimes linked to his political militancy. In fact, the Court rulings were not based on terrorist accusations, and therefore they could not be used by the European Union to justify his listing on the counter-terrorist list. Thus, the ECFI annulled the Council decisions insofar as they regard Sison (Sison vs Council 2009).

These decisions combined with the growing concern of further legal problems have created a tension between the need to improve sanctioning practices so as to avoid legal challenges and the discomfort created by the use of a foreign policy tool of doubtful efficacy and complex implementation. On the one hand, the EU has responded to the judgements of the Courts in a proactive way. For instance, the rights to be heard and the right of proper communications have been granted to those applicants who felt these rights were denied to them. Furthermore, the sole right to appeal against Council's decisions at the Court of First Instance and the European Court of Justice in Luxembourg is a fundamental step that was taken in order to guarantee the possibility to an effective remedy and to be delisted in case of wrongful listing. Nevertheless, on the other hand, the EU has shown a certain degree of reluctance to impose restrictive measures presumably to minimize the complexities linked to the imposition of targeted sanctions.

The Objectives in Theory: Why Does the EU Impose Sanctions?

As decisions taken under the CFSP umbrella, EU restrictive measures are adopted with the intent to achieve the objectives set by Art. 11 of the Treaty:

- to safeguard the common values, fundamental interests, independence and integrity of the Union in conformity with the principles of the United Nations Charter;
- to strengthen the security of the Union in all ways; to preserve peace and strengthen international security, in accordance with the principles of the United Nations Charter and the Helsinki Final Act, and the objectives of the Paris Charter, including those on external borders;
- to promote international cooperation;
- to develop and consolidate democracy and the rule of law and respect for human rights and fundamental freedoms.[10]

According to the Basic Principles, EU restrictive measures should be adopted in support of efforts to fight terrorism and the proliferation of weapons of mass destruction, to uphold respect for human rights, democracy, the rule of law and good governance (European Union 2004) and that they 'do not have an economic motivation' (Council of the European Union 2005: 4).

The 'Guidelines' deal more in depth with the objectives of the restrictive measures and states that 'In general terms, restrictive measures are imposed by the EU to bring about a change in policy or activity by the target country, part of country, government, entities or individuals, in line with the objectives set out in the Common Position' (Council of the European Union 2005: 4). However, a more appropriate analytical investigation would not limit the scope of sanctions to the sole behavioural change of targets, but it should assume that restrictive measures can, at least, serve three different purposes as coercing, constraining and signalling targets.

Coercive sanctions are imposed with the objective of making a target's behavioural change more likely by imposing a bearable cost on a certain course of action *vis-à-vis* another. Constraining sanctions aim at limiting the capabilities of a target in order to prevent him from achieving his goals or, in other words, it intends to make the life of targets 'more difficult'. Finally, signalling sanctions are designed to send messages to audiences, whether domestic or international, that can span from strong condemnation, to support or simply to symbolic consideration.[11]

The three purposes have a mainly analytical value and in the real world the same case of restrictive measures can play the three functions with a different intensity and in different moments. Nevertheless, this categorization emphasizes the differences across cases of the restrictive measures of the EU from which designing and implementation could greatly benefit.

---

10   The *Consolidated Versions of the Treaty on European Union and of the Treaty Establishing the European Community* is available at: http://eur-lex.europa.eu/LexUriServ/ LexUriServ.do?uri=OJ:C:2006:321E:0001:0331:EN:pdf.

11   Please note that signalling sanctions can also change the behaviour of the target, but the causal link is not based on the material loss undergone by the target.

An Empirical View: Where, When and Why the EU Adopts Restrictive Measures

The EU has decided to impose autonomous restrictive measures on 22 different occasions since the end of the Cold War. With regard to the geographical location of targets, the EU has resorted to restrictive measures in four different continents: North America, Europe, Asia and Africa. As illustrated by Figure 3.1, Latin America is the only geographical area that was not sanctioned by the EU under art. 15 of the Treaty.

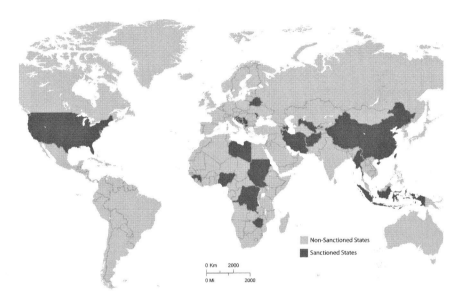

Figure 3.1   EU sanctions around the world

The importance of the European Union as an international actor has grown substantially in the past decade and the development of a sanctioning policy is one of the elements that have contributed to it (de Vries and Hazelzet 2005). Following a similar trend to the one experienced by the UN in the 1990s (Cortright and Lopez 2000), the frequency of sanctions has increased constantly over time since the end of the Cold War. As presented in Figure 3.2, the number of sanctions has varied from two cases in 1989 to 12 in 2009.

'Sanctions *a la carte*' could be a catchy label to describe how the EU has adopted different types of restrictive measures through a multiplicity of crises. Since the end of the Cold War, the Council has decided autonomously to impose 14 arms embargoes, 10 asset freezes, seven commodity and service boycotts, and 14 travel bans. However, the figures on ongoing regimes limit the strength of this finding as they show a more balanced picture with the EU currently handling six

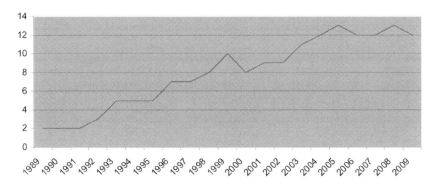

Figure 3.2   Frequency of EU restrictive measures – 1989/2009

arms embargoes, seven asset freezes, six commodity and service boycotts, and eight travel bans as summarized in the Table 3.1.

The evidence above leads to a further generalization on the EU sanctioning policy as the Council seems to prefer arms embargoes and travel bans to asset freezes and commodity and service boycotts. This could be related to the fact that arms embargoes and travel bans look 'softer' compared to the others, an affirmation that has further emerged in one interview with EU officials. Accordingly, the EU seemed to be inclined to use the freezing of assets and commodity boycotts only in extreme conditions or in presence of serious violations of international obligations.[12]

Finally, a relevant aspect is related to the triggering cause for the implementation of sanctions. In the timeframe considered, the EU has adopted restrictive measures in cases of human rights promotion, crisis management, the fight against terrorism and non-proliferation. Overall, the most frequent imposition of restrictive measures happened as a response to human rights violations or attempts to undermine democratization processes, which would further confirm that the EU behaves as a normative power using normative means (targeted measures to minimize the humanitarian consequences) with normative ends (promote democracy and human rights).

Crisis management is the second most frequent context in which the EU decided to use sanctions, and it should be underlined that this category includes the compensatory measures imposed on the US and Libya to protect European companies from the possible consequences of the Helms-Burton act and UN Security Council Resolution 883. The following table offers the details for both concluded and ongoing EU restrictive measures.

The current situation confirms the trend of the past 17 years since the EU handles five sanctions regimes for human rights protection, five to manage crises,

12   Interview with EU official, April 2008.

Table 3.1   EU restrictive measures by type

	Arms embargo	Freezing of funds	Comm. or serv. boyc.	Travel ban
ONGOING				
Belarus		X		X
US			X	
Libya			X	
Moldova				X
Zimbabwe	X	X	X	X
Iran	X	X	X	X
Ex-Yugoslavia		X		X
Macedonia		X		X
Terrorist list	X	X	X	X
Burma/Myanmar	X	X	X	X
China	X			
Uzbekistan	X			
TOTAL	6	7	6	8
CONCLUDED				
Belarus				X
Indonesia	X		X	
Comoros		X		X
Afghanistan	X	X		X
Azerbaijan	X			
DRC	X	X		X
Nigeria	X			X
Sudan (1)	X			
Sudan (2)	X			
Libya	X			X
CONCL.	8	3	1	6
TOTAL	14	10	7	14

and only two to counter terrorism and the proliferation of nuclear weapons. While the aggregate data can offer the general overview on the EU sanctioning policy, a narrative description of ongoing and recently concluded sanctions' cases – classified according to the tripartite typology of coercing, constraining and signalling illustrated above[13] – help to clarify further the rationale of EU restrictive measures.

---

13   For an extensive explanation of this typology, see Giumelli 2009a, 175–80.

Table 3.2   EU restrictive measures by crisis

	Human rights	Crisis management	Non-proliferation	Terrorism
ONGOING				
Belarus	X			
US		X		
Libya		X		
Moldova		X		
Zimbabwe	X			
Iran			X	
Ex-Yugoslavia		X		
Macedonia		X		
Terrorist list				X
Burma/ Myanmar	X			
China	X			
Uzbekistan	X			
TOTAL	5	5	1	1
CONCLUDED				
Indonesia		X		
Comoros	X			
Afghanistan				X
Azerbaijan		X		
DRC	X			
Nigeria	X			
Sudan (1)				X
Sudan (2)	X			
Libya				X
CONCLUDED	4	2	0	3
TOTAL	9	7	1	4

Coercing Belarus

The European Union and Belarus had multiple disagreements since Lukashenka's rise to power. Sanctions have been imposed in 1996 and 1998, but it is only from 2004 that the restrictive measures took a coercive form. Initially, Lukashenka paid little attention to EU concerns regarding his human rights records because of the perspective of forming a political union with Russia, which was launched in 1993 when the Belarusian Prime Minister Vyacheslav Kebich and the Russian Prime

Minister Viktor Chernomyrdin established a monetary union between the two countries (Ambrosio 2006: 413).

The unconditional support from Russia, which had shouldered the cost of sustaining the Belarusian economy through the granting of special oil and gas subsidies, allowed Lukashenka to stand firm before EU measures and, most importantly, to avoid their costs altogether. Lukashenka was able to consolidate his power by nurturing the collective memory of the Soviet past especially through important sectors of the population by resorting to effective propaganda and through the administrative apparatus (Jarabik and Silitski 2008: 28). The human rights record of Lukashenka's regime was not an issue in the country's relationship with Moscow, thus allowing for violations to continue. After a visa-related problem in 2002, the crisis escalated in 2004 when Lukashenka's victory in rigged elections led the EU to impose new restrictive measures on the country's leadership. Such measures were also linked to the lack of investigation on the disappearance of four people in 1999 and 2000 for which the Pourgourides Report blamed government authorities (Council of Europe 2004).

On 24 September 2004, the Council imposed a travel ban on the four people indicated by the Report as responsible for not carrying out the investigation together with Common Position 661. On 13 December of the same year, additional names were added to the list. On 18 May 2006, the assets and economic resources of those banned from entering the Union were frozen. The freeing of three political prisoners and the critical positioning against Russia during the post-war crisis with Georgia led the EU to suspend the travel ban on 'certain leading figures with the exception of those involved in the disappearances' of 1999/2000 'and of the President of the Central Electoral Commission' with Common Position 844 in November 2008. This position was confirmed by Common Position 314 on April 2009, which suspended the travel ban for further nine months 'with a view to encouraging dialogue with the Belarusian authorities and the adoption of measures to strengthen democracy and respect for human rights' (Jarabik and Silitski 2008: 110–17, European Commission 2006).

Coercing the US and Libya

EU restrictive measures against the US and Libya do not resemble the other cases that have been presented, but they meet all the requirements to be included in this analysis since they were approved by the Council under art. 15 of the TEU. In both cases, the measures compensate for previous decisions and aim at discouraging or annulling the effects of possible actions against European companies.

In 1996, the US approved the Cuban Liberty and Democratic Solidarity Act (known as Helms-Burton Act) that intended to strengthen the sanctions regime on Cuba by authorizing the US government to punish companies located around the world that were trading with Cuba. According to the WTO, the extra-territorial application of this law violated the norms of international trade. The EU claimed that this law could have damaged its companies and passed Joint Action 668 of 22 November 1996, to protect EU companies that were damaged by US regulations. An agreement was reached in early 1997 between the EU and the US (Roy 1997), but the measure remains in force as indicated in Council Regulation 807 of 14 April 2003.

The case of the EU in Libya follows a similar logic, as the EU had an autonomous position towards Libya after the Lockerbie incident in 1998. Since 1986, Libya became a target of the international community for its support to international terrorism. In the early 1990s, when the regime in Tripoli was accused of sheltering the two responsible for the Lockerbie bombing, the United Nations imposed a wide set of restrictions with Resolution 883, and therefore by the EU as well. In 1998, when a deal between Libya, the US and the UK was struck, the UN suspended its sanctions, which were lifted in 2003. However, the EU decided to lift the measures implemented with UNSCR 883 (with the exception of paragraph 8), but also maintained certain measures that were imposed by 'Member States on 27 January and 14 April 1986' as an arms embargo and a travel ban as indicated by art. 2 of Common Position 261 of 16 April 1999.

In 2004, as a confirmation of the improved relations between Libya and the EU, the Member States lifted the 1986 sanctions, but decided to protect 'economic operators against claims affected by measures taken in accordance with UN Security Council Resolution 883 (1993)' with Common Position 698 of 14 October 2004 as indicated by paragraph 8 of UNSCR 883, which states that all states shall take the necessary measures to prevent any claims related to the losses determined by the resolution. The measure is still in force and, even in this case, it is tailored to companies and non-state actors.

Constraining Zimbabwe

The European Union began its sanctioning regime on Zimbabwe in 2002, when President Mugabe, in power since 1980, took advantage of the country's volatile land reform situation in order to eliminate his political opponents and strengthen his hold on power (Eriksson 2007: 7–8).

The crisis in Zimbabwe is linked to its colonial past, when the white ruling minority took over most of the fertile lands of the country, generating strong resentment among the majority of the population. Taking advantage of these deep social cleavages, Robert Mugabe rose to power defending a political platform that included the promise of land redistribution. However, the process of re-equilibration has proceeded very slowly (Neil 2003).

In 2000, a referendum was held to amend the constitution in order to simplify the acquisition of land by Zimbabweans, but the negative outcome triggered the anger of war veterans who forcefully occupied farms. Mugabe was accused of backing the turmoil and although the Supreme Court ruled against the occupants, he confirmed his sympathy towards the veterans. The unstable situation continued until elections in 2002, for which Mugabe justified his violent methods to secure his victory, also by harassing the political opposition of the Movement for Democratic Change (MDC) led by Morgan Tsvangirai (International Crisis Group 2002: 2–5).

Immediately before the elections, the EU decided to suspend its Partnership Agreement talks and to threaten Zimbabwe with sanctions had the conditions not changed and had Mugabe prevented the entry of electoral observers and free media. After the elections, the Council passed Common Position 145 followed by a prohibition on the supply of arms and technical assistance or training and the supply of equipment that might be used for internal repression. It also imposed a travel ban and a freezing of funds on 20 people who bore responsibility for serious violations of human rights in the county. Subsequent Common Positions better defined the measures and raised the number of listed individuals up to 131 in June 2007. After tightening the travel ban in July 2008 with Common Position 632, the list of targets, both individuals and entities, went up to 243 with Common Position 68 of 26 January 2009 (Graham 2006: 114; MacFarquhar 2008).

Constraining Transnistria

The Transnistrian conflict in Moldova is geographically the closest secessionist case to the EU. After the collapse of the Soviet Union, Moldova declared independence in 1991 and a conflict erupted in the east part of the country causing 1500 casualties. Transnistria broke away from Moldova because of its desire to remain part of the Soviet Block. The conflict was suspended thanks to the intervention of the Russian army and it has been frozen since 1992. The security zone created between Moldova and Transnistria is ruled by the Joint Control Command, while the OSCE has participated in the creation of the 3+2 (now 5+2) mechanism that aims at solving the conflict.

The conflict has remained silent for a few years, but in recent years Brussels has increased its level of attention on the conflict since EU enlargement stretched all the way to the Moldovan border. The EU imposed a travel ban on 17 leaders of Transnistria for the first time on 23 February 2003, due to their 'lack of cooperation to promote a political settlement of the conflict'. The stated objective of the European Union was to support its 'more active involvement in the political process' and to encourage those listed 'to make substantial progress in negotiations on the settlement of Transnistria's political status within Moldova' (Council of the European Union 2003). In 2004, the list was updated by Common Position 179 with additional names that were indicated as responsible for the attempt to close down Latin-script schools in Transnistria

Common Position 160 of 15 February 2008 deserves attention as the Council updated the list by removing six names and adding other six both in regard to the obstruction to the settlement of the conflict and to the intimidation campaign against the Latin-script schools. Among the names of those who were delisted is Evgeny Shevchuk, leader of the political party *Obnovlenie* (Renewal) that is battling to decrease the power of the President. Many have described this as a political move to empower more accommodating forces in Transnistria and to open a breakthrough in the negotiations (Giumelli 2009b).

The most recent Common Position was passed by the Council on 16 February 2009, and it renewed the travel ban on 13 people who are accused of obstructing the settlement of the conflict and on six people who are accused of organizing the intimidation campaign against the Latinscript schools in Transnistria (Council of the European Union 2009).

Signalling Myanmar/Burma

Sanctions on Burma/Myanmar are among the longest case of autonomous restrictive measures imposed by the European Union, given that a variety of measures to promote democracy and protect humans rights have been in force in this Southeast Asian country since 1988.

The crisis began when a military junta – which called itself the State Law and Order Restoration Council (SLORC), later renamed State Peace and Development Council (SPDC) – went into power in order to fill the power vacuum left by General Ne Win who was ousted from power by massive popular demonstrations against the regime and in favour of political and economic reforms. The army took control of the country with the objective of restoring order and created a multiparty system. In 1990, the National League for Democracy (NLD), led by Dan Aung San Suu Kyi, won the elections against the party backed by the junta, which refused to release power with the motivation that the country needed a constitutional reform to function in a plural democracy. Ever since, the military junta has first renamed the country in Union of Myanmar, moved the capital from Yangoon to Rangoon, and ruled by extensive use of violent means and violations of human rights.

The EU followed the events in Burma from the very beginning. After the 1988 Uprising, during which thousands of people lost their lives due to the government repression, the Council halted non-humanitarian aid, imposed an arms embargo and withdrew the military staff from embassies (between 1988 and 1991) (King 1999, Smith 2002). In 1996, the first Common Position was approved by the Council and travel bans were imposed on the leaders of the military junta. The measures have been renewed ever since, and they have also subsequently been strengthened. In 2000, the assets of the members of the military junta were frozen, and in 2004, European banks were banned from lending money to Burma/Myanmar. Beyond these measures, the misconduct of the junta was also sanctioned by denying the Generalized System of Preference through the WTO. The ILO as well has been involved in proving that Burma/Myanmar violated the rights of the workers, which is the first case recorded in which sanctions are imposed also because of workers' rights violations (Pedersen 2008).

After the military junta's harsh repression protests carried out by monks in the autumn of 2007, the European Union has strengthen its sanctions further by banning the imports of logs, timber and gems, and by prohibiting new investment in the country with Common Position 750 of 15 November. In the summer of 2009, travel bans and asset freezes have been extended to the members of the judiciary responsible for the verdict against Daw Aung San Suu Kyi. To date, Commission Regulation 747 of August 2009 lists 539 individuals and 109 entities.

Signalling Uzbekistan

On 13 May 2005, a large crowd gathered in Andijan, the fourth largest city in Uzbekistan located in the eastern part of the country, to manifest their discontent towards the government of Islom Karimov. The events that triggered the rally occurred earlier in the morning, when a group of people assailed a prison in order to free 23 individuals jailed under the accusation of being members of a radical Islamic group. The authoritarian practices that were attributed to the government materialized when the rally was dispersed brutally by the police, an action that caused the deaths of hundreds of people (International Crisis Group 2005, Hill and Jones 2006: 111–12).

On 23 May 2005, the EU condemned 'the excessive, disproportionate and indiscriminate use of force by the Uzbek security forces' and urged the government to carry out a proper investigation of the facts in order to bring those responsible to trial. The government in Tashkent failed to address the UN's request for an international investigation (United Nations 2006), and on November 2005 the Council passed Common Position 792, which imposed an arms embargo on equipment that could have been used for internal repression and a travel ban on the member officials who were both allegedly involved in the act of repression and responsible for not carrying out the investigation. By means of the Common Position adopted, 12 people were included in the list of targets. Originally imposed for 12 months, the restrictive measures were renewed and the list was reduced to eight people in 2007. In April 2008, the Council decided to suspend the travel ban 'with a view to encouraging the Uzbek authorities to take positive steps to improve the human rights situation and taking into account the commitments of the Uzbek authorities' which were lifted in November since 'the Council welcomed the progress achieved in Uzbekistan in the previous year with regard to respect for the rule of law and protection of human rights' with Common Position 734. However, since 'the council [remains] concerned about the situation of human rights in a number of subject areas in Uzbekistan' the arms embargo has been renewed until November 2009 (Council of the European Union 2008, Human Rights Watch 2006).

Conclusions

Together with states and international organizations, individuals participate actively in events as both causes of order and disorder in the twenty-first century's complex international system. The development of targeted sanctioning is caused by this trend since they concentrate their effects on those responsible for wrongdoings and minimize their adverse impacts on innocent civilians. Either way, the effects on individuals and non-state entities determine the design, implementation and monitoring of targeted sanctions.

The analysis of the EU practice as an international sanctioner confirms these points and highlights its postmodern dimension. The EU seems to have taken up the challenges of this post-Westphalian order through strategies that interpret the changing nature of the international system, taking into account the growing role of individuals and the importance of international law in maintaining stability and promoting justice in the world. All the case studies presented above show the mutated character of the international system as individuals and non-state entities fill the Common Positions of the Council. That is the case of the EU in Moldova or in Uzbekistan, where violators of human rights were personally affected by the decisions taken in Brussels by the 27 governments. It is certainly the case of Pye Phyo Tav Za, son of the Burmese Managing Director of Trading Co. Tav Za, who could raise a legitimate complaint based on his inclusion in the EU sanctions list against Myanmnar/Burma because of his father's support to the military junta. Certainly, his complaint would be legitimate as he was only 18 months old when the 8888 Uprising took place.

An international institutionalization of the practice of targeted sanctions could open a Pandora's Box, unleashing a re-defining force in the international system. Indeed, the transition from the Westphalian system constructed on the centrality of nation-states to a post-Westphalian world characterized by the international actorness of individuals and non-state entities alike could be traumatic. Robert Kaplan's 'The Coming Anarchy' (1994) is a clear warning about some of the possible effects of this transition.

Certainly, the growing role of individuals and non-state entities that made possible the isolation of those responsible for crimes and human rights violations bolstered the expectations of those who believed that targeted sanctions could minimize the humanitarian consequences of comprehensive embargoes and to secure targets deemed as wrongdoers to justice. More order would be the outcome of this process, but the implementations of targeted sanctions poses relevant challenges to the international legal system that could lead to disorder rather than order. Individuals and non-state entities claim international rights that could be claimed in liberal democratic systems basing their demands also on international treaties. Furthermore, since a proper implementation of targeted sanctions requires higher skills and competence, disorder would be also bolstered by the burden imposed on targets as the deterrent effect would disappear when there is no consequence to certain misconducts.

Nevertheless, a balanced integration of targeted sanctions with the current state-centred practices could be an effective tool to contribute to international order. The EU represents a successful story in this regard as it was able to combine the need to meet the new challenges of the twenty-first century with the necessity to guarantee and preserve a series of rights that characterized the previous century.

The EU policy on restrictive measure represents an important instrument to dealing with current foreign policy issues that, however, presents pitfalls that should be avoided in order to maximize the benefits from the adoption of targeted measures. First, better coordination among the actors responsible for implementing, monitoring and enforcing the measures is needed. Today, the states are responsible for implementing and enforcing directly arms embargoes and travel bans, but there is no knowledge on visa denials or arms transfers towards targeted entities. National reports on the status of sanctions regimes should be adopted and shared with the delegations of Member States in Brussels and with EU institutions in order to facilitate the comprehension of what can be achieved and how certain mechanisms can be improved. A similar reasoning can be used for financial and economic measures.

Second, restrictive measures should have a dedicated Unit at the Council to allow for better coordination and the creation of an institutional memory. Today, a long list of actors contributes – COREPER, geographical group, national ministries, etc. – to the implementation and monitoring of restrictive measures, but only the Commission has a dedicated Unit on sanctions – Unit A2 of Crisis Response and Peace Building in the DG External Relations – while the Council relies only on a specific formation of the RELEX Group that is not sufficient to gather all the information needed to produce a coherent sanctioning strategy. The Treaty of Lisbon could contribute to the resolution of this problem, but a solid political will is necessary to accomplish this objective.

The application of analytical tools such as the tripartite taxonomy of purpose influences the design, implementation and monitoring of restrictive measures. First, the demands have to be properly designed in order to allow compliance from the target's side for coercive types of sanctions. Demands have to be clear and unambiguous. While ambiguity is a potent element in diplomacy, the effectiveness of coercive sanctions would benefit from providing targets with a checklist of what is allowed, what is forbidden and what is expected. Furthermore, it is clear that a material impact has to follow the imposition of constraining sanctions that aim at undermining the existence of a policy or of a target itself, therefore only measures that can be implemented should be adopted. Pre-assessment analysis could limit this problem and prevent the empty imposition of a sanction that aims at limiting a target's policy. Finally, ambiguity and vagueness in the demands should be the principles to follow allowing for multiple exit strategies from situations wherein senders can play a marginal role, run the risk of being pulled by the warring parties or, realistically, not be interested *per se*.

For instance, targets such as President Mugabe, the leadership of Transnistria, Osama Bin Laden or the USA will react in profoundly different manners to European sanctions. Indeed, it can be assumed that the sensitivity to costs of the American president would be lower than that of members of radical terrorist organizations, therefore the criteria for success and for understanding the adoption of sanctions must be drawn accordingly. Whereas expecting a behavioural change in the case of the EU sanctions on the USA would be a well-grounded hope, the objective of imposing sanctions on terrorist organizations should be either to prevent or, more realistically, to decrease the likelihood of any further attacks against civilians.

The EU has devoted increasing attention to targeted sanctions as a foreign policy tool that was vested with the expectations of punishing the bad guys without harming the innocent. Unfortunately, the adoption of this tool presents not only opportunities, but also challenges that might undermine the legitimacy of targeted sanctions in their entirety. Overall, targeted sanctions are not a universal remedy for the shadows cast by the new challenges of the twenty-first century, but they could offer a greater lever to policy makers in dealing with the new security complexities in the coming decade.

Bibliography

Ali, Mohamed M., and Shah H. Iqbal. 2000. Sanctions and Childhood Mortality in Iraq. *Lancet*, 27 May, 1851–7.

Alnasrawi, A. 2001. Iraq: Economic Sanctions and Consequences, 1990–2000. *Third World Quarterly* 2, 205–18.

Ambrosio, T. 2006. The Political Success of Russia-Belarus Relations: Insulating Minsk from a Color Revolution. *Demokratizatsiya: The Journal of Post-Soviet Democratization* 14(3), 407–34.

Baldwin, D.A. 1985. *Economic Statecraft*. Princeton, NJ: Princeton University Press.

Biersteker, T.J. and Eckert S.E. 2006. *Strengthening Targeted Sanctions through Fair and Clear Procedures*. Providence, RI: Watson Institute for International Studies.

Clawson, P. 1993. *How has Saddam Hussein Survived? Economic Sanctions, 1990–1993*. Washington, DC: Institute for National Strategic Studies, National Defense University.

Cortright, D. and Lopez G.A. 1995. *Economic Sanctions: Panacea or Peacebuilding in a Post-Cold War World?* Boulder, CO: Westview Press.

———. 2000. *The Sanctions Decade: Assessing UN Strategies in the 1990s*. Boulder, CO: Lynne Reiner Publishers.

———. 2002. *Smart Sanctions: Targeting Economic Statecraft*. Lanham, MD: Rowman and Littlefield Publishers.

Council of Europe: Parliamentary Assembly. 2004. *Disappeared Persons in Belarus, Report by the Committee on Legal Affairs and Human Rights, Rapporteur: Mr Christos Pourgourides, Cyprus, Group of the European*

People's Party, 4 February. Doc. 10062, available at: http://www.unhcr.org/refworld/docid/4162a4654.html [accessed 16 November 2009].

Council of the European Union, European Union. 2003. *Council Common Position 2003/139/CFSP of 27 February 2003 concerning Restrictive Measures against the Leadership of the Transnistrian Region of the Moldovan Republic*, 2003/139/CFSP.

———. 2004. Basic Principles on the Use of Restrictive Measures (Sanctions). 10198/1/04. Brussels.

———, European Union. 2005. Guidelines on Implementation and Evaluation of Restrictive Measures (sanctions) in the Framework of the EU Common Foreign and Security Policy. 15114/05. Brussels.

———. 2008. Update of the EU Best Practices for the Effective Implementation of Restrictive Measures. 8666/1/08. Brussels.

———. 2009. Council Common Position 2009/139/CFSP of 16 February 2009 Renewing Restrictive Measures against the Leadership of the Transnistrian Region of the Republic of Moldova, 2009/139/CFSP.

———. 2006. What the European Union Could Bring to Belarus. [Online]. Available at: http://ec.europa.eu/external_relations/belarus/intro/non_paper_1106.pdf [accessed: 16 November 2009].

de Vries, A.W. and Hazelzet, H. 2005. The EU as a New Actor on the Sanctions Scene, in *International Sanctions: Between Words and Wars in The Global System*, edited by P. Wallensteen and C. Staibano. London, New York, NY: Frank Cass, 95–107.

Eriksson, M. 2007. *Targeting Zimbabwe's Leadership*. Department of Peace and Conflict Research, Uppsala University.

Galtung, J. 1967. On the Effects of International Economic Sanctions: With Examples from the Case of Rhodesia. *World Politics* 19(3), 378–416.

Giumelli, F. 2009a. Coercing, Signaling: Explaining UN and EU Sanctions After the Cold War. PhD Dissertation. University of Florence.

Giumelli, F. 2009b. Measuring the Success of Sanctions. The Case of the EU in Moldova. Paper to the Annual Meeting of the American Political Science Association: Politics in Motion: Change and Complexity in the Contemporary Era, Toronto, 3–6 September.

Graham, V. 2006. How Firm the Handshake? South Africa's Use of Quiet Diplomacy in Zimbabwe from 1999 to 2006. *African Security Review* 15(4), 114–27.

Hill, F. and Jones K. 2006. Fear of Democracy of Revolution: The Reaction to Andijon. *The Washington Quarterly* 29(3), 111–25.

Hufbauer, G.C., Schott, J.J. and Elliott, K.A. 1990. *Economic Sanctions Reconsidered: History and Current Policy*, 2nd edn. Washington, DC: Institute for International Economics.

———. 2007. *Economic Sanctions Reconsidered: History and Current Policy*, 3rd edn. Washington, DC: Institute for International Economics.

Human Rights Watch. 2006. *The Andijan Trials*. [Online: May]. Available at: http://www.hrw.org/backgrounder/eca/uzbekistan0506/3.htm#_Toc134868086 [accessed: 16 November 2009].

International Crisis Group. 2002. *Zimbabwe at the Crossroads: Transition or Conflict?* [Online: 22 March]. Available at: http://www.crisisgroup.org/home/index.cfm?l=1andid=1481 [accessed: 16 November 2009].

————. 2005. *Uzbekistan: The Andijon Uprising*. [Online: 25 May]. Available at: http://www.crisisgroup.org/home/index.cfm?id=3469 [accessed: 16 November 2009].

Jarabik, B. and Silitski, V. 2008. Belarus, in *Is the European Union Supporting Democracy in its Neighbourhood?* edited by R. Youngs. Madrid: Fride, 101–20.

Jones, S.G. 2007. *The Rise of European Security Cooperation*. Cambridge: Cambridge University Press.

Kadi and Al Barakaat vs Council. [2008]. Joined Cases C-402/05 and C-415/05 P. *Court of Justice*. 3 September.

Kaplan, R. 1994. The Coming Anarchy. *Atlantic Monthly* 273(2), 44–76.

King, T. 1999. Human Rights in European Foreign Policy: Success or Failure for Post-modern Diplomacy? *European Journal of International Law* 2, 313–37.

Kirshner, J. 1997. The Microfoundations of Economic Sanctions. *Security Studies* 6(3), 32–64.

Kreutz, J. 2005. Hard Measures by a Soft Power? Sanctions Policy of the European Union 1981–2004. *Bonn International Center for Conversion*, Paper 45.

MacFarquhar, N. 2008. Two Vetoes Quash UN Sanctions on Zimbabwe. *New York Times*, 12 July.

Morgan, C.T. and Schwebach, V.L. 1996. Economic Sanctions as an Instrument of Foreign Policy: The Role of Domestic Politics. *International Interactions* 36(3), 25–52.

Mueller, J. and Mueller, K. 1999. Sanctions of Mass Destruction. *Foreign Affairs* 78(3), 43–53.

Naylor, T.R. 2001. *Economic Warfare: Sanctions, Embargo Busting and their Human Cost*. Boston, MA: Northeastern University Press.

Neil, T.H. 2003. Land Reform in Zimbabwe. *Third World Quarterly* 24(4), 691–712.

Partnership Agreement ACP-EC. 2000. [Online]. Available at: http://ec.europa.eu/development/icenter/repository/Cotonou_EN_2006_en.pdf [accessed: 16 November 2009].

Pedersen, M. 2008. *Promoting Human Rights in Burma: A Critique of Western Sanctions Policy*. Lanham, MD: Rowman and Littlefield Publishers.

PMOI vs Council. [2008]. Case T-284/08. *The Court of First Instance of the European Communities*, 4 December.

Roy, J. 1997. The Helms-Burton Law: Development, Consequences, and Legacy for Inter-American and European-US relations. *Journal of Interamerican Studies and World Affairs* 39(3), 77–108.

Runner, P. 2008. EU Ministers Drop Iran Group from Terror List. *Euobserver.com*, 26 January.

Sison vs. Council. [2009] Case T-341/07. *Court of First Instance of the European Communities* (Seventh Chamber), 30 November.

Smith, M. 2002. Army Politics as a Historical Legacy: The Experience of Burma, in *Political Armies: The Military and Nation Building in the Age of Democracy*, edited by K. Koonings and D. Kruijt. London: Zed Books, 270–96.

Stetter, S. 2004. Cross-pillar Politics: Functional Unity and Institutional Fragmentation of EU Foreign Policies. *Journal of European Public Policy* 11(4), 720–39.

United Nations, Economic and Social Council. 1997. *The Relationship between Economic Sanctions and Respect for Economic, Social and Cultural Rights*. [Online: 12 December] Available at: http://www.unhchr.ch/tbs/doc.nsf/ 0/974080d2db3ec66d802565c5003b2f57?Opendocument [accessed: 16 November 2009].

———. Commission on Human Rights. 2006. *Report of the United Nations High Commissioner for Human Rights and Follow Up to the World Conference on Human Rights. Report of the Mission to Kyrgyzstan by the Office of the United Nations High Commission for Human Rights (OHCHR) Concerning the Events in Andijan, Uzbekistan, 13–14 May 2005*, edited by High Commissioner of Human Rights. E/CN.4/2006/119.

Uzbekistan Surprised by EU Move to Extend Sanction. (2006). *Eurorasianet.org*, 14 November.

Wagner, H.R. 1988. Economic Interdependence, Bargaining Power, and Political Influence. *International Organization* 42(3), 461–83.

Walker, P. 1995. How to Keep Sanctions in Proportion. *Financial Times*, 18 May.

Wallensteen, P. and Staibano, C., 2005. *International Sanctions: Between Words and Wars in the Global System*. London, New York, NY: Frank Cass.

Weiss, T.G., Cortright, D., Lopez, G.A. and Minear, L. 1997. *Political Gain and Civilian Pain. Humanitarian Impact of Economic Sanctions*. Lanham, MD: Rowman and Littlefield Publishers.

Chapter 4

International Order and Global Leadership

Tian Jia-Dong

Introduction: Connectivism – A Way Beyond Realism and Idealism

At this moment in human history and for a long period of time in the foreseeable future, one of the key themes for human society is and will be international order. A revolutionary era has ended; the underlying fundamental interests of major players have settled and a global power structure has been shaped. The mood among the leading actors is a craving for peace and order on their terms. In a global village, international order depends on effective global leadership. Global leadership is called for because there are immanent threats to an orderly 'village' life, or even a potential 'war of all against all'. The goal of global leadership is to establish a global governance system without the Morgenthau sense of world government (Morgenthau 2006: 512–16). The global governance system is supposed to achieve what a national government is charged with but has failed to accomplish: social order, societal stability, individual sense of security, increased trust between people/nation-states, financial prosperity, and sensible and responsible government/global governance system. In the mean time, its function is to prevent the following from happening: widespread government corruption, international and domestic violence, a decline in the social order, civil unrest, a reduced living standard, and lack of trust between people/nation-states as well as global insecurity.

The question that arises is what type of global leadership has such a potential to generate and maintain the desirable international order in a Westphalian nation-state system? The two dominant schools – realism and idealism – in international studies (it would be assumed that constructivism, the English School, as well as neo-liberalism are equally important but less distinctive in theory and less dominant in practice) are not very effective in answering this question. For realism, the focus is on 'national interests' and the power to actualize them. Can a 'leader' build leadership based on its self-constructed national interests and pursue them with power, hard or soft or the combination of the two? Generally speaking, to be a global leader, power is necessary and national interests are inevitable. But in the present, when power and interest structures are roughly set and the space for manoeuvre is limited, power must be exercised in relational and contextual interactions. 'National interests' have become less rigid and intrinsic; they are more relational and contextual and less individualistic. 'Smart power' is a smart notion but is rather an individualistic tactic and therefore has little chance of succeeding in this relational and contextual environment.

For idealism, the thoughts are oriented towards universal values and institutional constructions. If it is genuine without intention to use the values and institutions as clubs to beat others into line with one's own interests, its fundamental mentality is rather revolutionary – the leaders in the developed nations try to mobilize the people in the developing nations in a revolutionary fashion to reshape the institutions in those nations. It is true that we have universal values. But we cannot assume that people who share the same values will be automatically connected and mobilized to fight for them. These values are only visible, meaningful, powerful and effective in concrete social relationships – they can only be known not in themselves but in concrete human relations and interactions. It is also true that no international institutions can work without embedding within national connections. The effort to use universal values to upset existing social connections inside nations are too revolutionary for the leaders as well as the people in those nations to accept, despite the fact that they might accept the values *per se*. Therefore, when the values reach the ordinary people inside the nations, they are more likely to be regarded as empty words – especially when the people who do the talking are regarded as self-serving. A working order of any national or international institutions is not so much as the order of itself, but as the order of national connections in which it is embedded. The 'democratic peace' argument is false because both 'democratic institutions' and 'peace' are only possible when a more authentic third factor, the power of the live, energetic and concrete human social connection is present (Dong 2008: 58–9).

The essence here is human togetherness and there are three logics that create and shape human togetherness. The first is the logic of conquest, which is based on planned order backed by superior force; the second is the logic of interdependence, which is a result of exchange between or among acceptable system insiders and safeguarded by international institutions. The third and most fundamental one is the logic of togetherness. It highlights a fact that just as individuals are born into a family and it is basically inescapable, individual nation-states were born into a set structure of international society and no one can escape from it. We cannot selectively attach ourselves to someone we like and intentionally detach ourselves from the ones we don't like. Our freedom is very limited in terms of our social association, despite our claimed sovereignty. The global society is indeed a 'village' and nation-states have to live with a life that has everybody sailing in the same boat on the high seas, that we hold each other 'hostage', that mutuality and connection is a must instead of a choice (Dong 2008: 16–19).

However, just as it is not easy to make selfish individuals come together and stay together, individual nation-states strive for their self-defined interests and values. These interests and values are generally a reflection of their unique national characteristics, specific historical experiences, unstable emotional interactions among the different social groups within the nations, fluctuating and unsustainable power of volitions and unreliable and constantly misperceived rationality. Nation-states' individual drives are therefore often at odds with the logics that enable their own survival and ability to thrive in the human community. They hurt themselves and most of the time without realizing the source of the hurt. Therefore, the task of an effective global leadership is to act upon the three fundamental logics of human togetherness and bring individual nation-states together. This is what effective global leadership has accomplished and is set out to accomplish more.

This chapter attempts to pinpoint a connective type of international leadership and highlights it as an intrinsic part of a meaningful international order at this historical moment. The connective leadership in the international setting can be defined as the follows:

Connective leadership is a power of social change that generates leader-follower relationship between/among nation-states through involving and empowering nation-states to change patterns of interaction between/among them, as well as the patterns of interaction between individual nation-states and the global society in general. It includes, but is not limited to and not same as, power of political change, which means the change of the institutionalized power system; it also includes, but not limited to and not same as, power of economic change, which means the change in the systems of production, exchange, distribution and consumption.

The key concept of connective leadership is empowerment. It is defined as follows:

Empowerment is a process that enables each independent nation-state to do things they would otherwise not be able to do. Power is generally defined as the ability to make others do things they would otherwise not do. It clearly has a negative side in its practice. But empowerment as we define it is an enabling process. It differs from our common understanding about power in the following senses:

a. It is an interactive process instead of an individualistic ability. It is based on a dynamic mutuality among the independent nation-states that involve in the process. Individual ability of each of them is only a part of it because it can become bigger or smaller qualitatively or quantitatively in the process.

b. The enabling process can be hierarchical – some nation-states play more significant role and are more dominating. The hierarchy is a fluid system which is based on both the initial power, hard and soft, and its accumulation in the interactive process.

c. The ideal that connective leadership strives for is inter-national harmony through mutual enabling, instead of individual nation's sovereignty and freedom. The Hobbes sense of 'giving up' some of individual sovereignty would be common. But the individual sovereignty is not handed over to a global government but to a mutually enabling web of social connections.

The driving force behind this mutually enabling web of social connections among nation-states is social capital between/among individual nation-states. In an era of peace and order, social capital is more vital than any other types of capital. Social capital is generally defined as social connections between or among people that have value. Social capital is different from financial capital, which means money; it is different from physical capital, which means materials; it is also different from human capital, which means education, training and skill. Social capital regards social connections as valuable similar to money, materials and skills. And more significantly, unlike money, materials and skill, which can only be possessed as individual assets, social capital is the only valuable asset that can be shared and collectively owned. Interpersonally, social capital indicates and enables the paramount role of social relationship in human life. It ensures that trusting individual's life to social relationships is the only certainty people can get in an otherwise volatile human life. It is the most reliable way for human individuals to survive and thrive in human society; and therefore, it regards social isolation as the most dangerous symptom of deep-rooted social and individual problems (Granovetter 1973, 1985, 1979, 1983, Lin 2001, Burt 1992, Putnam 2000). Internationally, social capital highlights a path that is beyond hard power vs soft power dichotomy. Social connection between or among nation-states is a more authentic description of international order than individualistic power. It can be an independent type of power – the more mutually enabling connections a nation-state builds, the more powerful it is.

The Three Dominant Theories on Global Leadership: A Critical Review

Striving for leadership, global leadership included, is a common pursuit of human collectivities. However, people have different views about how to achieve this purpose. Basically, there are three theories that have been dictating the practice of global leadership in different directions. These three theories are: the individualistic view, the institutional view, and the systemic view.

The Individualistic View

The first one is the individualistic view. This view first formulated by Thucydides (Thucydides 2006), developed by Machiavelli (Machiavelli 1952) and further elaborated by many influential scholars of international relations today.

As Machiavelli mentioned (Machiavelli 1952: Book 18), a leader must be two animals at the same time: a lion and a fox. He needs to possess the lion's strength and power as well as the fox's smarts and ability of manipulation. The contemporary representation of this view does not actually go beyond it too much (Lukes 1974). In the field of international studies, there are the balance of power view (Gilpin 1981, Modelski 1987, Waltz 1979, 2001, Mearsheimer 1994, 2001) and the hard/soft power (or power plus social purpose) approach (Nye 2005, 1990,

Ikenberry 1996, 1989). Both views regard 'power' as an individual possession and it is composed of resources and capabilities (the major difference between these two views is on what constitute resources and capabilities). Therefore, socially in the process of interaction with others, national power is no different from wealth – the more you use it, the less you own it. Based upon examining each nation-state's national power, these two views reached a similar conclusion: the global power structure is balanced at this point. In this global power structure, American hard power in terms of resource mobilization and military might is unparalleled since the Roman empire. And in terms of soft power, it would assume that American culture is unique and the best around the world; American political, cultural and economic systems are the beacon of hope and city upon the hill; American society is the enviable example everybody the world over is trying to emulate. The US therefore has the capacity to be a benevolent hegemonic power. The most recent development is the so-called 'smart power' approach coined by Joseph Nye (Nye 2008) and accepted by the Obama administration. It is clearly reflected in President Obama and Secretary of State Clinton's new foreign policies across the globe. But, still, national power is regarded as an individually possessed 'thing'.

The connectivist approach agrees with this view that individually possessed power does play a significant role in leadership and the US is the most likely global leader at this point in history. However, power cannot be too individualistically perceived and constructed. It can be a fluid process and its effectiveness has the potential to diminish as its individualistic power expansion increased. Imagine a scenario: in an enclosed room there is no window and door is completely locked, a group of people live together with a very smart and strong animal, a combination of fox and lion, smarter and stronger than any individual human. This animal meets all the qualifications set by the individualistic view: strength, capability, possession of resources, smartness, ability of manipulation, behavioural attractiveness, and so forth. But, how is it possible for this animal to be a leader among a group of people? The more likely result would be: under a perceived constant threat of being eaten by this animal, the only and natural way for this group of people to safely survive would be to work collectively to kill this animal. People cannot feel safe without eliminating this kind of power, which is too distinctive, too different, too alien, too threatening, and too disempowering. No matter how strong and how smart this animal is, it cannot resist the collective power of all the people who are in a perceived desperate situation to fight. And no matter how well intentioned this animal is, its very distinctiveness would alienate people and make all the people feel under threat and therefore unite all the people. In a global village in which everyone is tightly tied together with one another, the fate of an individualistic power, no matter how strong, how smart, how benevolent it is, would be same as this fox + lion animal. International leadership is therefore not possible. In fact, the essence of American leadership when it succeeded in the past does not mirror this view.

We usually regard the theoretical school anchored on Thucydides and Machiavelli, as well as many contemporaries, as realism because they are assumed to be talking about reality instead of norms and they are more realistic instead of idealistic. But in fact, what they illustrated as 'reality', as well as what they proposed as a prescription of leadership, is far from reality. It might be better termed as idealist individualism instead of realism. They started with a false assumption about the individualistic nature of human life and completely overlooked an essential reality of human social existence: we are social animals and our very survival depends on how well we socially connect to one another. The very fact that human beings became who we are today in a million year journey towards humanness is a revelation of the power of the human pack, not human individuals. We are pack animals to begin with and we survive and thrive in and through our pack all along. The naturally existing and developed human packs, like family, clan, nation, so on and so forth, are much more fundamental to each individual human being than his/her own strength plus smarts. It is no doubt that there are countless conflicts and struggles within this human pack. But from a long-term historical view, the winners and leaders have been the ones who can best mobilize the 'pack' power, instead of those who are individually strong and smart. It should be clear that we need to add a third animal to Machiavelli's combination of a lion and a fox. This third animal is a wolf (Dong 2008: 114–15).

The Institutional View

The second theory is the institutional view. Unlike the individualistic view, the institutional view does not regard power as an individualistic possession – it does not have to be a zero-sum game. Power can be shared and collectively owned. International institutions are the foundation and vehicle that make this happen. Global leadership thus gains its strength through international institutionalization. The view starts with the discussion of legitimacy and regards it as the essential part of leadership. It therefore introduces the concept 'authority' and uses it as the theoretical foundation to go beyond the discussion of 'power'. The representative of this school of thinking is Max Weber (Weber 1958). He defines authority as 'legitimated power' or 'accepted power'. In the field of international studies, he has a large following (Ruggie 1982, Beetham 1991).

According to Weber, there are three ways for a power to be legitimized as authority – the influential three ideal types of authority: legal, traditional and charismatic. The first two depend completely on institutional constructions as their foundation. Legal or rational authority is based on bureaucratic institutions and traditional authority the institutionalized norms and 'the way things are'. Only the last one, charismatic authority, starts with individual characteristics, the perceived possession of 'divine' power of the leader. But first, this is a very rare case because very few individuals are regarded as 'god' by others – even fewer nation-states can expect others regard them as 'divine' nations. Second, and more importantly, Weber pointed out that this type of authority can only survive by routinizing its practice into either one of the other two types (Weber 1958: 295–6, 299).

In terms of global leadership, the contemporary followers of the institutional view focus on rational/legal constructions of political and economic systems across national borders (so-called 'nation-building'). It also attempts to institutionalize cultural values and norms of some dominating nation-states onto both the global system and the dominated nation-states. The global institutional constructions such as the UN, the World Bank, the IMF, etc., which are also emphasized, thus emerged. The idea is that global order is based on political, economic, and cultural institutions. Global leadership is reflected by an assumption that one, or a few, most powerful nation-state(s) can successfully establish these institutions, in both legal and, hopefully, traditional ways (Young 1991, 1992, Maier 1989, Krasner 1983, Bergsten 1994, Keohane 1984, 1988).

The connectivist approach agrees with the institutional view on the importance of legitimacy and institutionalization. However, its major problem is its inability to see the fundamental significance of the natural order of human society. It therefore has to place its trust too heavily on planned systems. First of all, it pays overwhelming attention to the logic of conquest by focusing on institutional control but overlooked the logic of togetherness. As we all know, there are always gaps and loopholes in legal constructions. Rationality can help set up standards and prescribe scripts for our daily activities. But it cannot cover all the ground in our day-to-day social life. Our cognitive capability is simply not sufficient to understand, foresee and construct the natural and spontaneous human social interactions. We have limited capability to receive and process information; we have limited capability to make sense of others in a natural and spontaneous setting. As has been well documented, human togetherness starts with a natural order (family) and survives in other natural orders (clan, nation, etc.). As Friedrich Hayek pointed out (Hayek 1978), for these natural orders ('kosmos'), people's daily interactions create social connections in which spontaneity and uncertainty are the signature nature. A planned system, government included, cannot achieve much before it reaches its limit in a complicated and interactive system. A global reach of global leadership must be a social reach, which incorporates all the naturally formed and maintained social units. Planned formal institutions, as well as the process of institutionalization, function in only a limited area where rigid rules can be developed and enforced. In an international setting, this precondition is difficult to meet.

Secondly, the institutional theory's over-emphasis on the role of international institutions is also based on the misunderstanding of the logic of interdependence (Dong 2008: 17, 58–9). The successful leadership role-playing of the international institutions depends on the dependability of the actors involved – the performance of the institutional insiders in particular and the actions of all the people involved in general must be measurable and predictable. But a 'nation-building' practice is like a powerful family going to another family and attempting to 'build' it. Can it expect the members of the 'built' family to be dependable? Can it even expect its own behaviour to be predictable and measurable? So how can it 'institutionalize' its 'building' practice which is so uncertain and fluid? In terms of the global leadership played through international institutions and institutionalization, it can succeed only when it can safely exclude the not-so-dependable groups/nation-states. However, the fact is that the logic of interdependence is highly exclusive. It only happens among/between the people who are equals and who can be mutually dependable in an exchange situation. An institution whose success depends on the working of the logic of interdependence must meet this condition.

The Systemic View

The third theory is the systemic view. It portrays global leadership as an organic part, or to be more accurate, an agent, of the global expansion of the capitalist system. Global leadership therefore is rooted in the systematic power of the global capitalist system. This system includes the following: financial capital accumulation through banking and investment activities; material capital monopolization through dominating the top end of the production and the consumption chain; an educational system that trains useful workers ready for the capitalist exploitation; cultural hegemony with dominating capitalist values and norms; and a political system in each nation-state which is controlled by the international and domestic capitalist alliance and disguised under the ideological cover of representative democracy. All the sub-systems function as part of the chain of command of the global capitalist economic system. Karl Marx inaugurated this view (Marx 1978) and Immanuel Wallerstein reframed it and applied it in contemporary international studies (Wallerstein 1979, 1974).

According to this view, no global leadership can achieve positive results without fundamentally changing the capitalist economic system – from profit-oriented production and investment system, to market-oriented models of business operation, to tax and tariff systems through which the states serve the need of the capitalists, to individualistic culture that supports the capitalist system. The only hope is a revolution by the underprivileged nation-states or social groups to set up an entirely new system. They cannot depict a clear picture about this new system. All their designs are based on the faith in the organization of the current underprivileged nation-states/social groups and whatever they would do after they obtain sufficient power on a global scale.

The connectivist approach agrees with this view that there are some fundamental problems in the global capitalist system. Socially speaking, its main problem lies in the fundamental logic it follows: the logic of interdependence is naturally exclusive. Only those who are perceived as 'dependable', as capital providers, as exchange partners, as possessors of useful skills, or as exploitable workers, are included as the system insiders. All the others are excluded. This not only causes a huge gap between the rich and poor, but also generates a huge social gap and cultural gap between the system insiders and outsiders. The resentment rooted in this system among the system outsiders will only grow deeper and more intense. However, this perspective only highlighted the impact of the logic of interdependence and overlooked the logic of togetherness. It also paid attention to the negative side of the logic of conquest and overlooked its positive side. On the one hand, the logic of togetherness ensures the expansion of the capitalist system as a dynamic process. It, after all, has included more and more people into its system through its global expansion. To join and be a part of the system, the underprivileged might be transformed and advanced by the spontaneous and dynamic connections. On the other hand, the global capitalist system has generated many planned and spontaneous social connections that enable mutual empowerment under the logic of togetherness. Even Marx recognized this fact. For everybody affected by this system, including the underprivileged, it is not necessarily a zero-sum game. Global capitalism in general and global corporations in particular can be effective vehicles for social connections and social capital accumulations.

A Connectivist View on Global Leadership

Global leadership fits into the connectivist frame and is therefore prescribed by connectivism as an empowering leader, a superhero who creates heroes. It is therefore described as 'connective leadership'. Connective leadership is based on the connective power dynamics generated by all the three logics of human togetherness but the logic of togetherness is the most fundamental: all of us are in a lifeboat with nowhere to go. We only have limited space to be shared with friends as well as enemies at the same time. Like it or not, we have to stay together for the time being, or even forever. In a situation like this, the best strategy would be to have a long-term view with the possibility of sacrificing immediate interests for a better relationship. A necessary mentality would have to focus on the good and tolerate all the imperfections. The most effective leaders are those who seek to change 'them' and 'us' in a dynamic process and make efforts to construct an inclusive, but hierarchical, system in which its leadership role is reflected by its instrumentality.

In this system, a relational web works as the fundamental structure of world order. The social fabric depends less on planned institutional constructions and more on natural and spontaneous social connection. Relationship is paramount and national interests become a by-product. An individualistic view is not relevant because national interest or national identity are not fixed and predetermined without referring it to the specific relationships constructed by the nation-states involved. Relationship has become more valuable than specific interest. The approach 'my way or the highway' is doomed to be punished by the collective power dynamics. The inescapable connections facilitate a hierarchical system that enables the well connected nation-states to possess stronger power than the less connected ones. To make something happen despite resistance, leadership therefore derives from the quality and quantity of connections. The more connected nation-states are the more dynamic power they obtain to share with others, to empower others, to shape the world order by enabling others to do the things they would not do otherwise.

Cognitively speaking, connective leadership is based on the understanding of relationality and contextuality, in addition to rationality. Rationality is a reflection of a sense of control. It is based on an 'everything-can-be-under-control' mentality. Its assumption is as follows: as long as we can get enough information, our rationality has the capacity to enable us to reach an ideal decision. Therefore, it pushes the leaders to focus on individually rationalizing the situation and try to make themselves smarter as individuals. Relationality, however, is based on the recognition of our vulnerability. It highlights the significance of shared vulnerability and the need of mutual empowerment. It pushes the leaders to gain strength through sharing their weakness with the people they have relationships with. The strategy is to 'make relationships work' instead of 'making myself smarter'. Once the relationship works, the leaders will enable others to do what they otherwise would not be able to do and, in the mean time, the leaders would be enabled to do what they otherwise would not be able to do.

Contextuality, as John Dewey pointed out, highlights the fact that a leader is an aspect of something bigger. S/he is not only relationally one among many, but also an incomplete one (Dong 2008: 34). Without co-existing with others, even powerful leaders are not able to exist at all. Contextuality pushes leaders onto a path of thinking that always orients towards actively constructing and actively responding to the surrounding context. Contrary to a rationalist way of thinking, which assumes that leaders know their needs and want and are capable of fulfilling these needs and wants through cost-benefit calculation, contextual thinking does not assume they know the cost-benefit through rational reasoning. The leaders' very needs and wants are fluid and shaped by the social context. Only by actively responding to others can a leader know and fulfil their needs and wants. If relationality regards other individuals we have relationships with as resources of mutual empowerment, contextuality would regard all those people as the part of ourselves and we are inseparable from them. In the mean time, we are an organic and inseparable part of them and our power, therefore, is based on our function in this organic 'whole' (Dong 2008: 54–7). Specifically, the connective leadership in international settings possesses two fundamental characteristics: instrumentality and inclusiveness.

First, as a power holder with a purpose of constructing an authority system, instrumental/inclusive leadership does not want to impose an institution with a formal authority system onto the led and hopes to use this institutionalized authority to overpower them. A constant mistake a leader makes is to subjectively decide the significance of the different forces in a structure and artificially set up a leadership system upon the led based on an artificial plan. It is common for this practice to easily cause a mismatch between the real powerful social forces in a society and the artificial structure the leader sets up. The leader would end up in depending on the social forces that do not have genuine power and real impact on that society. The institution would be an empty one.

An instrumental/inclusive leadership wants to connect to those led, in a natural and spontaneous way, in order to maximize the involvement of the genuine powers and stretch individual wisdom beyond its ultimate limits through a collective process. Here, weak ties, or social connections, to the naturally formed and pre-existing social units, like family, clan, etc., are the essential mechanism. Therefore, instrumental/inclusive leadership addresses a key issue: 'instrumental' to whom? Who are supposed to be included in the governance system? The answer is: the leadership is instrumental to the forces that have naturally grown into significant positions and therefore to guide and facilitate their positive functioning in the society as a whole.

Second, the instrumental/inclusive leader occupies a strategic position in the structure and plays a key functional role to lead the direction of this structure and to make the structure work. The leader sets out to transform each party's pursuit of individual interests into part of a structure and makes it possible that only through this structure can the led fulfil their interests. Here, the most difficult task for the instrumental/inclusive leadership is not how to lead others, but how to change itself. It has to clearly demonstrate to the led that, to the leader, the relationship between the leader and the led is more critical than the leader's self interests – the leader's individual pursuit of interests has been transformed by the construction of the relationships. For this purpose, the instrumental/inclusive leadership itself regards relationship as paramount and avoids single-mindedly pursuing its pre-fixed interests.

Third, it is difficult to lead forces who have nothing to lose and who don't care about their rationalized interests. If they want to die in order to make your life miserable, your rational construction of interests through relationship will not work. Here, instrumental/inclusive leadership sets up a pure relationship without involving considerations of interests. Social connection is the only effective weapon to lead those emotional, faithful to something else and 'selfless' people. To connect to the network they have connection with and share that connection is the most effective way to guide, influence, transform and lead these people. For the purpose of social connections, the instrumental/inclusive leadership gives up its 'either/or' world view. It cannot see the world as either black or white. Connection is paramount. Moral standards and values, as well as material interests, must serve the purpose of connection. It should be clear that connection can change 'them' more, although 'we' might have to change, too. In a difficult situation like this, sensitivity toward others and transformation of itself in a relational and contextual way is critical for the success of an instrumental/inclusive leadership.

A little easier but no less significant situation also needs an instrumental/inclusive leadership to deal with: there are a lot of nation-states or social groups that are not 'dependable'. Only through 'sailing with everybody' and including all the parties that can exercise some power on the global issues, can the instrumental/inclusive leadership gain access to the possibility of transforming those who are not dependable and push these undependable nation-states to be more dependable in an interdependent system.

The instrument/inclusive leadership practices the 'doing with' instead of 'doing for' strategy: joining closely and doing good are very directly related. The more a nation is involved and included, the more altruistic behaviour it tends to display. Altruistic behaviours are more likely to happen when nations are together. By 'doing with', an instrumental/inclusive leadership has the greatest potential to transform an individual nation's beliefs, its financial capital and its military might for a good purpose.

The empowering function of 'doing with' can be viewed in the following ways. First, it is instructional/educational through enforcing a process of socialization. To individual nation-states, especially to those which cannot smoothly integrate into mainstream global society, the key issue is not providing them freedom under the notion of national sovereignty. Instead, the most important is to empower them to go through a process of socialization to become a qualified member of global society. Even to the well-established global powers, they also need a continuous process of socialization. In a dynamic global village, 'we transform, therefore, we are'. Instrumental/inclusive leadership with its power to generate social connections creates and enforces the most effective ways for nation-states to achieve positive socialization. Ikenberry and Kupchan also mentioned this approach in their article (Ikenberry and Kupchan 1990).

The second empowering function of inclusive 'doing with' is the function of bonding (see the idea of 'bonding' and 'bridging' in Putnam 2000: 22–4). An orderly society depends on naturally developed social binding inside each social group of people. It is essential for any leadership if it can manage to become a part of this natural process, instead of staying in an institutionalized political cocoon above this process. The 'doing with' strategy fosters the ability of the leading nation-states to participate in the binding process of the led and therefore to guide the natural process. Through working inside social groups/nation-states, fostering positive social connections among people in the groups and giving people identity that enables them to properly fit in the groups they belong, the inclusive 'doing with' strategy can be very powerful. This approach was successful for the US, working together with the existing domestic forces inside Germany or Japan to reconstruct their respective after-war social-political-economic systems (Schwartz 1995, 1991, Ward and Yoshikazu 1987).

The third empowering function is bridging. We are more divided than united across the globe. How can a leading nation-state minimize the dividing factors and maximize the uniting ones on the global scene? It has to have power, but individualistic power is far from sufficient. It has to have established institutions to fall back on and to institutionalize new systems, but it cannot cocoon itself inside its own institutional construction. It has to be aware of the 'long-wave' global system currently and, in the foreseeable future, the capitalist system, but cannot be passively driven by its single logic of interdependence – a longer-term view is necessary to include the other logics of human society: the logic of conquest and the logic of togetherness. The connectivist instrumental and inclusive leadership is the only type of leadership that has the potential of 'bridging'. Its connective power enables it to go beyond the common practice prescribed by the other theories and to generate sufficient social capital to bridge the gaps between/among the dividing factors across the globe. The success of the US connective leadership was especially reflected in the period immediately after World War II when the US reshaped the patterns of interaction between and among nation-states, as well as each nation-state's patterns of interaction with the global society (Ruggie 1982, 1991, Auerbach 1993, Bailey 1969: 743–833, Herring 2008: 538–650, Montgomery 1957, Hertz 1982).

Two Dilemmas

As with everything in social life, nothing is perfect; in the process of making things closer to perfection, nothing is simple, easy and straightforward. We always have to deal with all kinds of dilemmas. With all its strengths, connective leadership has the potential to generate at least two dilemmas in the process of its practice.

The first dilemma the connective leadership has to deal with is between global, top-down, hierarchical professionalism and local/national bottom-up grassroots democracy. It might be legitimate to worry about the potential of a hierarchical oligarchy and about ordinary men and women forsaking participation and being reduced to spectatorship and leisure. It is supposed that social capital accumulation and investment is a dynamic process. One-sided efforts would hardly achieve the desired results. The essence is social connection and it must be rooted in mutual accommodation and adjustment. But this scenario is true only if we look at the agency side of the story when nation-states have free choice about whether to engage and how much resource and energy to engage in social connections. However, in reality, nation-states, as well as social groups, have different access to social capital just as they have different access to financial capital or physical capital. It all depends on their structural positions in the global system. The higher their position is, the more opportunities there are for them to accumulate and invest social capital. The structural 'Matthew Effect' is clear there. Even from the agency perspective, the potential for a formation of a hierarchical oligarchy still looms. The reason is simple: the more powerful nation-states are more dynamic and they potentially gain more power in the dynamic process they create and facilitate. If the nation-states on the higher positions, especially the ones at the top, do not initiate the process and lead the way, it would be hard for the process of social connection to begin. In its essence, the connective leadership is a top-down process.

The driving force of social connections is the national elites in the most powerful nation-states and their drive for a global order. The grassroots participation is something out there waiting to be mobilized. It is the elites' job to 'connect' to other 'lesser' nations-states. By connection, these national elites would become global elites or work together with national elites and find ways to penetrate in local/national politics, religion and all other areas of social life. It would be clear that to reach people socially, the elites would penetrate into all different areas like social service, public health, community design, basic education, neighbourhood organization, philanthropy, and all the forms of communal and cultural activities.

They work 'efficiently' as proxies to guide and represent people in where formerly ordinary people participate as actors. Therefore, an ironic disempowering process could happen: ordinary folks' voluntary activities are likely to be shaped by the global elites and they could eventually and gradually diminish grassroots civic engagement and foster oligarchy.

The second dilemma can be boiled down to freedom/equality vs harmony. On the one side is the sovereign nation-state's individual freedom, the equally unconstrained pursuit of self-interests, individual responsibility and efforts. On the other, a harmonious global order with authoritative guarantee for a secure and intimate community. Connective leadership sets out for global community and its goal is to promote community. It wants a global life of intimacy as in a close-knit neighbourhood without being broken up by the growth of an intricate mesh of wider contacts on a global scale. To promote community, connective leadership sets out to transform strangers into social, economic and spiritual community – the process of empowerment is also one of transformation.

It would be assumed that if connective leadership gets its way and achieves what it sets out to achieve, the remarkable purpose of countering the trend of individualistic pursuit of national self-interests and countering institutionally supported freedom and equality among nation-states would be advanced. However, it would have to answer a key question: without individualistic national responsibility and efforts rooted in individual pursuit of self-interests in an established institutional framework, who is responsible for global justice that guarantees equal opportunities for all? If there must be someone on the offering end and others on the receiving end, the people on the receiving end would have to depend on the people on the offering end; the latter would have power over the former and they might be sacrificed in the interests of global harmony. Equality would be an illusion. Once equality is gone, how can the connective leadership make sure a harmonious community is sustainable?

Related to the freedom/equality vs harmony dilemma is the issue between communal 'mutualism', likely to be the aim of connective leadership and individualistic multiculturalism, likely to be insisted on by most individual nation-states. A connective leadership might set out to empower individual cultural entities to pursue a goal they otherwise would be unable to do. However, in the process of reaching out to as many people as possible and involving them and engaging them, how could connective leadership accommodate different and distinctive cultures and ways of life? The dilemma is clear: should connective leadership accept them as what they are or process them and reshape them into a global culture? Should the global culture be a 'melting pot' or a 'salad bowl' or a 'soup basin'? Who needs to change what in the process? Realistically, can mutualism survive in the sandwich between Big-Brother-ist globalism and multiculturalism? How does mutualism itself avoid becoming Big Brother-ism, an overdone communitarianism?

Conclusion

Contrary to the way it is conventionally regarded, global leadership is not only about individual strength or smartness; not only about established institutional positions; not only about systemic locations in a historical 'long wave'. In addition to all the above, it is also about functional positions and strategic locations in global social connections, a web of international and transnational ties. Based on the understanding of the three logics of human togetherness, especially the logic of togetherness, a successful connective leadership should be functional in role playing through inclusive leadership. Its success is also based on its strategic network positioning through instrumental leadership. The essence can be boiled down to one word – empowerment – and to one sentence – be a superhero who creates heroes. There are plenty of examples to highlight the effectiveness of connective leadership throughout the history of US foreign relations. However, the theoretical abstraction and generalization have lagged far behind our historical experience. Scholars have failed in theorizing the successful stories. Without correct theories about the binocular and microscope, practitioners would be guided either by wrong perceptions with wrong vision, or by their own limited experience through trial and error. Some of them happened to be right so are regarded as 'brilliant'. But without sufficient theorizing, these 'brilliant' practitioners' 'doctrines' were not apparent to others and were obscure even to themselves; that is why many of them acted inconsistently. The unlucky people thus tragically failed by following the doctrines that were successful at one time. In these circumstances the consequences can be seriously tragic.

Bibliography

Auerbach, S, 1993. The Ironies that Built Japan. *Washington Post*, 18 July.

Bailey, T. 1969. *A Diplomatic History of the American People*, 8th edn. New York: Appleton-Century-Crofts.

Beetham, D. 1991. *The Legitimation of Power*. London: Macmillan.

Bergsten, C.F. 1994. Managing the World Economy of the Future, in *Managing the World Economy: Fifty Years after Bretton Woods*, edited by P. Kenan. Washington, DC: Institute for International Economics.

Burt, R. 1992. *Structure Holes: The Social Structure of Competition*. Cambridge, MA: Harvard University Press.

Dong, T. 2008, *Social Reach: A Connectivist Approach to American Identity and Global Governance*. Lanham, MD: University Press of America.

Gilpin, R. 1981. *War and Change in World Politics*. New York: Cambridge University Press.

Granovetter, M. 1973. The Strength of Weak Ties. *American Journal of Sociology* 78, No. 6: 1360–80.

Granovetter, M. 1979. The Theory-Gap in Social Network Analysis in *Perspectives on Social Network Research*, edited by Paul Holland and Samuel Leinhardt. New York: Academic Press.

Granovetter, M. 1983. The Strength of Weak Ties: A Network Theory Revisited. *Sociological Theory*, No. 1: 201–33.

Granovetter, M. 1985. Economic Action and Social Structure: The Problem of Embeddedness. *American Journal of Sociology* 91, No. 3: 481–510.

Hayek, F. 1978. *Law, Legislation and Liberty, vol. 1: Rules and Order.* Chicago: University of Chicago Press.

Herring, G. 2008. *From Colony to Superpower: US Foreign Relations Since 1776.* Oxford: Oxford University Press.

Herz, J. ed. 1982. *From Dictatorship to Democracy: Coping with the Legacies of Authoritarianism and Totalitarianism.* Westport, CT: Greenwood.

Ikenberry, J. 1989. Rethinking the Origins of American Hegemony. *Political Science Quarterly*, 104, 375–400.

Ikenberry, J. 1996. The Future of International Leadership. *Political Science Quarterly*, 111: 385–402.

Ikenberry, G.J. and Charles A. Kupchan. 1990. Socialization and Hegemonic Power. *International Organization*, 44, 283–315.

Keohane, R. 1984. *After Hegemony: Cooperation and Discord in the World Political Economy.* Princeton, NJ: Princeton University Press.

Keohane, R. 1988. International Institutions: Two Approaches. *International Studies Quarterly*, 32, No. 4: 379–96.

Krasner, S. ed. 1983. *International Regimes.* Ithaca, NY: Cornell University Press.

Lin, N. 2001. *Social Capital – A Theory of Social Structure and Action.* New York: Cambridge University Press.

Lukes, S. 1974. *Power: A Radical Perspective.* London: Macmillan.

Machiavelli, N. 1952. *The Prince.* New York: The New American Library of World Literature Inc.

Maier, C. 1989. Alliance and Autonomy: European Identity and US Foreign Policy Objectives in the Truman Years, in *The Truman Presidency*, edited by M. Lacy. New York: Cambridge University Press.

Marx, K. and Engels, F. 1978. Manifesto of the Communist Party, in *The Marx-Engles Reader*, second edition, ed. Robert C. Tucker, New York: W.W Norton.

Mearsheimer, J. 1994/95. The False Promise of International Institutions. *International Security*, 19: 5–49.

Mearsheimer, J. 2001. *The Tragedy of Great Power Politics.* New York: W.W. Norton.

Modelski, G. 1987. *Long Cycles in World Politics.* Seattle: University of Washington Press.

Modelski, G. 1990. Is World Politics a Learning Process? *International Organization*, 44: 1–24.

Montgomery, J. 1957. *Forced to be Free: The Artificial Revolution in Germany and Japan.* Chicago: University of Chicago Press.

Morgenthau, H.J. 2006. *Politics Among Nations: The Struggle for Power and Peace,* 7th edn. Boston: McGraw Hill Higher Education.

Nye, J. Jr. 1990. *Bound to Lead.* New York: Basic Books.

Nye, J. Jr. 2005. *Soft Power: The Means to Success in World Politics.* New York: Public Affairs.

Nye, J. Jr. 2008. *Power to Lead.* New York: Oxford University Press.

Putnam, R. 2000. *Bowling Alone.* New York: Simon & Schuster Paperbacks.

Ruggie, J. 1982. International Regimes, Transactions, and Change: Embedded Liberalism in the Postwar Economic Order. *International Organization,* 36, 379–416.

Ruggie, J. 1991. Embedded Liberalism Revisited: Institutions and Progress, in *International Economic Relations in* Progress in International Relations, edited by E. Adler and B. Crawford. New York: Columbia University Press.

Schwartz, T. 1991. *America's Germany: John J. McCloy and the Federal Republic of Germany.* Cambridge, MA: Harvard University Press.

Schwartz, T. 1995. The United States and Germany after 1945: Alliances, Transnational Relations, and the Legacy of the Cold War. *Diplomacy History,* 19, No. 4: 549–68.

Thucydides. 2006. *The History of the Peloponnesian War.* New York: Barns and Noble Books.

Wallerstein, I. 1974. The Rise and Future Demise of the World Capitalist System. *Comparative Studies in Society and History,* 16: 387–415.

Wallerstein, I. 1979. *The Capitalist World-Economy.* New York: Cambridge University Press.

Waltz, K.N. 1979. *Theory of International Politics.* Reading, MA: Addison-Wesley.

Waltz, K.N. 2001. *Man, the State, and War: A Theoretical Analysis.* New York: Columbia University Press.

Ward, R. and Yoshikazu, S. eds. 1987. *Democratizing Japan: The Allied Occupation.* Honolulu: University of Hawaii Press.

Weber, M. 1958. *From Max Weber: Essays in Sociology,* (paperback edition), Hans H. Gerth and C. Wright Mills, eds, New York: Oxford University Press.

Young, O. 1991. Political Leadership and Regime Formation: On the Development of Institutions in International Society. *International Organization,* 45, No. 3: 281–308.

Young, O. 1992. The Effectiveness of International Institutions: Hard Cases and Critical Variables' in *Governance without Government: Order and Change in World Politics,* edited by J.N. Rosenau and E. Czempiel. New York: Cambridge University Press.

Chapter 5

One World – Many 'Orders'?

Paweł Frankowski

The subject of a new world order gathered momentum after the fall of the Berlin Wall. The narrative of a new international arrangement has been told in terms of liberalism, a struggle between democracy and the rest of world, the war with terrorism, and the North-South divide. Scholars have been unable to agree on a coherent vision of this order for over 20 years and little progress has been made to this date. This raises the question of whether order really exists. Can we discuss 'one world and one order' when times are changing, everything is fluid and international relations (IR) are undergoing rapid change rather stabilizing? Undertakings that aim to order reality have two dimensions. First, scholars, societal leaders and politicians promote some desired visions. The second category of actions, aiming to explain regularities in the world order, are characteristic of those scholars who do not subscribe to a normative function of IR. We delineate this as a 'value free' assumption and it describes the period between 1989 and 2009 as a 20 years' crisis.

This chapter addresses the question whether the issue of international order can be examined, because an interpretation of significance of such a notion has sparked a debate centred on an international system, where economic globalization, regional integration, and the unconstrained spread of ideas have changed our perception of global reality. When some authors suggest that globalization is a first step in modernity's demise (Harvey 1990), others perceive that process as a transformation of the Westphalian order, when the basic elements will be changed but not invalidated (Paul 1999). Globalization as an overall process causes the old order, created in the conditions of interacting nation states, to clash with a new, as yet undetermined order, whose shape and structure are inscrutable and disturbing as well. Thus, we have to deal simultaneously with the abrasion and the imposition of two orders: the modern (national) and the postmodern (cosmopolitan) reality. Beck refers to this as a situation of meta-game, where two different, though interlinked, groups of participants – the state and the non-state or out-state actors (Beck 2005) – interact in world politics. The first group, according to Beck, belongs to the system of world economy, where economic interests prevail, and where this represents a global civil society. This group of players encroaches into areas previously reserved for the state and undertakes economic activities which largely affect the sovereignty of nation states. Actors competing with the state for the same assets, increasingly raise their voice in world politics, while the neutralizing side effects accompanying the processes of globalization are left to the state. The state's role is negated by the transnational companies and is denied the right to vote on matters relating to the global economy.

The main endeavour of this chapter is to answer three fundamental questions: what is order; why do we try to limit the study of the international system to a traditional, state-based model; and which order will prevail in the twenty-first century? Accordingly, the first part is an effort to present a theoretical explanation of 'order', and point out the differences between the international and the world order. The second part is devoted to a description of the order that we are witnessing now (*cosmos*), and its relation to visions of world order, which is promoted by the most important actors in the world politics (*taxis*).

Acharaya aptly points out that many scholars use the term 'order' as self-evident and sometimes with the conviction that its meaning should be obvious to every student of International Relations. Order may carry many meanings. First, it could concern the empirical cognition of international relations, to describe relations between the main participants in the world system, both the states and out-state actors. The first usage of order, according to Acharaya, has a descriptive dimension when it focuses on the existing distribution of power, irrespective of consequences and outcomes; it describes the existing status quo rather than attempting an explanation of existing mechanisms, arrangements and institutions (Acharaya 2007: 637). But it could also be a normative vision, which denotes a desired 'state of world' and describes relations between all the elements in a plausible way. Lastly, 'order' may also refer to the vision promoted by different actors and to describe their efforts to establish a particular 'state of world'; these efforts are depicted in the last part of the article. It can be assumed that two types of order are always evaluated: self-organized order; and an order imposed from outside the centre of power, which is a part of system and its core element. The concept of self-organized, spontaneous order derives from the Greek where word '*cosmos*' (κόσμος) meaning natural order, organized by laws and rules, but none of them has been created by humans or gods. This idea is compellingly opposed to chaos, where laws don't exist. Some researchers used the term to describe the situation after 1989 (cf. Ikenberry 1996). *Cosmos*, as a state of world order where we live and act, is usually very hard to describe and understand because of the lack of perspective, and the inherent characteristics of the social sciences. *Cosmos*, spontaneous order, is formed before our eyes; we hardly discern its shape; and certainly we cannot understand it. We try to describe it, but we don't understand and even know the rules governing this order. *Taxis* – arrangement (artificially constructed order): has a specific purpose – using this order we try to subdue constituting order through norms, regimes and institutions, and make the reality more predictable. Of course, there is a problem of congruency of these two orders – to what extent *cosmos* can be organized and to what extent *taxis* responds to the reality, which one has to be subdued.

Thus, order can be perceived in two ways: as a system of relations between states, and as a state of humanity. According to Bull's definition, presented in a seminal book on the international order, the international system is 'a pattern or activity that sustains the elementary or primary goals of the society of states' (Bull 1977: 8). This society is based on a few fundamental premises like sovereignty, the state system, limiting violence, and role of regimes. It is worth noting that Bull has distinguished between the international system and the international order. A system of states (or international system), according to Bull, is formed when 'two or more states have sufficient contact between them and have sufficient impact on one another's decisions to cause them to behave – at least in some measure – as part of a whole' (Bull 1977: 10). The society of states (international society), on the other hand, exists when 'a group of states, conscious of certain common interests and common values, form a society in the sense that they conceive themselves to be bound by a common sets of rules in their relations with one another and share in the working of common institutions' (Bull 1977: 13). Thus, the international order is not identical with world order, where an emphasis is on morality, common values and solidarity, as well as, considering the interests of other actors. We can make an assumption that the evolution of international relations (and change of international order) should proceed from the international order to the world system. Of course, it is an optimistic premise because now we observe some undertakings whose aims are somehow opposed and separated when different actors try to build and present conflicting orders.

The starting point for opening the conceptual analysis is to identify the critical elements of world structure. The question of the structure of the world order is, first of all, a question of the meaning of the rules governing the existing order, which are generally derived by most students of international relations from Kant. Fundamental institutions, like sovereignty, the state, territory, international law, and also the institutions which fulfil procedural functions, like international trade or war, have been changing. In the emerging order, we can observe a growing number of contradictions which have been arising about the meaning of the fundamentals of international relations: territory and borders are still important, but the ties existing between citizen and state (individual, legal, cultural) are less sound and going to diminish (Zacher 2001). Territory gradually loses its organizational dimension of the political sphere because competitive centres of authority can exist in the same area and claim the right to rule over the same inhabitants. The history of states is the history of territorial divisions – the order, introduced by territorial division, and has started to mean less, even when it doesn't disappear. Zacher (2001: 243) suggests that the decreasing significance of territory can be explained also by the economic trends, because states are less motivated to increase their territorial expansion which is less profitable than trade. Moreover 'having strategically located territory is less important now ... in technologically advanced era' (Zacher 2001: 244), and it seems that that state should pay less attention to territorial integrity norm. March and Olsen remark that the nation-state order, based on this norm, is undergoing three changes: rapid change in national boundaries, increasing fragmentation and disintegration, and substantial increase in international and cross-national connections (March and Olsen 1998). These practices and institutions link states and build the structure of world politics, where decisions are taken outside the traditional nation-state. It seems that changes in the global order match with the demands of non-state actors who realize their interests outside the territorial discourse. Thus in recent years we have been witness to the debate regarding the capacity of the nation-state to conduct successful politics in the era of globalization. Some authors suggest that postmodern states operate as transnational corporations, and can even move beyond 'the territorial trap' to achieve particular goals (cf. Glassman 1999).

On the other hand it does not mean that states decided to leave the territorial integrity norm, and focus on the good aspects of globalization. Otherwise, the globalizing economy still requires a powerful state, also in the territorial dimension, because the state is responsible for maintaining global institutions. Moreover, territory forms a framework of global order, within which states, decision makers and citizens must learn to interact with each other. Territorial issues are so fundamental that the behaviour associated with their settlement literally constructs a world order (including a world of anarchy)' (Vazquez 1993: 151). Thus, the fundamental institutions of global order, like war, sovereignty and peace are shaped by a particular approach to territory. Within territory, we can trace different origins of diversified visions of regional and global orders. Because the 'state-form', as Deleuze and Guattari point out, operates through the processes of determining and acquiring borders (Deleuze and Guattari 1977) sometimes territory is synonymous with sovereignty – where it ends, when the border disappears the sovereignty of the state also disappears. On the contrary, in different parts of world, borders, precisely delimitated, are debilitated by less oppressive states, while in some regions the borders are just demarcated. Moreover, despite the rule of inviolability of territorial integrity, the protection of human beings provided by these borders is incomplete; also, very often this barrier is broken in the name of a solidaristic vision of the world system. The solidaristic approach is often connected with the promotion of domestic orders and institutions within other states. Owen points out that such a tendency has been observed since the dawn of modern states, and in the name of 'common values' states have used a variety of instruments to modify or maintain internal orders (Owen 2002). Even the great powers refer to common values and public goods, there is a question what kind of values should be preferred, and to what extent this promotion of values serves the global order. Owen finds that in most cases it is hard to point out a single, definitive factor and the majority of foreign involvement should be explained by an interaction of ideology and power. It is worth adding that most states who feel responsible for the maintenance of global or regional order repeatedly engage in such promoting practice. This practice is not an exception to the general rule or isolated incident; actions undertaken by the promoting states have a clear political and economic basis. In other words, the promoting states know they have to do something – this is their duty and obligation. Analysis of this promotion is more problematic if we try to narrow the concept of sovereignty to Westphalian sovereignty – any promotion of solidaristic vision should be treated as a violation of sovereignty. But if motives are virtuous (in the name of democracy, human rights, etc.) and the promoting state does not want to expand its influence and power, like the US and the case of Somalia in 1994, it seems that the sovereignty clause could be temporarily suspended.

The international system is less dominant, but its existence is a key element in domestic and international politics. States are changing, but don't disappear, despite some prophets who announce the end of nation-states (cf. Ohmae 1995). The twilight era of a nation-state is caused by the balance between nation and the state being unsettled at the level of regions. Postmodern states give more autonomy to supranational bodies (such as the European Union) and new communities are emerging against the state, against its territory and against its authority. These new actors are locating themselves in the same space where the power of the state 'falls', slipping away from hands of the state. At the same time, the state is 'at bay' because larger communities want to absorb it. This complex situation has caused sovereignty, as distinctive from the state, to be less obvious or robust, thus we are witnessing the de-territorialization of sovereignty. Borders are too porous for the state, and too open for other actors. In fact, states are 'at bay' by non-state actors and facing globalization, which cannot be controlled. Osiander remarked that growing interdependence is, to an extent, a result of industrialization. Thus for over a century this process seriously has undermined self-reliance of states and will diminish it further (Osiander 2001). He points out also that we can observe a shift from near-total autonomy of states toward 'proliferation of international institutions trying to 'get in' on the management of transborder politics' (Osiander 2001: 283). As a result, postmodern states are tangled in complex structure of governance, where we can observe a framework made from cooperation and mutual restraint, where supra-national actors, bit by bit, have expanded their political influence. Thus, even the sovereignty clause allows for non-participation in this framework, in practice the escape from the globalized world carries serious costs and consequences.

Domestic politics and international affairs still seem to be distinctive spheres of activity, but it's very hard to point out clearly the domestic or external character of political activity. Procedural institutions also seem to change, depending on the regions studied. The images of war in Asia, Africa and Europe are completely different – and the lack of congruency of these worlds means that high-tech loses against guerrilla or primitive weapons in the theatre of war. In the North, issues of security are also understood in the different ways – meaning that even in the same area or same 'order' we can expect some clashes over questions of security, threat and challenge. International trade, as a procedural institution, also differs from region to region – disproportions between rules imposed by strong states and rules which cannot be enforced by weak states are more than visible. Moreover, citizens are more sceptical towards the idea of the state while more active regarding their needs (Rosenau 1998).

Trying to depict the world order, it is worth stressing that disorder, existing in many African countries like Sudan or Somalia, is a disorder from the Westphalian point of view. When we take a perspective of these countries, the state of war is something normal and usual (albeit undesirable) characteristic for the pre-state era. But one thing differentiates these orders – when in the North war usually creates the state, in the global South war has a completely different meaning. War is not state-building by its nature, but a characteristic of environment, where imperfect states try to build their imperfect rule.

State borders, rules of law based on common consent are relatively unimportant in that environment. Law, rules and order, even from the North's perspective of being wrong, have been formed chaotically and spontaneously, and it is a mixture of primordial sentiments, modern tools of governing and an adapted form of post-colonial bureaucracy. The only solution is to make *cordon sanitaire* around these areas, but in that way tacit consent is given for ethnic cleansing and violent acts, which are in opposition to a solidaristic vision of the world order. In fact, the dispute about the international order is a dispute between a pluralistic and solidaristic concept of international relations. Because the concept of solidaristic order is, as mentioned earlier, desirable rather than neglected (while the concept of pluralistic is realized and actual), it is worth stopping for a moment on this issue. We can assume, according to realism, that the national states compete not only in military affairs but in other matters as well, especially in the economy. Competition is the consequence of anarchy, which forces a self-help system because it can assure their autonomy and possible survival. It does not mean that cooperation is impossible, but states decide to cooperate only when they see a clearly positive influence on their relative status (Mastanduno 1999). Also, Alderson and Hurrell propose that for the post Cold-War era, we should distinguish between consensual solidarism and coercive solidarism, when the key characteristic of first concept is characterized by an increase of norm creation resulted from spontaneous normative integration, the latter suggests coerced solidarism through the hegemonic power (Alderson and Hurrell 2000: 67). Approving the solidaristic vision of the world order, as desired, somehow raises questions automatically on the limits in its realization. Solidaristic arguments compel the powerful states to act against genocide or ethnic cleansing – but the question is whether these states are ready and able to devote their assets (and their citizens) in the name of protection of other, weaker states. (Wheeler 2000). According to Linklater (1998), the ethical obligations, which result from the solidaristic vision, come down to the assumption that wealthy societies are morally obliged to support people from poorer states. But the question is – how to coerce this vision and impose *taxis* on *cosmos* of an anarchical system?

Nowadays the international order is legitimized through sovereignty and non-intervention clauses, but what about the moral content of such legitimacy (cf. Smith 1999)? The answer, provided by Clark, is very simple – a basis for legitimized actions on the international arena is justified governance (Clark 2005, 174n.). Weak states or quasi-states, as Jackson (1990) proposes, are characterized by the external sovereignty like strong states (strong states are the UN members and other international organizations, which take part in the international agreements etc.), but internally they do not govern at all. That could be a main source for the approval on the solidaristic vision – to make an order inside the weak states

– because weak and unstable participants undermine the main rules of the system which is based on the premise of sovereignty.

When we try to describe the orders, proposed by some centres, it should be emphasized that the key difference in the proposed orders is a question of support for the solidaristic or pluralistic vision. This question is completely irrelevant without analysis of power in international relations, i.e. who can and wants to support this vision. Characteristic of the post-Second World War system is the America-centred world order that has emerged, which is built around institutional and multilateral structures (Ikenberry 2000). This order, with institutions, rules, rights which 'are widely agreed upon, highly institutionalized, and generally observed' (Ikenberry 2000: 36), markedly differs from previous arrangements, based generally on the zero-sum game, where traditional balance of power prevails and each party perceives others' gains as its own loss. This system, based on the multilateral structures, where stable and cooperative relations are the key element for all the participants, supports the United States, but on the other hand has institutional constraints that limit US power. Schweller suggests that the existence of institutions can be treated as a signal for other powers or potential partners that the US does not intend to use the power to find out the solution (Schweller 2001: 163), but it does not necessarily mean that the most powerful participant would restrain its power for others' sake. Moreover, binding institutions have to be based on a high degree of autonomy, which is rather unlikely. Thus, the postwar institutions, created and led by Americans, are part of a myth, invented to unify the West against the East and to secure America's supremacy.

Katzenstein suggests that US policy is tailored to support regional visions of order, based on the American guidelines. Accordingly, every change which results from globalization and the postmodern approach to the world politics, like the openness of borders, the vanishing strategic dimension of territory, and multiple citizenships and multiple loyalties, works 'in accordance with the power and purpose of the American empire' (Katzenstein 2005: 13). Katzenstein points out also that despite the fact that the US shapes the regional orders to a great extent, regional powers may still have an influence on American foreign policy. Analysis of the potentials and limitations of such influence, however, suggests that there is no genuine impact but rather feedback, and the US continues to expand and fine-tune its policies. Even though the world can react against US policy with 'admiration and resentment and occasionally with violent fury' it does not mean that regional orders may have an impact on the global arrangements. Dependence between the global player and regional powers is based on the one-way model, and short-range and long-range policies are unchangeable. This constancy serves as the important element of the world system – it gives predictability and kind of stability, but in fact it is a double-edged sword. American-centred order, in which the US has the dominant and hegemonic role, serves as a point of reference because most states try to support or build an opposite vision – but emphasize, to some extent, its institutional characteristics rather than structures, based on American domination which, even indirectly, they opposed. It is worth stressing that all the principal emerging powers, like Brazil, PRC or India, have been functioning mostly at the peripheries of the US-centred world politics. The roles of these states for over 50 years has been determined by American interests, even when they sometimes strongly opposed and, often, did not accept American dominance. Even benign hegemonic power is not a leader, but a dormant power which threatens and terrifies everyone.

Proponents of the theory of hegemonic stability (THS), consider that the hegemonic power also stabilizes the system through its material resources and secures the integrity of the basic principles of the system. The belief that an economically strong country stabilizes the world system emerged in the 1970s. Realists, who refer to this theory, argue that international order is created and maintained by a hegemonic power. This approach proposed by Kindleberger, referred to the economic sphere of international relations, and argued that 'for the world economy to be stabilized, there must be a stabilizer, one stabilizer' (Kindelberger 1973: 305). This proposition was based on the analysis of the years 1929–39, when the US was responsible for the reconstruction of the global economy. This theory gives a positive interpretation of aspects of hegemonic power and its impact on the creation of free trade. The main argument to confirm this theory would be, according to Kindleberger, that the hegemonic power actively creates 'public goods', in other words, undertakes actions to build global prosperity. This proposition is based mostly on the studies of Olson (1965) on collective actions – Kindleberger transferred its presumptions to the level of the world system. Arrighi (1982) identifies two types of goods that hegemonic power can bring to the world system: security (peace) and economy (prosperity). However, the states protect their own interests, and the common goods are less important. Thus the question regarding the extent to which hegemonic power operates benignly, and how much coercion is applied, has divided critics and proponents of the theory of hegemonic stability. Snidal (1986) points out that the hegemonic power cannot be benevolent and responsible for maintaining the system when other countries are exempted from this responsibility. It is in contradiction to the idea of hegemonic advantage over other countries – a hegemonic state, providing 'common goods' bears all the costs, and less powerful countries do not bear any costs at all. To properly understand this argument regarding America's role in the world system, it is important to distinguish between three concepts: leadership, domination and hegemony – all three are different forms of advantage. Dominance is characterized by present use of force against the less-powerful states. An example could be the American policy known as the 'Good Neighbour Policy' towards the Caribbean countries and Latin America. Strong states treat weaker countries as second class, although, according to Bull (1977), it is difficult nowadays to find a clear example of such domination in international relations. On the other hand, leadership is an advantage over other countries, assuming compliance with international standards. Primacy is characterized by advantage without violence, but accompanied by the recognition of international standards. Hegemony lies between domination and leadership, when we can observe a rare use of force, but a strong state reserves the right to use it. Hegemony produces a sort of order – countries which are in the sphere of influence are less prone to initiate a military action each other. Violation of rules, set by the hegemonic power, results in an immediate reaction by the powerful actor. According to Snidal, using the traditional view of hegemony turned the world upside down (Snidal 1986: 581) – it is difficult to imagine a country that abandons its interests for the good of the system. On the other hand, a hegemonic power cannot use coercion all the time to secure leadership in the system. The dispute about the nature of hegemony and the question of how much coercion the hegemonic power should use, divides proponents of hegemonic stability theory. To understand the modern meaning of hegemony it is worth noting the definition of hegemony proposed by Keohane and Nye – a hegemony is the state of world, when one power is strong enough to maintain the basic principles governing international relations and has the will to do so (Keohane and Nye 1977). In this context the hegemonic power is a state that creates the structure of the international system, sets itself at the top, but at the same time ensures stability and predictability for the system. This approach combines in the concept of 'hegemony' both the concepts of leadership and primacy in international relations. However, there are significant doubts about the legitimacy of such hegemony.

In an attempt to resolve the dispute about the nature of hegemony, Snidal (1986) distinguishes two models of hegemony: benevolent leadership and coercive leadership. In the first model, the power of the state is important because the hegemonic power provides 'common goods' for system, i.e. the more the powerful state the greater the expectations. In the latter model a powerful state shifts the burden of the system to weaker countries (burden sharing), and forces them to undertake particular actions. The result is that they participate in 'common goods', but also increase the advantage of the hegemonic state. The two models proposed by Snidal are rather extreme examples, and Hasenclever, Mayer and Rittberger (1997: 92) believe that a hegemony is a multidimensional phenomenon. The concept of hegemony must contain an element of coercive behaviour and rewards, and criticism made by Snidal regarding costs incurred by a hegemonic state also appears to have disadvantages. The costs incurred by hegemonic power are clearly much higher than the costs of less powerful countries, but in the long term the hegemonic state increases its power, because benefits from hegemony grow disproportionately to the costs. At the same time the profits of participating countries rise as well, although, as Snidal points out, some countries of the 'Third' and 'Fourth World' perceive American dominance as support for private rather than public goods.

Christopher Layne aptly points out that any scenario that assumes a shift toward multipolarity or bipolarity is misleading because international relations theory has not produced 'a unified theory of great power emergence' (Layne 2009: 163). We do know, however, that the great powers can emerge under certain conditions, but to get and keep great power status is not an easy task. Any prediction based on measuring state power should consider a variety of political and societal factors, and examples of Germany in 1914 and Japan in 1970s are the best proof of complexity in international relations. In most cases, state capacity, domestic stability and demographic trends, are omitted in such calculations.

After 1989 the American vision has paradoxically helped other visions to emerge and flourish. Visions of *taxis* differ, and most of them do not consider a solidaristic issue. States like India, the People's Republic of China (PRC), Russia, and even the European Union (EU), try to impose their own visions, and in the best case this is driven by the dominant state. It is possible to get the impression, that all these projects are an emanation of hegemony (on different levels, from different region in the world), concerning different spheres of human activity (economic and religious). The means for accomplishment and promotion of specific orders also differ – from temptation with cooperation (like the PRC in some African states), to enforcement of conditions (that could be a case of economic relations between the Russian Federation and Georgia or Ukraine). But there is no doubt that the US is the main element of the existing world order, and it is mainly against this actor that alliances and strategic cooperation are built (cf. Garver 2002).

The Chinese vision of the world order is a kind of paradox, based on the American vision – states freely fulfil their economic interests. The PRC uses the possibilities given by the American vision of world, and is actively engaged in many Asian and African states. In return for cheap goods of poor quality, they buy raw materials that drives the Chinese economy. This situation is reminiscent of Japanese-American relations when the Japanese economy outpaced the US economy in production of highly advanced technology products (cf. Raine 2009). The same situation makes the United States unable to cope with the challenge which confronts them: merger of many ties between the US economy and the Chinese economy. So, there is a direct threat for the US, that officials in Washington have underlined very often, that the PRC is the strategic competitor of the US (Kagan 2001: 12) whose aim is not to keep the status quo in the region, but to enlarge their power in the world (Rice 2000). A lack of vision concerning the PRC's role in the world is clearly seen in Brzezinski's (2000) observation that: China is neither an international adversary nor a strategic partner of the United States – if so, that leaves open the question of the role of the PRC in the world order. Chinese foreign policy, and the Chinese vision is centred on domestic affairs, and it is hard to disagree with Chen, who points out, that regarding China's capabilities and the country's approach to the international order it is 'impossible for China to pose a threat for current international order' (Chen 2007, 95). But even the PRC does not pose a direct threat on the global level; its *taxis* could be a considerable challenge for regional order. Shambaugh noticed that Chinese diplomacy is extremely active on the regional level (Shambaugh 2004), and the PRC has strengthened its image as a status quo power. China not only engages the peripheries of Asia, but it also engineers peripheries of the world system in Africa where a possibility of real dialogue, outside the post-colonial discourse, is much easier in comparison to European or American attempts. Africa is a profitable place for the PRC to invest reserves, and China plays the role of benevolent hegemon for the region (Carmody and Owusu 2007: 508). Zakaria argues that China, using skilful diplomacy and economic advantage, can present itself as 'an attractive partner, especially in a world in which the United States is seen as an overbearing hegemon' (Zakaria 2008: 127). It is worth stressing that Chinese diplomacy uses all these arguments and instruments that have been provided by the American order, i.e. multilateralism, primacy of self-determination, and free trade. Even China would try to undermine the American influence in Asia and the relative balance between the two powers will change. There is a lot of convergence between Chinese and American interests and approaches to the international system. Undoubtedly, China, to some extent, will oppose American power in the region. It will do that inside the limits set after World War II because it is much cheaper and more effective to use reliable *taxis* than to try and develop a new one.

The Chinese vision confronts the neoconservative vision – where freedom, but on the American principles and American power is a normal part of order (cf. Drexner 2007). The power should be used to shape the world in one's own image, and should prevent any possibility of the emergence of a competitor in the international arena. This vision is contrary to the vision of order proposed by Harry Truman after World War II, because it limits unilateral actions undertaken by the United States. Thus the US, according to Kupchan, should find a new strategy. Waiting for the moment when their power will be 'squandered' is 'missing a huge opportunity offered by the US position today' (Kupchan 2003: 208). This is a 'luxury' to select the desired strategy for regime change in the multipolar world, a luxury of choice of for one's own *taxis*, when *cosmos* allows for it. Accordingly, Krauthammer believes that this country, having such a big advantage, must expand its power and not 'turn away' from seemingly minor conflicts. This is for two reasons. Firstly, when the US will decide to not intervene in a relatively small conflict it could run the risk of a situation in which they are not ready to face a serious danger. Secondly, when they stop to intervene, another power will emerge very soon in their place, for example the Russian Federation. But some authors (Walt 2005) pose a question whether the US should intervene everywhere, export the ideas and actively prevent the emergence of competitor or rival states. It is to some extent a question of limits of and possibilities for American power and the American order and, as Reus-Smit argues, any misunderstanding of the nature of American power, by Washington policy-makers, can affect the structure of the international system (Reus-Smit 2004), which is based on the American principles. Thus, intervention in any conflict entails the danger of dispersal of power and the US will be unable to respond to a real threat to its national security. Therefore, as a realistic view, Krauthammer proposes to follow the principle of 'selective engagement', which consists of four elements: containment and deterrence of 'rogue states; to contain China; 'vigilance' against a resurgent Russia; and the preservation of order as a guarantee of peace and stability (Krauthammer 2000, 31). The question of preservation of order is always connected with the efficiency of institutions and procedures, which are at the disposal of strongest power. Organizations and institutions like the IMF, NATO, and GATT have reflected the dominance and preferences of the US and were designed to boost its power. In that case, institutions such as NATO or IMF serve as the linchpin of existing order – it means that any state that might try to undermine the existing order would have to replace these institutions. Otherwise, the remains of the previous '*taxis* drafter' would exist not only as the practical instruments of control, but also as an important part of a still vivid history. Moreover, many of the rising powers believe that the existing global order structures were created against them. Thus, any competitive or opposite vision should be as comprehensive as possible.

When we try to compare different visions and orders, it is inescapable that most Western scholars perceive this comparison through the lenses of the Western approach to the world order, which is based on the state-centric approach that has endured from the Treaty of Westphalia. The main organizing elements are the economy, idea of gains and losses, and interdependence which serves the most powerful state. But this approach should be broadened, to encompass other dimensions of human activity, and not always using the level of transactions or number of memberships in international organizations as the best 'markers' for predictability and accountability in the system. For example, a vision proposed by the Islamic community is not based on the exchange of goods, but on interactions based on a broad community of discourse, where Islam is identified as more than religion, but also as a civilization and specific *taxis*, which is much closer to the 'natural state of things' (cf. Voll 1994). Thus the political order, strengthened through the moral norms and obligations, widely accepted by African states, could be a challenge to Western order in the region, but does it pose a real threat for global order? *Taxis*, proposed by Muslims, who want to establish a world Caliphate, could be attractive on the regional level, but has only a tiny chance of acquiring the status of system stabilizer (Mahbubani 2006). First of all it is worth stressing that most states which aspire to promote the world order cannot manage their internal problems and social inequalities. In the case of China, traditionally inward-looking, any attempt to expand the Chinese vision on the world scale would be a violation of heritage, which inclines treating Great China as a separate system (i.e. with separate *taxis*). It is hard to find any natural aspiration to promote the Chinese vision abroad – it is rather a case of acceptance and soft hegemony. Regarding the Islamic vision, the main fault of this *taxis* is the lack of coherent vision, because different Islamic groups cannot arrange the one, single vision of the world order. Unfortunately some of them try to impose their vision of world society by force. For such a vision of the world, the US can oppose in only one way – using their military forces – but it is apparently not enough. But there is a kind of community of discourse, which is based not only on economic matters, but also on values and human rights – the European Union. The idea of a civilian power Europe, which has its origins in the 1970s, when one of the key advisers to Jean Monnet, François Duchêne, depicted a vision of the Community based on a sense of collective action, social values of equality and justice as well as civilian ends, opposed to military means. (Duchêne 1972). The concept of civilian power, developed by Duchêne followers, has been translated into a variety of ideas based on the European model of international relations. As Orbie aptly points out, 'each of them suggests that the Union is, and has, a particular kind of power in the world' (Orbie 2008: 2) – and thanks to this power the EU can transform the international system, acting like a model, not like a coercive power. But even the EU can be perceived as a postmodern state (Cooper 2003) or European superpower (McCormick 2007) the key characteristic of the proposed visions are built on the indirect negation of American *taxis*. Moreover, even where a vision of order proclaimed by the postmodern states (or regions, in fact), that is the EU, and even where the solidaristic vision of order, are partially implemented as a reflection of these assumptions, the proclaimed order hardly meets the aspirations of the EU member states because very often they cannot reach common ground. Thus a normative power could not be disseminated, and the possibility of a global order after the European fashion is rather questionable. It leads us to the conclusion that regional orders are much more important than a quest for a global and universal order. In fact, the power of regions, marginalized during the Cold War, that have been influenced by one of two major players, should be analyzed, and areas excluded from the discourse on the global order, should be reintegrated into discussion on the global order (Buzan and Wæver 2003). Particular visions of order are introduced by powerful states in South America. In this region, we can distinguish two trends: an attempt to determine the global role of the region's largest country, Brazil; and an attempt of integration around specific American values, such as the Andean Community (*La Comunidad Andina*). Importantly, the latter implies that, inter alia, the actors will create a common foreign policy, which would allow for wider participation in world politics, and it will offer them a chance to have an impact on global *taxis*. However, in fact this organization is constituted from relatively poor countries, where more than 50 per cent of citizens live below the poverty line (de Soto 2005). When poor states try to organize themselves, the regional power, Brazil, tries to obtain a permanent seat on the Security Council – it can be seen in the involvement of Brazil in stabilization or peacekeeping missions conducted under the aegis of the UN (for example, in Mozambique, Cyprus, Congo, Angola, East Timor and Haiti). But in principle, countries that aspire to the role of those who could present their visions of the world order cannot cope with internal inequalities. For example, GINI set the state of Brazil in 75th place among the states with the highest social inequality – PRC at 92nd, Russian Federation at 52nd, and India places at 134th (UNDP 2009). India, as well as Brazil, aspires to the title of one of the poles of the new order (although this is a vague term). Also it does not have a coherent vision of global governance, and pays more attention to regional relations and political practices than the idea of global *taxis*. India, despite its rich heritage and its more than one billion people, is unable to propose any significant regional, let alone global, proposition.

Thus, what kind of order we are witnessing now? What kind of distinction should be used to distinguish 'orders', which are mentioned in the title? The first and popular division is the distinction between democratic and undemocratic countries (Brown 1996). The assumption that democracies do not fight each other does not mean that they would not start to fight against undemocratic states, if they were less powerful. However, in the case of countries such as the Russian Federation, Azerbaijan and PRC, democracies do not take any action. This leads to the conclusion that this division is correct, but it does not move us any further to answer what is the shape and structure of the contemporary order. If so, maybe the division between liberal and illiberal states should be more specific. But, perhaps, this type of division should be abandoned also, because it could be hard to distinguish between states which obey the liberal rules on the international level, and at the same time violate a clause of liberty in their domestic affairs. That could be the case in China or Saudi Arabia, when we compare relations between these countries and the rest of the world. And thus we come to the conclusion that while a state may or may not be liberal, its potential determines vulnerability to the instruments used by the proponents of a particular order.

An interesting typology is proposed by Michael Mastanduno, who distinguishes three types of order: geo-economic competition, multipolar balance of power and American-centered order (Mastanduno 1999). According to Mastanduno, the current situation can be described though geo-economic competition, because idealistic assumption – promoted by realists in fact, that the unipolar order, controlled by the US, would be characterized by inclusion of new states without any resistance from other powers – has failed. Even US foreign policy under Clinton differed significantly from the foreign policy of G.W. Bush. But, after closer examination it is surprising that that the international community wanted to believe that the US adopted the role of the stabilizer without any expectations and profits in return (Layne 2009). Otherwise, since the end of the Cold War the United States has consistently pursued its own interests, and the idea that before 2001 the United States had a multilateral approach is rather a myth than fact which is reflected in the ongoing activities.

Heginbotham and Samuels claim that economic threats are equally important as military threats – it causes the strongest powers to engage in economic balancing, and geo-economic interests can be realized at the expense of political or security interests (Heginbotham and Samuels 1998). Thus, when the geopolitical interests are at stake, both regimes and international standards are unimportant. Accordingly, particular attention should be given to formation of sometimes quite surprising coalitions whose aim is to balance American power (for example, the agreement between Brazil and South Africa). At the same time, these coalitions comprise multi-level games and economic ties, when cultural and geostrategic ties intersect which results in a complex network of interdependence.

The main aim of the US, still the strongest power in the world system, is to prevent the emergence of new centres of power that are emerging in the south and east of the Eurasian subcontinent and South America. Russia, a natural challenger of the American order, which has innumerable natural resources on its territory, opposes American activities, and conducts hard realpolitik, which involves the weakening of potential or current US allies, while seeking to attract other centres. But in fact, the main reason is not to counterbalance American power but to build its own *taxis*, at least on the regional level. Moreover, this is no longer a clash of two ideologies, but a struggle over the economy, where the weapons are oil and gas. When the Russian-owned company Gazprom signs agreements with Algeria, Venezuela, Sudan, and is extremely active in Central Asia, Russia should not be surprised at US efforts to consolidate its interests in the 'soft underbelly of Russia' as it attempts to encroach on Ukraine or Georgia, or use the oil fields of the Caspian Sea. These efforts are 'proxy wars' of the modern age carried out by other means – political and economic – not always military.

The most important problem, for policymakers and scholars as well, is how to attain terms of cooperation between different actors functioning in the different 'orders'. Bull (1977) suggests that 'order' is possible among states which do not feel 'affiliate' to one civilization. John Vincent points out that the international society is functional or utilitarian in fact, not cultural or moral (Vincent 1984). But the order that we are witnessing nowadays (or more precisely a set of orders and narratives on the reality) is rather a clash between the hegemon and challengers, who are countered by the US in different ways, mostly by promise of cooperation or reward. Policymakers in Washington are aware of their dependence on China, but their actions can be described as a typical gridlock, which they cannot deal with. There is no illusion that both the Chinese and the Russians welcomed the US intervention in Afghanistan and Iraq, hoping for a replay of Vietnam. At the same time, it gave the US legitimacy to treat other countries, once again, according to American standards. In conclusion, at the moment, there are seemingly many orders which result from unequal regional development. Studies on the regional orders are rather unpopular and most scholars try to find some set of defining characteristics for global order. Even in seminal books, such as *Regions and Powers* by Buzan and Wæver (2003), or *A World of Regions* by Katzenstein (2005), we cannot find a coherent definition of regional order *vis-à-vis* global order, and there are more differences than similarities between regions to build a conceptual model for analysis. In most cases the most powerful state in the region defines its structure, institutions, and relations with other regions. These powerful regional states create small poles of the system, and it is justified to talk about an archipelago called the international order, consisting of overlapping and partially covered irregular islets of order (or regularity). The world that we observe now consists of 'emerging fragments of international security communities alongside the traditional war system that continues elsewhere' (Ruggie 1993: 174). The *cosmos* definitely does not equate to international order and *taxis*.

Bibliography

Acharaya, A. 2007. The Emerging Regional Architecture of World Politics. *World Politics*, 59(4), 629–52.
Alderson K. and Hurrell A. 2000. Introduction in *Hedley Bull on International Society*, edited by K. Alderson and A. Hurrell, London, Palgrave

Arrighi, G. 1982. A Crisis of Hegemony, in, *Dynamics of Global Crisis*, edited by S. Amin et al. London: Macmillan.

Beck, U. 2005. *Power in the Global Age*. Cambridge: Polity.

Brown, M.E. et al. (eds) 1996. *Debating the Democratic Peace*. Cambridge: MIT Press

Brzezinski, Z. 2000. Living with China. *National Interest*, 59, 5–21.

Bull, H. 1977. *Anarchical Society: A Study of World Order in World Politics*. New York: Columbia University Press.

Buzan, B. and Wæver, O. 2003. *Regions and Power: The Structure of International Security*. Cambridge: Cambridge University Press.

Carmody, P.R. and Owusu, F.Y. 2007. Competing Hegemons? Chinese versus American Geo-economic Strategies in Africa. *Political Geography*, 26(5), 504–24.

Chen Y. 2007. China's Foreign Policy Dynamics and International Order, in *International Order in Globalizing World*, edited by Y.A. Stivachtis, Aldershot: Ashgate

Clark, I. 2005. *Legitimacy in International Society*. New York: Oxford University Press.

Cooper R. 2003. *The Breaking of Nations: Order and Chaos in the Twenty-first Century*. London: Atlantic Books.

Deleuze, G. and Guattari, F. 1977. *Anti-Oedipus: Capitalism and Schizophrenia*. New York: Library of America.

Drexner, D.W. 2007. The New New World Order. *Foreign Affairs*, 86(2), 34–46.

Duchêne F. 1972. Europe's Role in World Peace, in *Europe Tomorrow: Sixteen Europeans Look Ahead*, edited by R. Mayne. London: Fontana, 32–47.

Garver, J.W. 2002. *Protracted Contest: Sino-Indian Rivalry in the Twentieth Century*. Seattle: University of Washington Press.

Glassman, J. 1999. State Power beyond the 'Territorial Trap': The Internationalization of the State. *Political Geography*, 18(6), 669–96.

Harvey, D. 1990. *The Condition of Postmodernity*. Cambridge: Basil Blackwell.

Hasenclever A., Mayer P., Rittberger V. 1997. *Theories of International Regimes*. Cambridge: Cambridge University Press.

Heginbotham, E. and Samuels, R. 1998 Mercantile Realism and Japanese Foreign Policy. *International Security*, 22(4), 171–203.

Hettne, B. and Söderbaum, F. 2005. Civilian Power or Soft Imperialism? The EU as a Global Actor and the Role of Interregionalism. *European Foreign Affairs Review*, 10(4), 538–9.

Ikenberry, G.I. 1996. The Myth of Post-Cold War Chaos. *Foreign Affairs*, 75(3), 79–92.

Ikenberry, G.I. 2000. *After Victory: Institutions, Strategic Restraint and the Rebuilding of Order After Major Wars*. Princeton, NJ: Princeton University Press.

Jackson, R. 1990. *Quasi-States: Sovereignty, International Relations and the Third World*. Cambridge: Cambridge University Press.

Kagen, R. 2001. The World and President Bush, *Survival*, 43(1), 7–16.

Katzenstein, P.J. 2005. *A World of Regions: Asia and Europe in the American Imperium*. Ithaca, NY: Cornell University Press.

Keohane, R.O. and Nye, J. 1977. *Power and Interdependence: World Politics in Transition*. Boston: Little, Brown and Company.

Kindleberger, Charles P. 1973. *World in Depression 1929–1939*. Berkeley and Los Angeles: University of California Press.

Krauthammer, C. 2000. American Power – For What? A Symposium, *Commentary*, 109(1), 21–43.

Kupchan, C.A. 2003. The Rise of Europe, America's Changing Internationalism, and the end of US Primacy. *Political Science Quarterly*, 118(2) 205–31.

Layne, Christopher. 2009. The Waning of US Hegemony – Myth or Reality? A Review Essay. *International Security*, 34(1), 147–72.

Linklater, A. 1998. *The Transformation of Political Community: Ethical Foundation of the Post-Westphalian Era.* Columbia, SC: University of South Carolina Press.

Mahbubani, K. 2006. The Impending Demise of the Postwar System. *Survival*, 47(4), 7–18.

March, J.G. and Olsen, J.P. 1998. The Institutional Dynamics of International Political Orders. *International Organization*, 52(4), 943–69.

Mastanduno M. 1999. A Realist View: Three Images of the Coming International Order, in *International Order and the Future of World Politics*, edited by T.V. Paul and J.A. Hall, Cambridge: Cambridge University Press.

McCormick J. 2007. *The European Superpower*. Basingstoke and New York: Palgrave Macmillan.

Miller, B. 2005. When and How Regions Become Peaceful: Potential Theoretical Pathways to Peace. *International Studies Review*, 7(2), 229–67.

Ohmae, K. 1995. *The End of the Nation State: The Rise of Regional Economies*. New York: Free Press.

Olson, M. 1965. *The Logic of Collective Action. Public Goods and Theory of Groups*. Cambridge and London: Harvard University Press.

Orbie, J. 2008. A Civilian Power in the World? Instruments and Objectives in European Union External Policies, in *Europe's Global Role. External Policies of the European Union*, edited by J. Orbie. Aldershot: Ashgate.

Osiander, A. 2001. Sovereignty, International Relations, and the Westphalian Myth. *International Organization*, 55(2), 251–87.

Owen, J.M. 2002. The Foreign Imposition of Domestic Institutions. *International Organization*, 56(2), 375–409.

Paul, D.E. 1999. Sovereignty, Survival and the Westphalian Blind Alley in International Relations. *Review of International Studies*, 25(2), 217–31.

Raine, S. 2009. China's African Challenges. *Adelphi Papers*, 404–5.

Rice, C. 2000. Promoting National Interest. *Foreign Affairs*, 79(1), 45–62.

Rosenau, J.N. 1998. States and Sovereignty in a Globalizing World. *DUPI Working Papers*. Copenhagen: DUPI.

Ruggie, J.G. 1993. Territoriality and Beyond: Problematizing Modernity in International Relations. *International Organization*, 47(1), 139–74.

Schweller, R.L. 2001. The Problem of International Order Revisited. *International Security*, 26(1), 161–86.

Shambaugh D. 2004. China Engages Asia. *International Security*, 29(3), 64–99.

Smith, S. 1999. Is the Truth Out There? Eight Questions about International Order, in *International Order and the Future of World Politics*, edited by T.V. Paul and J.A. Hall. Cambridge: Cambridge University Press.

Snidal, D. 1986. The Limits of Hegemonic Stability Theory. *International Organization*, 39(4), 579–614.

Soto, G.F. de. 2005. Past, Present And Future Of Andean Integration – Towards the Strengthening of the Andean Community: Challenges, Achievements and Perspectives for the Future. *Studia Diplomatica*, LVIII(3), 11–28.

UNDP 2009. *Human Development Report 2009*. [Online] Available at http://hdrstats.undp.org/en/indicators/161.html [accessed: 1 December 2009].

Vasquez, J.A. 1993. *The War Puzzle*. Cambridge: Cambridge University Press.

Vincent, R.J. 1984. Edmund Burke and the Theory of International Relations. *Review of International Studies*, 10, 205–18.

Voll, J.O. 1994. Islam as a Special World-System. *Journal of World History*, 5(2), 213–26.

Walt, S. 2005. *Taming American Power: The Global Response to US Primacy*. New York: W.W. Norton and Company.

Wheeler, N.J. 2000. *Saving Strangers: Humanitarian Intervention in International Society*. New York: Oxford University Press.

Zacher, M.W. 2001. The Territorial Integrity Norm: International Boundaries and the Use of Force. *International Organization*, 55(2), 215–50.

Zakaria, F. 2008. *The Post-American World*. New York: W.W. Norton.

Chapter 6

State Failure in the Contemporary International System: New Trends, New Threats[1]

Natalia Piskunova

Introduction

The ongoing discussion on the role of the state as a safeguard of security in a modern system of International Relations offers contrasting views on the problem of state failure. This chapter presents an examination of the current political situation in a failed state of Somalia. From 1990 to 2010 political-territorial developments in Somalia challenged the established approaches to state formation; today it is relevant to examine the developing local trends of state-building under conditions of negative configuration of security.

The present state of the art in the academic discipline of International Relations suggests challenges posed to the international system. These challenges are caused by the gradual modification of the role of the state on the chessboard of international affairs. The classic domain of state dominance – security – is now likely to come to the hands of new players. As a result, several regions of the world are defined by the abundance of de-facto cases of weak governance and state failure. Examples of failed states in various regions of the world demonstrate that failure of the state as a key player in contemporary international relations to carry out its duties in political process in most cases leads to humanitarian failure.

There is a pressing need to scrutinize recent ongoing processes in a failed state in order to prevent humanitarian tragedies. Moreover, the examination of the factors that distort state rule is necessary in order to account for the new possible global threats that state failure/collapse may bring. This can demonstrate how the local poor governance and, eventually, state failure are transferred to a higher level of threat hierarchy (Rotberg 2004; Eizenstat, Porter and Weinstein 2005; Clapham 1996).

A preliminary hypothesis is that the modern security configuration in an underdeveloped region poses challenges to governance, which the states can not overcome. Poor governance, which results from this process, generates a sustained

---

1 A previous version of this chapter appeared in the *Central European Journal of International & Security Studies*, and parts of that article have been used here with kind permission of CEJISS.

internal conflict within the states of the region. This provokes a spiral of internal violence, which may be viewed as a threat to the existence of states.

Approaching State Failure in Post-Westphalia Conditions

The phenomenon of state failure has attracted attention of scholars of the International Relations discipline in the 1990s with the dissolution of the Yalta-Potsdam system and the end of the Cold War. In the two decades since that pivotal moment in International Relations, the issue of a failed state remains unresolved. This poses a new challenge to scholars, given the new system of International Relations that is emerging. In fact, the issue of state failure has been viewed as a local phenomenon with no significance for the global political development attached to it. However, an almost 20-year period of unsuccessful attempts to resolve, or to create a viable theoretical and practical framework to address this issue calls for a revision of state failure and its current trends.

Previously, state failure has been addressed retrospectively from a historical perspective, where chronologies of failure were demonstrated. Various policy implications were offered to address this problem; however, none of them was implemented successfully (Yannis 2002). Today, several new approaches to this phenomenon are developing.

One of the new approaches to analyzing state failure is offered by the Mo Ibrahim Foundation and the World Peace Foundation. The Ibrahim Index of African Governance offers data for African governance 2000–2008, and presents a cumulative set of indices of governance performance in Africa, i.e. making a hierarchy of failed states and showing the areas of state failure. According to the authors of the Index, it

> ... uniquely defines 'good governance' as the delivery of key political goods, which we specify in terms of five categories, fifteen sub-categories, and fifty-eight sub-sub-categories. We argue that this definition is comprehensive and common to all countries. Good government means the supply of those core political goods, whatever the culture and whatever else the government might undertake. The delivery of those core political goods can be measured with basic figures and statistics on poverty, infrastructure, the free and fairness of elections, the absence of war, and so on. Such statistics can be defined, operationalized, and measured in an objective way and, if done correctly, verified and reproduced by others. (Rotberg and Gisselquist 2008: 40)

As the authors of the Ibrahim Index of African Governance explain, 'The Index is composed of 57 separate markers capturing the performance of individual countries' (Rotberg and Gisselquist 2008: 20–21). The outcome of the calculations performed by the authors of the Index is presented in the form of a ranking chart for all African countries. The governance assessment criteria are then evaluated:

'The essential political goods can be summarized and gathered under five categories: 1) Safety and Security; 2) Rule of Law, Transparency and Corruption; 3) Participation and Human Rights; 4) Sustainable Economic Opportunity; 5) Human Development' (Rotberg and Gisselquist 2008: 20). The authors of the Index stress:

> The Index of African Governance is unique ... in a number of key ways. First, it is one of the few to measure 'governance' broadly defined. Most other work focuses on *components* of good governance – peace and security, the rule of law, corruption, political participation, human rights, sustainable development, etc. (Rotberg and Gisselquist 2008: 40)

In parallel, the Fund for Peace organization, founded in 1957, presents annual Failed States Index, which covers governance performance in all countries of the world from 2005. This index demonstrates a mathematically-based approach to assessing state failure, based on a number of formulas, which allows calculating and visualizing the existing situation in terms of state failure, as well as the prospect of failure in various countries, and to observe the contrasting cases of countries with almost no potential of state failure. The calculation of the Index is based on assessing social, political and economic indicators of state failure:

Social Indicators:
I-1. Mounting Demographic Pressures;
I-2. Massive Movement of Refugees or Internally Displaced Persons creating complex Humanitarian Emergencies;
I-3. Legacy of Vengeance-Seeking Group Grievance or Group Paranoia;
I-4. Chronic and Sustained Human Flight; Economic Indicators;
I-5. Uneven Economic Development along Group Lines;
I-6. Sharp and/or Severe Economic Decline; Political Indicators;
I-7. Criminalization and/or Delegitimization of the State;
I-8. Progressive Deterioration of Public Services;
I-9. Suspension or Arbitrary Application of the Rule of Law and Widespread Violation of Human Rights;
I-10. Security Apparatus Operates as a 'State Within a State';
I-11. Rise of Factionalized Elites;
I-12. Intervention of Other States or External Political Actors. (Fund for Peace 2010)

As for 2008, the highest rank for state failure was accredited to Somalia with a total of 114.2 score, and the lowest rank – to Norway with a total of 16.8 score. The ranking allows visualizing the 'red zone' countries with highest prospects for state failure (including 35 countries) and making comparisons between them on a series of indicators, mentioned above.

However, there are certain drawbacks to this developing Index-based approach. The prime shortcoming seems to be the impossibility to use these indices for making an overview of failed states in a dynamic and/or regional perspective. The problem is that the number of analyzed country cases in these indices varies from year to year, so the position and rating of a given country would be different each year. For example, the Failed State Index includes available data from 2005 to 2008, while the Index of African Governance contains data from 2000 to 2008, with reports and rankings for 2000, 2002, 2005, 2006, 2007 and 2008 available. This carries a potential of misjudgement, partially acknowledged by the authors of the indices: 'Scores for each country cannot be compared meaningfully year to year, but may unfortunately be interpreted in that way by those who do not fully understand the Index methodology' (Rotberg and Gisselquist 2008: 34). Given these drawbacks, the Indices, however consistent, do not allow to assess State failure as a regional phenomenon.

Another approach to state failure may be derived from the International Law discipline. In international legal terms, paradoxically, there is no such officially recognized term as 'failed state'. However, there is a growing debate about whether it is possible to recognize any political and territorial unit as a state, if it does not correspond with the basic UN provisions for the declaration of an independent state. In the UN tradition, a self-governing territory was recognized as an independent state if it could match certain criteria. Generally, an entity could be granted a status of an independent state if it proved possession of a defined territory, permanent population, and effective government, capacity to enter into relations with other states, independence and sovereignty. Moreover, there exists an international practice of recognizing seceding entities/autonomies as newly-created states.

From the perspective of modern international law, failed states pose a challenge to the established system of recognition of states as system units. Moreover, international legal system is not able to cope with this phenomena, as there is no mechanism of 'denouncing' the state, or withdrawal of the status of the state from a given unit. This was acknowledged by International Relations scholars in 1996, when Jeffrey Herbst suggested applying a mechanism of 'decertification' to de-facto failed states: 'Decertification would be a strong signal that something has gone wrong in an African country, and that parts of the international community are no longer willing to continue the myth that every state is always exercising sovereign authority' (Herbst 1996/1997: 142). In his opinion, this procedure would further a multidisciplinary approach, allowing us to take into consideration structural factors, which have long been ignored in analyzing state failure: 'Unfortunately, the international community, in its response to state failure in Africa, has refused to acknowledge the structural factors at work, despite mounting evidence that the loss of sovereign control is becoming a pattern in at least parts of Africa' (Herbst 1996/1997: 125).

There is a line of reasoning which views state failure as a process, which is inherent in the global political system, and which contributes to state formation: 'Depending on one's understanding of "collapse" and the political dynamics that give rise to it, it is indeed conceivable to regard collapse as part of processes of state reconfiguration and formation' (Doornboos 2002: 798). This, in its turn, calls for a question whether this reasoning applies to the failed state situation, visualized in case of former Somalia. The question is whether it is possible to regard the emerging self-proclaimed entities on the territory of the former Somalia as non-recognized states, and thus, actors in the international system with an effective internal structure of government: 'the right to be a State is dependent at least in the first instance upon the exercise of full governmental powers with respect to some area of territory' (Crawford 2007: 46). In relation to security conditions these circumstances create a situation when it is hard to distinguish politically viable entities, which maintain the mechanisms of effective control and management of domestic and external security of self-proclaimed autonomies. This can be seen as a threat to the security environment of the Horn of Africa: the whole system of political interactions exists under conditions of a partial power vacuum (since a structurally coherent national system player of Somalia de-facto does not exist).

Another point is that in case of any failed state there is a collision of two fundamental principles of international law. On the one hand, the internationally-recognized principle (and a corresponding right) of self-determination provides an official opportunity for any territorial and political unit to proclaim independence and seek international recognition. In case of failing or failed states, where certain territorial units seek secession from a failing entity (or a 'dissolving' state), in legal terms,

> The secession of a self-determination unit, where self-determination is forcibly prevented … will normally be reinforced by the principle of self-determination, so that the degree of effectiveness required as a precondition of recognition will be much less extensive than in the case of secession. (Crawford 2007: 383)

This presents another potential threat to the regional security environment, as in conditions of territorial demise of a failed state there is a strong tendency for fragmentation, which leads to local spiral of violence and inter-ethnic clashes.

On the other hand, international law protects the principle of territorial integrity of the state 'at least so far as external use of force and intervention are concerned – though not to the point of providing a guarantee' (Crawford 2007: 384). Another point is that actually possessing a formal ownership (or claim) of territory does not support the claims of self-proclaimed entities to be regarded as states, as only the effectiveness of governance is regarded as the criteria of state in its right:

> The requirement that a putative State have an effective government might be regarded as central to its claim to statehood. 'Governance' or 'effective government' is evidently a basis for the other central criterion of independence'. (Crawford 2007: 55)

Territorial sovereignty is not ownership of but governing power with respect to territory (Crawford 2007: 56):

> The right to be a State is dependent at least in the first instance upon the exercise
> of full governmental powers with respect to some area of territory. (Crawford
> 2007: 46)

As a result of this collision of two fundamental principles of international law,
especially in the case of failed states, there is no clear understanding of norms that
are applicable in the case of failed state and 'there is no longer one single test for
secessionary independence' (Crawford 2007: 384).

In cases of countries, where civil strife continues, a notion of a 'belligerent
recognition' may be applicable:

> Where a secessionary movement had achieved a certain degree of governmental
> and military organization, issues of responsibility ... impelled a certain de
> facto recognition of the situation even though the conflict was continuing ...
> By virtue of recognition of belligerency third States were entitled to maintain
> strict neutrality between the parties to the conflict and the insurgents achieved a
> separate though temporary status. (Crawford 2007: 380)

In this sense, the phenomenon of state failure in conditions of an emerging
post-Westphalia system creates a certain window of opportunity for maintaining
security at local levels: if the notion of a 'belligerent recognition' is officially
granted to warring local entities, which possess a viable level of territorial and
political organization, it may arouse a certain degree of stabilization of the political
situation on ground. This may be seen as a small step towards progressing to peace
negotiations.

However, one notion on behalf of state failure in legal understanding should
be remarked:

> It is necessary to distinguish unilateral secession of part of a State and the outright
> dissolution of the predecessor State as a whole. In the latter case there is, by
> definition, no predecessor State continuing in existence whose consent to any
> new arrangements can be sought ... The dissolution of a State may be initially
> triggered by the secession or attempted secession of one part of that State. If the
> process goes beyond that and involves a general withdrawal of all or most of the
> territories concerned, and no substantial central or federal component remains
> behind, it may be evident that the predecessor State as a whole has ceased to
> exist. (Crawford 2007: 390–91)

In case of a failed state of Somalia, there exist a number of self-proclaimed,
diplomatically unrecognized units, some of which have been exercising a de-facto
power in their territories for several decades. In particular, this is the case with
Somaliland and Puntland, and to a lesser extent with Maakhir and Galmudug. To
date, none of these self-proclaimed self-determination units has been recognized
internationally *de jure*. Moreover, the situation with the exercise of power over the

territories and, as a consequence, the maintenance of security, is largely dependent on the activization of new sub-state actors within the general configuration of a 'failed state' scheme. These sub-state actors in case of Somali are represented by the ethnic clans and networks, which may be considered patronate-based local elites.

Trend 1: Patronate-based Elites: Internal Actors within a Failed State Configuration

Elites are considered to be a personalized type of market and economy players. It is common knowledge that the role of elites in the development of a country is projected in the economic sector, in political and social spheres. Elites exhibit their role as actors in a complex of intertwined economic, political and social interactions between citizens. Modern economic and political elites conduct activity in a new global configuration, produced by the emerging post-Westphalian world order. The present state of affairs suggests changes and challenges posed to the present international system – most evidently, by the gradual decline of state as a key player on the chessboard of international affairs. The shift of focus is thus evident, as domestic economy, which is one of the classic domains of state prevalence now is likely to come to the hands of new players.

The post-Westphalian era creates a new framework of action for elites, as the role of the state as a key player in the market has been decreased. The state as a player in the market gradually steps away from the intense market interactions in certain areas, and this gives way to the activization of alternative players. In developed economies, this new configuration contributed to the expansion of the role of political and economic elites in post-Westphalian conditions, whereas in underdeveloped economies the situation is not so obvious. In underdeveloped economies, the structure of industries and markets is still largely dependant on the state as a regulator of economic transactions. These markets exist in conditions of traditional society, where the component of personal interaction may at times be more important than the rule of conduct, introduced by the state.

Evidently, the type of economic and political elite in a given country depends largely on the regime type, which exists in it (Schedler 2002; Spears 2002). The type and essence of a regime predetermine the type of governance in the country, which, in its turn, influences the functioning of the country's economy in general.

In underdeveloped economies, major economic subjects – elites – conduct their economic activity under the strong influence of the system of interactions, which is typical for traditional societies. In these traditional economies, patronate-based elites play the role of key economic and political actors on both the economic market and the political arena.

Globalization increases elites' competition and widens the prospects of modernization in these economies. The governments are induced to 'maintain the "opening" of these societies, develop the economy and thus limit the regulating capacity in a country' (Kaiser 1998: 3). However, this entails a potential of fragmentation of a weak state, because, as Martin Doornboos noted, in many post-colonial African states 'their survival as independent states would have come to a halt had it not been for the international recognition of their sovereignty' (Doornboos 2002: 809; also see Jackson 1990).

Originally Africa was associated with particular political and economic development mechanisms. The internal security configuration in Africa remains under the strong influence of clientelism, which may be defined as dissemination of ethnic, religious, clan-based, family-based and other liaisons in the political sphere. Clientelism remains one of the basic principles of recruitment of elites in underdeveloped countries (such as Somalia and Ethiopia). Political and economic tradition still plays a foremost role in these societies. In countries of Africa in general the process of state-building has never been accomplished according to western standards. As a result, it is these countries where all mistakes and miscalculations of governance are most visible (see Zartman 1995). Studying elites as political and economic actors in Africa can be conducted within the framework of discussing personalized actors of intra-societal interaction. In Somalia, the analysis of elites is complicated, because a single economic subject may be represented in different elite strata. This results in constant internal uncertainty and hinders economic development. In underdeveloped societies polarized elites rest on the same social base, and this contributes to permanent instability in the political sphere.

One of the key differences between western and oriental practices of creating intra-state political structure is visualized in the tradition of recruiting the ruling elite through political parties' competition. Political parties in African societies are often formed on the basis of a 'patron-client' relationship, which excludes the consideration of political platforms and manifestos of the parties. The political relations between parties are substituted by the vulnerable system of personal and often family- or relative-based relations between leaders and party members. In certain cases, this system is based on relationship between ethnical clans, local communities and religious groups, which are related neither with party policy, nor with party manifesto.

Organizational structure in such societies is based on authoritarian principles. The key political leader (often an incumbent president) creates a ruling 'presidency clan' – an informal network of professional politicians and businessmen, who hold key posts in the government. This structure rests on the system of personal relations between its members, which may be based on religious, ethnic, family unity, as well as on connection in business liaisons and common political interests.

Internal security configuration in these countries is haunted by the problem of power distribution and means of adapting traditional institutions of regulating national economies to new formats. During the whole post-colonial period traditional economic and political institutions of these societies have been transforming in order to adapt to liberalized markets, fast-track democratization and structural transformation of political and economic systems of these countries. Nonetheless, political elites failed to deal with the focal problem of power transfer, which is crucial for maintaining the process of democratic liberalization and opening of national economies. Political elites were eventually substituted by alternative elites – that is, patronate-based elites, which were formed on the basis of clan relationships between different ethnic groups.

In Somalia, ethnic clans act as non-traditional non-state actors in the whole system of political controversies in this area (and even beyond the territory of former Somalia). Clans represent a type of an internal actor in the sub-state system, and they often perform their activities as mediators between local population, military bands and formations, economic enterprises and traditional general jurisdiction courts in form of a court of Sharia. As seen in Somalia, 'clans are determined by patrilineal descent and membership can be as large as several hundred thousand members. Within the larger clan structure, smaller groups, known as diya-paying groups, also exist' (Coyne 2006: 347).

Also, clans in former Somalia represent a type of the emerging patronate-based elite. It is visible that political parties in many failing societies are often formed on the basis of 'patron-client' relationship, which excludes the consideration of political platforms and manifestos of the parties. The political relations between parties are substituted by the vulnerable system of personal and often family- or relative-based relationships between leaders and party members. In certain cases, this system is based on relationship between ethnical clans, local communities and religious groups, which are related neither with party policy, nor with party manifesto (see Fortes and Evans-Pritchard 1940).

Several decades after gaining independence from colonial powers it becomes clear that in the majority of cases the first leaders of newly independent states did not realize that their states, in fact, were mere conglomerates of uncohesive local communities with diverging schemes of subjection (power-sharing); nor had they considered the limits of available resources and possibilities (for detailed discussion see Austin 1984). Attempts to ruin patronate-client-based system of governance, which appears to be natural for oriental societies, prove to be senseless, as they do not contribute to the dissemination of liberal market norms and principles. In this sense, colonialism, which induced the westernized system of governance and market interactions to African countries, failed to root these new systems into the basis of traditional-type governance, which was authentic to the colonized territory (Kreijen 2004: 66).

In modern conditions PBE (patronate-based elites) act as alternative elites, which substitute market-created elites. PBEs are based on deeply rooted interrelations between clans or ethnic groups in underdeveloped economies. The influence of PBEs on development of economy in these countries can be both positive and negative. Moreover, the impact of PBEs on economic development of underdeveloped countries is closely connected with political transformations in these states. In a failed state situation, PBEs act as alternative elites, or alternative market players. PBEs use the status quo of power vacuum and non-existence of state-imposed regulation to create new conditions for both economic and political markets.

Trend 2: Non-state Actors in a Failed State: A New Threat?

In the emerging international system the role of the non-state actors becomes significant. Some scholars believe in the positive impact of these actors in the process of state-building, whereas some critically object to it. It is interesting to look at how this new trend is demonstrated in the region of the Horn of Africa.

In this region, since 1990s, various radicalist organizations have been widening and intensifying the scope of their activities. Historically, the Horn of Africa countries have had a sustained relationship with the Islamic Middle East countries. However, in the 1990s the influence of radicalist organizations widened as a result of an emerging 'power vacuum' in the region. Since the 1990s, business groups from Saudi Arabia, Iran, Turkey and Malaysia have been widening investment inflows into strategically important Ethiopian economy sectors – i.e. mining, metal and food industries. Alongside, these business groups were investing into construction of mosques, thus helping to introduce Islam in traditionally non-Islamic regions. After Ethiopia-Eritrea war in 1998–2000, both countries were exhausted financially, which created a demand for loans and direct investment from the Arab countries. As a consequence, the government of Ethiopia had to adapt its confessional policy. With increasing foreign investment inflow from the Arab countries, several Muslim organizations were revived or newly created. These included the Supreme Council on Muslim Affairs, the Regional Association of Muslim Scholars and others. At present, these organizations operate as networked non-state actors on a sub-state level, aiming at widening the presence of Islamist organizations in all regions of the country. For instance, in the Afaria region of Ethiopia (Afaria is situated close to Ethiopia-Somalia and Ethiopia-Kenya borders) there is a sustained standoff between tigrai-amhara organizations (Tigrai Liberation National Front and Afar Liberation Front).

Other significant radicalist organizations include Al-Ittihad al-Islamiyya, the Islamic Front for Oromo Liberation, the National Front for Liberation of Ogaden, the Oromo Liberation Front and Muslim Brothers. These radical organizations aim at creating the 'Islamic Republic of Oromia' in the border region of Ethiopia, Kenya and Somalia. The government of Ethiopia has taken political, economic and military measures to weaken the activities of one of the most active radicalist organizations – the Oromo Liberation Front. However, the government fails to resist the radical activities of the other Fronts, as these organizations have exhibited attempts to unite their efforts against it.

The impact of radical and extremist organizations in the Horn of Africa is increasing. In general, it has several aims:

1. consistent geographic expansion of the Islamized regions;
2. providing financial support to local radical Islamic organizations;
3. fast-track transformation of Muslim communities into extremist organizations in several regions;

4. incorporation of sharia-based law in Muslim communities to the detriment of state-imposed law;
5. lobbying Islamist activists in government.

These organizations act as sub-state actors with an aim to provoke the local radical Muslim communities to open violent standoffs with other communities. Activities of these radical organizations are often well-coordinated: for example, they attempted to initiate clashes on the basis of religion in different regions of Ethiopia in 2002. Earlier, in 1999, the followers of the Oromo Liberation Front staged local clashes in the towns of Harar, Nazret and Addis-Ababa (http://news. bbc.co.uk/2/hi/world/monitoring/258640.stm).

An international radicalist organization, Al-Ittihad al-Islamiyya, has a history of involvement in the Horn of Africa. This organization, which acts as an independent non-state actor in the region, coordinates its activities with the local extremist and radicalist organizations (including Fronts supporting the activity of Oromo, Afar and Tigrai political groups) and with Somalian military and political groupings. Alongside with Al-Ittihad al-Islamiyya, there are other non-state radicalist organizations, which aim at promoting extremism from their bases in Somalia, such as Al-Majmaa al-Islam, Al-Sunna ba al-Djamaa, Ansar al-Sunna. The activity of these organizations is a telling example of potential threats which may be cast on countries neighbouring the former state of Somalia. It is reasonable to expect that in conditions of continuing civil war and political instability in the territories of former Somalia, the potential role and impact of the radicalized organizations will gradually increase. In its turn, this activization of non-state actors in the form of violent radicalized organizations may contribute to the worsening of conditions not only in the failed state of Somalia, but in countries of the Horn of Africa in general, thus enhancing the prospect of a regional failure.

Trend 3: Local Perspectives of Recent Developments in Somalia

As noted previously, in war-torn Somalia, the substitution of elites by clans in political sphere reveals the most acute political problems. In fact, this substitution has contributed to the process of state failure by creating a parochial mechanism of resource distribution:

> In the Somali case, it was inability to accommodate conflicting interests, often articulated on a clan basis, and the instrumental use to which the state apparatus was put in the pursuit of this inter-clan violence, that caused the disintegration of the fragile system. For all its repressive qualities, the Somali state had a relatively weak presence within the society, which meant that it could all the more easily collapse and be thrown off when inter-clan conflict and repression came to a head. (Doornboos 2002: 801)

In Somalia, in 1991–1999 the patronate-based elites applied for international financial and humanitarian aid on behalf of the state of Somalia. International funds and agencies provided the requested aid to these recipients; however, there was no outcome in terms of development of the country. As the United Nations Development Programme does not assess the Human Development Index for Somalia, it is difficult to consider the exact data of aid inflow and redistribution of foreign aid between the leading clans in former Somalia.

In 1991–1993 the recipients of international aid distributed these resources between different clans according to the hierarchy of clans. The extensive scale of this 'distribution' is obvious, since the whole of Somalian society is based on a hierarchy of ethnic clans. Practically the whole amount of international aid has gone to clans, which formed the patronate-based elites in Somalia. These elites used the power vacuum which was created in conditions of state failure to establish a scheme of acquiring international financial aid without providing any warrants. As credits and loans to Somalian agencies have thus been abstracted from any state guarantees, the investment climate in the country has deteriorated. Major international investors started to abandon the country and eventually the majority of international assets were withdrawn from Somalia. This led to the decrease of social spending and, as a result, the level of poverty soared.

The political configuration of state failure is largely triggered by the de-facto creation and development of independent proto-state units, which claimed authority over several territories of Somalia. This was partly endowed by the government of former Somali Republic in 1960, when 'political affiliations quickly developed along clan-based lines ... The majoritarian parliament created a set of incentives that led to constant struggles where clans would attempt to form coalitions and then create disputes among other clans in order to control a majority' (Coyne 2006: 348). In 1991 the northern territories of Somalia (former British Somaliland) claimed independence from Somaliland. (http://news.bbc.co.uk/2/hi/africa/country_profiles/1072611.stm). In 1998 in the north-eastern parts of Somalia the Majeerteen ethnic clan claimed independence for the autonomy of Puntland. (http://news.bbc.co.uk/2/hi/africa/country_profiles/1072611.stm) In south-western Somalia territories including Bay, Bakuul, Jubbada Dexe, Gedo, Shabeelaha Hoose and Jubbada Hoose declared independence from Somalia and in 1998 the creation of independent Jubaland was declared. All these independent units were created by clans, or patronate-based elites, which also established limited markets for the exchange of goods and services on these territories. Some of these attempts were rather successful, and they were noted in the Report of the Secretary-General of the UN as prerequisites for 'calm conditions' in the situation of a 'chaos and anarchy' in the rest of the former Somalia (Report of the Secretary-General of the UN S/2001/1211, 19 December 2000, paragraph 34; Report of the Secretary-General of the UN S/2001/1201, 25 October 2002, paragraph 55). One of these successful attempts was exercised by Somaliland, which 'while not recognized by any foreign government as a legitimate state ... has remained stable with the creation of a constitution' (Coyne 2006: 349).

An ongoing standoff between Somaliland and Puntland, fostered by competition for power and resources between patronate-based elites, resulted in the status-quo of non-recognition of neither of these units as states on the international arena. An ongoing territorial dispute, fostered by the struggle for power in the territories of the former state of Somalia, is actually developing as a full-scale war with new political entities emerging as a result of it (Conflict Barometer 2007: 31). This creates another inherent security threat for the regional system of inter-state interactions, as what is seen in these circumstances is in fact a 'process of state-building which appears consistently to exacerbate instability and armed conflict' (Menkhaus 2004: 18).

Both sides claimed the provinces of Sanaag and Sool as part of their respective territories. The conflict started in 2003, when Puntland took control of Sool's provincial capital, Las Anod. In April, both sides engaged in skirmishes in the province of Sanaag, which later declared its independence from Puntland as well as its allegiance to the Transitional Federal Government of Somalia, forming the autonomous entity of Maakhir.

Another example may be drawn from other non-recognized proto-state units on the territory of former Somalia – the regions of Sanaag and Bari, where the Maakhir ethnic clan has declared autonomy over their territories in 2007. In Maakhir-controlled lands, the political and business markets exist as a result of constant conflict (and bargaining) between Somaliland and Puntland.

However, the territory of south-eastern and southern Somalia, where the majority of population is concentrated, remains in political and economic chaos, sustained by the competition between patronate-based elites. In structural terms, this territory is a 'vacuum of power' territory, with no elements of sustained governance even in local communities. In this way, patronate-based elites, which control the local markets and communities in view of an ongoing civil strife, prevent the inflow of investors to these territories and restrict normal business and political interactions with the international environment.

Activization of non-state actors, such as clans (patronate-based elites) and radicalized religious organizations in newly created proto-state units has contributed to the sustaining of a situation of a de-facto absence of a unified central government in Somalia for the last 10 years. The interim (transitional) government tries to control parts of southern Somalia from its capital in Baidoa; however, it is not deemed legitimate by the majority of Somalians. In this situation of chaos, the future of security configuration in a failed state of Somalia remains an open question. However, at this stage it is evident that new developments, demonstrated by the Somalia case, show the rise of new actors and trends, which may have an ambiguous influence on the process of state-building in these territories. It is visible that the current condition of state failure remains a threat to the system of regional inter-state system, given the conditions of the emerging post-Westphalian order.

Conclusions

Despite a growing need to address the current trends of political and territorial development in situation of state failure, there is a lack of a multidisciplinary approach that would merge disperse views on state-building attempts under negative security conditions. As demonstrated in the case of former Somalia, self-proclaimed territorial and political entities may exhibit a potential of advancing to self-governance. However, these attempts are hindered by the negative conditions of security configuration, largely dependent on the ongoing civil strife.

The case of Somalia reflects a growing need of a realistic assessment of the patterns of governance in the countries of the underdeveloped regions of the world and of widening the debate on the mechanisms of prediction of potential threats to sustained governance in modern conditions.

Changes in the contemporary system of International Relations impose new challenges to the process of state-building under negative security conditions. The role of non-state actors, both internal and external, is intensified by the instability, caused by the continuing inter-clan war in territories of former state of Somalia. On the internal (sub-state) level, the patronate-based elites attempt to get hold of the authority of the state in managing security in a failed state. On the external level, the rise of the radicalized non-governmental organizations provokes additional violence and thus sustains chaos in a failed state. This ruins attempts to consolidate the self-proclaimed autonomies on the territories of former Somalia.

These trends carry both positive and negative consequences not only for the failed state, but for the region in general. A positive consequence may be the development of new forms of statehood with patronate-based elites being the pioneers of the process. A negative consequence may be the intensification of activities of radicalized organizations, which may hinder the process of stabilization of the political situation in this region.

Finally, the complicated process of initial state-building in a situation of the negative security environment of a failed state may be viewed as a first and unique attempt to create states in a modern configuration of the system of International Relations. This calls for a response of the scholars of the International Relations discipline, in order to offer a theoretical comprehension of these practical developments.

Bibliography

Austin, D. (1984). *Politics in Africa*, 2nd edn. Hannover: University Press of New England.

Clapham, C. (1996). *Africa and the International System: The Politics of State Survival*. New York: Cambridge University Press.

Conflict Barometer (2008). Heidelberg Institute for International Conflict Research, retrieved 10 June 2009, from http://hiik.de/en/konfliktbarometer/pdf/ConflictBarometer_2007.pdf.

Coyne, C. (2006). Reconstructing Weak and Failed States: Foreign intervention and the Nirvana fallacy. *Foreign Policy Analysis*, 2, 343–60.

Crawford, Y. (2007). *The Creation of States in International Law*. Oxford: Oxford University Press.

Doornboos, M. (2002). State Collapse and Fresh Starts: Some Critical Reflections. *Development and Change* 33(5), 797–815.

Doornboos, M. and Markakis, J. (1994). Society and State in Crisis: What Went Wrong in Somalia? In Mohammed Salih, M.A. and Wohlgemuth, L. (eds), *Crisis Management and the Politics of Reconciliation in Somalia*, pp. 12–18. Uppsala: Nordiska Afrikainstitutet.

Eizenstat, S., Porter, J.E. and Weinstein, J.M. (2005). Rebuilding Weak States. *Foreign Affairs*, 84, 134–46.

Fortes, M. and Evans-Pritchard, E. (eds) (1940). *African Political Systems*. Oxford: Oxford University Press.

Fund for Peace (2010). The Failed State Index, retrieved 15 June 2009 from http://www.fundforpeace.org/web/index.php?option=com_content&task=view&id=99&Itemid=323.

Herbst, J. (1996/1997). Responding to State Failure in Africa. *International Security*, 21(3) (Winter 1996/97), 120–44.

Jackson, R. (1990). *Quasi-states' Sovereignty, International Relations and the Third World*. Cambridge: Cambridge University Press.

Kaiser, K. (1998). Globalization as a Problem of Democracy. *Internationale Politik*, 4, April.

Kreijen, G. (2004). *State Failure, Sovereignty and Effectiveness*. Leiden-Boston: Martinus Nijhoff Publishers.

Menkhaus, K. (2004). *Somalia: State Collapse and the Threat of Terrorism*. London: International Institute of Strategic Studies.

The Mo Ibrahim Foundation (2006). Background Briefing, retrieved 12 May 2009, from http://www.moibrahimfoundation.org/index2008/pdf/english_briefing_note.pdf.

Rotberg, R. (2004). *When States Fail: Causes and Consequences*. Princeton, NJ: Princeton University Press.

Rotberg, R. and Gisselquist, R. (2008), Ibrahim Index of African Governance, retrieved on 13 November 2008 from http://www.moibrahimfoundation.org/The%20full%202008%20Ibrahim%20Index.pdf.

Schedler, A. (2002). The Menu of Manipulation. *Journal of Democracy*, V.13, #2, April 2002, 36–50.

Spears, I. (2002). Africa: The Limits of Power-Sharing. *Journal of Democracy*, 13(3), July, 123–36.

United Nations (2000). Report of the Secretary-General of the UN S/2001/1211, retrieved 15 April 2009, from http://daccessdds.un.org/doc/UNDOC/GEN/N00/785/22/PDF/N0078522.pdf?OpenElement.

United Nations (2002). Report of the Secretary-General of the UN (2002). S/2001/1201, retrieved 15 April 2009, from http://daccessdds.un.org/doc/UNDOC/GEN/N02/658/73/PDF/N0265873.pdf?OpenElement.

Yannis, A. (2002). State Collapse and its Implications for Peace-Building and Reconstruction. *Development and Change* 33(5), 817–35.

Zartman, W. (ed.) (1995). *Collapsed States: The Disintegration and Restoration of Legitimate Authority*. Boulder, CO: Lynne Rienner.

Chapter 7

NATO's First Mission to Africa – Darfur

Glen Segell

Introduction

The complex international system of the twenty-first century has seen an increase in bilateral inter-regionalism and trans-regionalism. This is seen as an element of globalisation where regional organisations now act outside of their originally defined regions. This chapter will examine NATO's answer to a call for assistance from the African Union in their AMIS mission in the Darfur region of Sudan in April 2005, providing airlift and training until the end of the AMIS mission in December 2007. This was the first time that NATO entertained a task on the African continent. NATO undertook the mission on humanitarian grounds without invoking any treaty and without any member state's security being under any direct threat. This was a milestone in NATO's history. The Darfur mission set the milestone for further missions to assist the African Union in Somalia and in general in such matters as training. Missions of this type suggest that the question on the future of NATO as a global actor is in the making. Such a mission also provides a case to understanding regional alliances, regionalism and the development of trans-regionalism as the process of globalisation in an international system which is not solely typified by international relations between sovereign states. Such an international system labelled as being post-Westphalia is characterised by interactions across sovereign borders in security alliances (NATO) or in regional structures such as the European Union or African Union (EU or AU).

To understand the uniqueness covered in this chapter is to define NATO as a regional alliance of the North Atlantic area consisting of member states from North America and Europe. Each member state has a treaty agreement to assist other member states in matters relating to their security – one for all and all for one. In recent years the treaty interpretation has broadened from the initial Cold War intent of the Soviet military threat to include civil defence assistance as well as extra-regional deployment of armed forces, to Afghanistan for example, to take the battle to the territory of the adversary. Not mentioned in any NATO treaty is assistance for another regional alliance on a continent not covered by NATO's remit in order to provide assistance for a peace-support mission, based upon humanitarian grounds and not on the basis of any threat to any NATO member state. Yet this is exactly what took place. NATO in April 2005 agreed to provide airlift, logistics, training and related support to assist the African Union Mission in Sudan (AMIS) force deployed to the Darfur region of Sudan based upon humanitarian grounds. In the deployment of NATO forces there was no mention of which article of which treaty was being invoked.

This chapter will attempt to provide a survey of the policy formulation and implementation of NATO as a trans-regional actor in Africa, from April 2005 to December 2007 – the date from which NATO provided assistance to the date that the AMIS force was disbanded. Trans-regional activities of the type that NATO engaged in have been identified by Jürgen Rüland (2005) as falling into two groups: bilateral inter-regionalism and trans-regionalism The former is defined by Rüland as group-to-group exchanges of information and cooperation (projects) in specific policy, based on a low level of institutionalisation, with no common overarching institutions, both sides exclusively relying on their own institutional infrastructure. This typifies the specific NATO-AMIS interactions in Darfur where NATO (states from the North American and European region) assisted the AU (states from the African region) and where each was a regional organisation in its own right. The policy of the contributing NATO member states, predominately the United States and the United Kingdom, as well as Norway, the Netherlands and Germany is important to consider when evaluating the decision making and policy implementation of NATO.

The latter (trans-regionalism) is defined by Rüland as being found where the agenda grows in complexity requiring trans-regional fora, comprising states from more than one region with its own organisational infrastructure (secretariat for research, policy planning, preparation and coordination of meetings and implementation of decisions). Such processes of institutional evolution vest trans-regional fora with some form of independent agency and distinguish them from bilateral inter-regionalism. This typifies the post-Cold War trans-regionalism interest in such institutions as the Asia-Europe Meeting (ASEM), the Asia-Pacific Cooperation (APEC) and the ASEAN-EU dialogue and is often linked to debates on globalisation. The specific NATO-AMIS mission was not of this type yet after its conclusion subsequent NATO-AU interactions and EU-AU interactions have moved in this direction.

This chapter offers the NATO-AMIS mission, as bilateral inter-regionalism, showing that its successes enabled subsequent NATO-AU bilateral inter-regionalism for example NATO assistance to the AU Mission in Somalia, to the Africa Standby Force brigades and most recently NATO naval assistance to deter and apprehend pirates off the coast of Somalia. The growing complexity of interactions suggests the potential for NATO-AU relations to evolve to the stage of trans-regionalism with a unique secretariat for research, policy planning, preparation and coordination of meetings and implementation of decisions.

By considering this unique case of NATO's first trans-regional mission in Africa, this chapter will make three contributions. These will be to contribute to understanding the role of regional alliances for example the AU, about regional alliances supporting other regional alliances, for example NATO supporting the AU, and specifically about NATO as a trans-regional actor. The case study is so new that as of yet, no definitive study has been published on the topic of NATO-

AU relations nor on that of NATO's role in Darfur. There is barely coverage of this in short monographs, edited books, articles and conference papers where the sparse yet notable mentions are by Richard (2007: 272), Van Ardenne, Salih, Grono and Mendez (2006), Feinstein (2007: 33), Hauser and Kernic (2006: 27), House of Commons Defence Committee (2007: 28), Raftopoulos and Alexander (2008: 84) and Reeves and Brassard (2007: 292).

The Formulation of Policy

Darfur is no different from other parts of Africa, or indeed the world, that have faced tribal conflict for centuries over the territorial imperatives of the ownership, settlement or usage of land and water. The British colonial rule over the region centuries ago was unable to ameliorate this conflict. In recent times, conflict erupted in Darfur in February 2003 when rebels from ethnic African tribes took up arms, complaining of discrimination and oppression by Sudan's Arab-dominated government. The government is accused of unleashing Arab tribal militia known as the Janjaweed against civilians in a campaign of murder, rape and arson. The president of Sudan now (in 2009) faces indictment from the International Criminal Court (ICC) for genocide and crimes against humanity. During the period of NATO assistance to the AU, between 2005 and 2007, the conflict could be described as of low-intensity in military terms between local armed groups, militias, the armed forces of Sudan and Chad and bandit groups sponsored by both sides. Most of the weaponry used was personal weapons dominated by the Soviet era AK-47 assault rifle and rocket propelled grenades (RPG). Transport on the ground was by four-wheel drives and trucks – few are armoured plated. Artillery has not been used though the Sudanese government has used two Soviet era Antonov manufactured transport aircraft converted for ground attack role in mass bombing – mainly of civilian villages. There has been no aerial combat between Chad and Sudan. Accurate figures are hard to come by but there is no doubt that by 2005 when the AU requested NATO assistance that there was not much left in Darfur that had not felt the conflict. The international attention in 2005 focused predominately on internally displaced people (IDP), refugees in neighbouring Chad, and atrocities inflicted on civilians on a scale and magnitude that required outside intervention.

The unique milestone in the history of NATO that initiated its involvement in this conflict commenced on 26 April 2005. It was well known at the time that western states, including NATO member states, were expressing deep concern over the conflict in Darfur and at atrocities against civilians. They were uncertain as to how to ameliorate the situation but were engaged in ongoing diplomatic efforts especially at the United Nations (UN). Numerous debates took place and an embargo and sanctions were levelled at the Sudanese government yet consensus on a Security Council Resolution for a mandate on the use of armed intervention was not forthcoming. A permanent member of the Council, China, had shown reluctance to see such a resolution and would probably have vetoed it if one had been tabled. China has substantial trade with Sudan dominated by the acquisition of raw materials for Chinese industry such as oil and iron ore. In turn China provides infrastructure development such as tele-communications and road construction without any of the pre-requisites often called for by European governments such as human rights. However, a regional alliance, the African Union (AU), had reached agreement amongst its members to send a force for peacekeeping, based on its constitutive articles that permitted it to do so. So the African Union Mission in Sudan (AMIS) was created. However, as Segell (2008) has pointed out, the fact that the AU lacked the capabilities to deploy this force and its forces lacked the necessary training to undertake the mission was problematic.

It was therefore no surprise that on 26 April 2005 the African Union requested assistance, by letter from the Chairperson of the Commission of the African Union, Mr Alpha Oumar Konaré, to the NATO Secretary General. The request was for NATO logistics assistance in the deployment of the AMIS force aimed to end violence and improve the humanitarian situation in a region that has been suffering from conflict since 2003. At the same time the European Union (EU) received a similar request. In clarification of the letter of request the Chairperson of the African Union Commission, Alpha Oumar Konaré, visited NATO Headquarters on 17 May 2005 – the first ever visit of an AU official to NATO HQ.

It is important to stress that this was the first time in NATO's history that another regional political-security alliance had requested such humanitarian assistance where there no were common member states with NATO. At first glance it therefore appeared that no NATO member state had any obligation to commit forces to NATO and NATO had no Treaty obligation to provide any assistance. This was especially since Sudan was not within the regional remit of NATO's operations and because no NATO member state faced any direct security or defence threat from what was taking place in Darfur. However, it was also apparent at the time that NATO would be hard pressed to resist providing some form of assistance to the AU given the magnitude of atrocities and inability or lack of willingness of anyone else to take action.

It could be assumed that the leadership of NATO would be intricately involved. A study of NATO Secretary General Jaap de Hoop Scheffer by Hendrickson (2005) has shown that he was a cautious public advocate for extensive and sustained NATO operations in Darfur. This is despite his openly favoured position that the world could not turn a blind eye to atrocities against civilians in Darfur. The study has analysed his speeches and his focus of attention on public diplomacy. Despite being cautious he was instrumental as being an arbiter in the ongoing debate amongst European states that NATO should not be the sole forum and that the EU should assume a more prominent role. Interestingly, the analysis of his speeches shows that he was active in this regard before the AU made its formal request but chose not to challenge NATO member states to formulate their individual policies. In sum it appears that he has been successful in finding consensus between and amongst NATO member states and with other regional organisations such as the AU and EU.

When the formal request of the AU was made known to NATO member states they expressed their opinion, which had been well known for many years. This was the notion that the best way to deliver security to Darfur was to get those with primary responsibility for it to do it – the Government of Sudan. The pressing issue was that it was known that the Government of Sudan was not going to do this and indeed was the cause of the problem. The issue then was deciding when other international actors and which other international actors should assume responsibility for protecting civilians from being killed as a direct result of the policy of the Government of Sudan. After the Iraq debacle no state gave voice to such phrases as 'regime change'.

Hence on 27 April 2005, the North Atlantic Council tasked the Alliance's military authorities to provide, as a matter of urgency, advice on possible NATO support and whether this could be in co-ordination not only with the AU but also with the European Union (EU). This advice was prepared in full consultation, transparency and complementarity with the African Union, the European Union and the United Nations.

On 24 May 2005 the North Atlantic Council, after receiving advice from NATO military authorities, agreed on initial military options for possible NATO support (NATO, May 2005). These options included support to the African Union in the areas of: strategic airlift deployment; training, for example in command and control and operational planning; and improvement of ability of the AU's mission in Darfur to use intelligence. NATO support did not imply the provision of combat troops. In announcing this, the Secretary General of NATO (NATO, June 2005) said that NATO 'will consult in the coming days with the AU and others on how to transform these initial offers into concrete proposals responding to a specific request'. The NATO Secretary General (NATO, June 2005) stressed that the African Union remained 'in the driving seat to solve this difficult conflict and that the Alliance's role is to contribute to strengthening the African Union's capability to meet this challenge.'

An elaboration of Mr de Hoop Scheffer's thinking and NATO's policy and strategy towards trans-regionalism in Africa highlighted that NATO member states no longer believed that they were constrained by their Treaty obligations that had been formulated during the Cold War. NATO member states had voiced their intent to undertake some sort of action in the forum of UN and EU in support of the AU as all were concerned about the plight of civilians in Darfur. NATO member states, especially the United States, saw NATO as a means to implement what they stood for as sovereign states caring for humanity at large. Mr de Hoop Scheffer explained that Darfur showed the need for close cooperation between international organisations that is also an element of what he calls modern security; and that Darfur shows that the international community is ready to support the African Union. So it came to be that NATO commenced a non-combatant military operation in close consultation and in coordination with the European Union, with the United Nations and with the African Union.

The lessons of Iraq were well learnt and it was clear that any military operation would have to take into account the Government of Sudan. The situation in Darfur was a direct consequence of the Sudanese government policy. NATO was not intending to embark on a change of regime in Sudan. Yet NATO would airlift foreign forces onto the sovereign territory of Sudan to protect and engage in efforts against the policy of the Government of Sudan and its implementation by the Sudanese armed forces. So NATO made clear that it would only implement its policy once the Government of Sudan had given the green light to the African Union. This was a difficult issue since there was no direct relationship between NATO and the government in Khartoum and there was no intention of establishing one. Raftopoulos and Alexander (2008: 84) have analysed this, suggesting that the largest potential contributor, the United States had a dichotomy of interests as 1) it wished to maintain Khartoum as an ally in the war on terror and 2) it believed that genocide was being perpetrated in Darfur.

These factors were not considerations for the AU. The founding act of the AU (African Union 2000) concluded in 2000 establishes 'the right of the Union to intervene in a Member State pursuant to a decision of the Assembly in respect to grave circumstances namely: war crimes, genocide and crimes against humanity'. Although the AU favours African solutions to African problems, it is pragmatic and this was one such situation where it recognised that it needed help from other international and regional organisations.

When NATO made the public announcement to provide non-combatant military support to the AU AMIS mission on 25 May 2005 six former foreign ministers from different countries wrote a joint article for the *International Herald Tribune* (Albright et al. 2005) in a show of moral support for the ethics of NATO's intended action. They were astute to point out a fact that would be well versed three years later when the AMIS force was disbanded, NATO assistance ceased to AMIS and the AMIS force was replaced by a hybrid UN-AU force called UNAMID. Albright (USA), Cook (UK), Dini (Italy), Axworthy (Canada), Palacio (Spain), Derycke (Belgium), and Pitsuwan (Thailand), stated that 'the AU force is currently too small to cover an area the size of France and lacks critical logistical capacities; the militias continue to burn villages and besiege refugees in their camps'. They further called for 'NATO to immediately provide the AU with helicopters; command, control and support capabilities; and strategic and tactical lift'. Six months into the UNAMID mission on 1 January 2008 the new UNAMID force lacked exactly this – helicopters. The six former foreign ministers also called for NATO to draw on its Response Force, which at the time had an operational capacity of 17,000, and for NATO to put a brigade-sized element at the disposal of the United Nations to augment the AU force until it could build up sufficient strength of its own. This was not beyond the will of NATO member states but it would require authority from the UN Security Council for a Chapter VII resolution that would need to include a no-flight zone over Darfur. It was, however, clear that some states on the UN Security Council, notably China, would oppose such measures on the grounds that the Sudanese government should be given time to resolve the conflict in Darfur through a new political process. So NATO pursued the basic option of logistic air lift support and training. Only time will tell in historical hindsight if this was too little too late or if it was a significant turning point.

Whilst the diplomatic process pressed on the North Atlantic Council (NAC) turned to General James Jones, who held the most senior military position of NATO forces in Europe (SACEUR), and asked him to take the lead and put a liaison team on the ground to support this mission. A NATO press release (NATO, May 2005) informed that General Jones looked to his command centre in Heidelberg Germany and asked Allied Land Component Command Headquarters (ALCC HQ HD) to take the lead in providing a liaison team on the ground. He chose Brigadier General Andre Defawe, Deputy Chief of Staff for Operations, (ALCC HQ HD), to be his Senior Military Liaison Officer (SMLO). The other Heidelberg members of the liaison team were Sergeant Major Pascal Wijkman (Senior NCOIC), Lieutenant Colonel Carsten Petersen (Operations Cell Director) and Lieutenant Colonel Ed Mead (Military Assistant to the SMLO).

Operationally the NATO mission was undertaken by Joint Command Lisbon, Portugal – under the overall command of Allied Command Operations – where the local responsibility for the NATO Senior Military Liaison Officer (SMLO) team operated out of Addis Ababa, Ethiopia. The SMLO team was the NATO's single military point of contact in Addis Ababa with the African Union. In addition, it was the NATO military point of contact with the representatives of the countries contributing troops to the AMIS operation, the representatives of the donor nations pledging support to the African Union, the United Nations, the European Union and various embassies.

While the military machinery was being put into place, predominately US Air Force transport aircraft, the diplomatic process continued. The NATO Secretary General participated in a meeting in Addis Ababa on 26 May 2005 chaired by UN Secretary General Annan and AU Commission President Konaré where he pledged international support for the African Union's mission in Darfur.

Following that meeting, and based on further clarification and confirmation of the AU's requirements, as well as consultations with the African Union, the European Union and the United Nations, NATO's North Atlantic Council agreed on 8 June on the detailed modalities and extent of Alliance support. The decision to support the AU with strategic deployment and staff capacity building was formally announced on 9 June, at the meeting of NATO Ministers of Defence in Brussels and reported by the NATO Press Office (NATO, June 2005).

Implementing the Strategy and the Policy

Despite the agreement in principle to provide support to the AU it was not as straight forward in implementing it. A few days before the 9 June NATO announcement an open split was reported by many newspapers, including by Dombey (2005: 4) writing in the *Financial Times*. The split had occurred between members states of the EU and NATO on the decision on which organisation should coordinate measures in support of AMIS. A local Kenyan newspaper, *The East Standard* (2005), reported that the United States and Canada preferred NATO (through SHAPE) given that they were not EU members while France preferred the EU. The United Kingdom was already providing direct assistance to AMIS, such as financial aid noted in a DFID report (2006) which had been £32 million in 2004 and which had increased to £52 million in 2006. Also the UK's Foreign and Commonwealth Office chief police expert advised the AU's police commissioner on civil policing aspects of the AU's AMIS mission. Hence the United Kingdom wanted to continue direct assistance, as well as use both the EU and NATO. Other countries, for example, Germany, the Netherlands and Norway, remained undecided. An important factor for the European members of NATO who preferred the EU over that of NATO was that, unlike NATO, the EU Rapid Reaction Force had a defined purpose that included humanitarian, rescue and peacekeeping operations. The EU had been helping the AU since 2004 when NATO had not appeared particularly interested in Africa. Feinstein (2007: 42) informs that the EU also had recent experience on the African continent – Operation Artemis in June–September 2003 to the Democratic Republic of the Congo that had entailed sending 1,700 troops to secure a town (Bunia) to allow the return of some 60,000 refugees.

An international news wire service (AFP 2005) reported that pressure on the ground in Darfur was the deciding factor which shortened the spat leading both the EU and NATO to provide support to the AU-led military cell in Addis Ababa with the choice of organisations (EU or NATO) being left to individual member states of both regional organisations. Given that the main airlift aircraft would be from the United States, which is not an EU member, it was clear that NATO would be the main airlift supporting organisation to AMIS. The London-based ISIS research group (2006) informed that France used solely the EU while the UK used both the EU and NATO. Other countries like Norway and the Netherlands provided vehicles and equipment as part of their commitment to both the EU and NATO.

There was open relief in NATO over the quick resolve to the spat and throughout the mission there was complete transparency between the EU and NATO. Despite this there remained the niggling apprehension that the Berlin Plus framework had not been invoked – this being the agreement reached on 16 December 2002 where the EU and NATO had reached agreement on cooperation on international security. The Berlin Plus agreement was seen as essential since the EU's Rapid Reaction Force and NATO's Rapid Reaction Force would draw from the same limited pool of deployable European forces and equipment. This given that the membership of both organisations overlapped to a great extent. This was exampled by the commitment, if not over-commitment, to other ongoing conflicts that included Afghanistan and Iraq and peace-support operations in the Balkans.

Hence there was apprehension in 2005 that the Berlin Plus Agreement had fallen by the wayside as an essential initial element would be a common planning centre or a joint chain of command that had not yet been established. At the time NATO planned through SHAPE while the EU used the Strategic Airlift Coordination

Centre (SALCC) in Eindhoven, Netherlands. Establishing the centre or command would have distracted and delayed assisting the AU by months or even years. This lead to further apprehension, that without such a centre or command both EU and NATO support to the AU might be doomed from the start.

This apprehension was short-lived since on the ground the military effected tactical cooperation to ensure mission success. Within a few weeks Darfur was being presented as a perfect example of EU–NATO cooperation by the Secretary General of NATO Mr Jaap de Hoop Scheffer (2005), in a speech in June 2005 at Bratislavia to NATO leaders. The longer-term ramifications are still be to be evaluated on this, especially on whether both the EU and NATO could have done more at the time and how they could do better in the future in other circumstances. This is a moot point since despite AU, EU, NATO and UN intervention the Sudan government has not stopped its activities and civilian atrocities and armed conflict persist in the Darfur region. Only time will tell if NATO trans-regionalism was a turning point for the better.

Turning back to the case it is clear that cooperation on the ground between the AU, EU and NATO meant that the NATO liaison team from ALCC HQ HD arrived in Addis Ababa, Ethiopia in mid June 2005 and immediately began to set up the NATO/AMIS Liaison headquarters. NATO documentation (NATO, July 2005) shows that the mandate from the NATO SACEUR headquarters in Europe was to liaise with the African Union and Darfur Integrated Task Force (DITF), which was co-located with the AU Headquarters in Addis Abba, Ethiopia and to coordinate for NATO support in three specific areas: 1) strategic airlift (deployment of AU force protection soldiers into Darfur, Sudan); 2) support to the United Nations (UN) led map exercise (MAPEX) and 3) execution of staff capacity building training for the DITF staff and the force headquarters.

In a rapid display of capability NATO was able to launch its airlift operations in support of the African Union Mission in Sudan (AMIS), with the first movement of Nigerian troops on 1 July. This was achieved by having NATO personnel deployed on the ground to coordinate NATO's airlift support. In reality this only required eight people – seven to Addis Ababa and one to Nigeria. These were later transferred to other countries based on the airlift schedule. Airlifts of personnel from Gambia, Kenya, Nigeria, Rwanda, Senegal and South Africa continued through July, August and September. NATO documentation issued on 3 August 2005 (NATO, August 2005), describes the initial airlift undertaken by United States C-130 and C-17 aircraft that moved approximately 680 troops to the region, while the United Kingdom later supported the airlift of another 680 troops.

Thus the first task of NATO support to the AU, immediate and decisive strategic airlift was successful within a three-month period. Integral to the success was the movement and control specialists and the NATO Senior Military Liaison Officer team. They succeeded in the main task of co-ordinating the planning and execution of cargo and troops between the troop contributing nations (TCN), the DITF Headquarters and various NATO air movement centres. On paper, as can be seen in NATO Documents on July 2005 (NATO, July 2005), the task seemed easy and the numbers seemed relatively small. However, it was a complex task because the troop movements had to be coordinated around 11 different Aerial Ports of Embarkation (APOEs) and three different Aerial Ports of Debarkation (APODs). However, the success of the mission proved that NATO was able to engage in a trans-regional military support operation in Africa without previous expertise.

This foray into Africa intrigued the world and NATO was publicly questioned by the press over which NATO Treaty was being invoked, which NATO member state was being threatened and, if none, then why was NATO becoming involved in Africa. Jamie Shea (Deputy Assistant Secretary General for External Relations, Division of Public Diplomacy, NATO) responded as reported in NATO Speeches (NATO Speeches, July 2005), 'NATO needs to use its forces in a reasoned manner with clear objectives which might not only include active conflict but also situations to address human indignities certainly as in Darfur, and I think that it's very appropriate that we do have that involvement in a contingency like Darfur'.

Whilst the airlift was in progress NATO commenced its second task – that of staff capacity building training. The NATO liaison team for this task worked with the DITF staff leadership and the tactical commanders on the ground to collect the staff capacity building training requirements. A plan was formulated, and NATO responded by providing two phases of training – targeting two different training audiences that were detailed in NATO documents in July 2005 (NATO Documents, July 2005).

The first phase was conducted in August 2005 in Addis Ababa, Ethiopia at the DITF Headquarters and was designed to train the DITF staff members on strategic level tasks. The second phase of the training was conducted in El-Fashir, Sudan at the AMIS Force Headquarters compound and was designed to train the Force Headquarters on operational and tactical level tasks. This training was widely accepted and in total there were 114 Force Headquarters and Sector Headquarters staff officers trained from all the combined Force HQ components (military, civilian police, CIMIC, and NGOs).

NATO support was not confined to solely supporting the AU directly. As part of the initial diplomacy it was clear that NATO would support UN initiatives to the AU as well as the EU in its assistance to the AU. So given the successes in direct airlift support and training to the AU, NATO then turned to the third critical mission that was requested. This was NATO support to the United Nations (UN) led map exercise (MAPEX) designed to help AU personnel to understand and operate effectively in the theatre of operations, as well as build their capacity to manage strategic operations.

Towards the end of August 2005, staff capacity-building activities started in Nairobi, Kenya. NATO helped to train AU personnel in key headquarters functions such as command and control, logistics and planning. The UN asked NATO for assistance in helping write the scenarios for the exercise and then to provide exercise controllers both in the Force Headquarters and the Sector headquarters. In a cost-effective operation only 16 NATO personnel were deployed to conduct the map exercise and another eight to organise the staff capability-building. In the words of both the AU and UN leadership during the exercise and in the after action review as informed in NATO Speeches (2006), 'the NATO involvement and participation in the MAPEX was pinnacle to the success of the entire operation'. With regard to NATO support to the EU in its assistance to the AU, it was on 7 August that NATO airlifted the first team of 49 African Union civilian police as well as an additional 533 military peacekeepers into Darfur, which was reported the next day in NATO Documentation (NATO, August 2005).

Thus within six months of the initial request and within three months of the start of operations a unique milestone was established. This was the first time that NATO had been involved in an operation on the African continent where the NATO contingent was accepted as a full partner by the AU leadership and the collective group of partner nations from the AU, EU and UN. This resulted in the appointment of a NATO Civilian Senior Representative (NCSR) from the Norwegian embassy in Ethiopia to assist with the political contacts and to work directly with NATO Headquarters. Clearly this particular NATO mission opened a whole new array of opportunities for the NATO Alliance and cast a very positive light on its member states intentions to the international community.

Given this state of affairs it was no surprise that on 21 September 2005 that the North Atlantic Council agreed to extend the duration of NATO's airlift support in order to ensure the airlift of the remaining peacekeeping reinforcements in Darfur until 31 October 2005.

Sustaining the Strategy and the Policy

The rapidity of the policy decision and initial implementation of trans-regional action by NATO into Africa in support of the AU had left no time for in-depth thought and discussion into the consequences and ramifications. There was a necessity for an internal and introspective review of the decision and the initial implementation successes. There was also a necessity to justify the policy decision and actions to an eager public audience. So in a show of transparency an open debate was organised on 30 September 2005 with the topic 'NATO, the African Union, the United Nations and Darfur'. The debate was chaired by Jamie Shea (Deputy Assistant Secretary General for External Relations, Division of Public Diplomacy, NATO) and the panel consisted of Eirini Lemos, resident UN expert on the NATO international staff, Dr Klaus Becher, Associate Director of the Foreign and Common Wealth Offices Wilton Park Agency in the United Kingdom and Professor Mats Berdal, Department of War Studies, Kings College, London.

It was clear from this debate, whose transcript was made available in NATO STOPWATCH (2005), that the policy was not a spontaneous off-the-cuff decision but had been clearly defined in political terms and the military had participated in the formulation of the strategy and had been given the ability and capability to undertake the mission. Strategic and tactical goals were clearly defined and limitations were clearly demarcated. All the participants in the debate agreed that this was a unique milestone in NATO's history and that 10 years previously NATO member states would have been more sceptical about undertaking such a mission. In envisaging 10 years hence, the panel noted that UN delegates had produced a commitment to a 10-year work plan to strengthen African peacekeeping capabilities within the AU context where NATO seemed to be a natural candidate to assist. Understandably it was questioned whether NATO could do more given that the AU accepted NATO presence, such as placing troops on the ground to operate bases, or running supply lines. However this was rejected given that NATO presence was limited to supporting another regional organisation's mission in meeting its challenge and not to taking it over. Africa was the region and the regional alliance was the AU – NATO was a trans-regional support actor to the AU.

The panel accepted that NATO's success meant that it could expect more such requests in the future and it would be hard-pressed to reject them given this precedence. The panel agreed that NATO's main mission is to protect its member states from attack from the outside but it could not turn its back and watch genocide – no matter where this was taking place. For that NATO would need to be prepared for global deployment based on a UN mandate. Part and parcel of such preparation would be local knowledge, building up networks of cooperation with other regional organisations, with countries in the region, and with various social and political groups in regions where NATO countries did not have sufficient knowledge and understanding of what was actually going on. For such a learning process NATO would need to engage more in trans-regionalism.

Following this debate, having suffered no casualties and having gained immense public support for having contributed to the AU mission, the North Atlantic Council (NAC) agreed on 30 September 2005 to continue to offer support to the African Union until 31 March 2006. The policy and strategy remained the same – for the coordination of strategic airlift during further troop rotations of the peacekeeping forces as well as additional staff capacity building, in order to add to the military skills of the African Union's officers. Having reviewed the African Union's troop rotation schedule on 9 November 2005 the NAC amended this until the end of May 2006.

Ultimately NATO relies on its member states commitments and such decisions required high level political consent. Clearly the pressure was on for more to be attempted in Darfur. For example Van deHei, and Lynch (2006) wrote in the *Washington Post* newspaper that on 17 February 2006 President Bush called for a sizeable UN force and a bigger role for NATO in the peacekeeping effort. Similarly United Nations Documents (2005, paras 138–40) quote the United Kingdom's International Development Secretary as having stated that Darfur 'represented the most serious humanitarian emergency in the world today'.

Hence by mid-March 2006 Pentagon authorities had completed a review of various options and were ready to back a large team of NATO advisers into Darfur. Secretary of Defense Donald H. Rumsfeld was briefed on the proposal and approved it for discussion with the White House and State Department. However a larger force with a different mandate was not to be. A number of reasons were cited. The first was described by Van deHei and Lynch (2006) in a *Washington Post* Editorial, that foremost NATO relies solely on contributing member states where no single member state was willing to make a significant increase in forces. They cited NATO member states as having informed that the NATO alliance had a growing role in securing Afghanistan and an increased force to Darfur might distract from this role. A further reluctance was the fear of sending significant numbers of Europeans and North Americans, which could inflame regional sensitivities – particularly if the mainly Muslim Sudanese government opposed a NATO deployment. This fear in part emanated from an Osama bin Laden tape that accused the United States of igniting strife in Darfur. Last but not least was the minimal domestic interest in western countries about Darfur in the sense that political elites perceived that they would neither gain nor lose any electoral or popular support by either invoking a smaller or larger military commitment through NATO or unilaterally. Hence it was no surprise that Reeves and Brassard (2007: 57) wrote that the word from NATO HQ on 29 March 2006 was that NATO was not planning, discussing or considering a NATO force on the ground in Darfur though NATO would continue to provide what it was already providing.

It was at this stage that the UN escalated its efforts. Firstly the UN Security Council imposed sanctions for the first time. This was on four men in the Sudanese military and government believed to be the main architects of the atrocities in Sudan's Darfur region. Secondly UN Secretary General Kofi Annan formally appealed to NATO by way of a phone call to the NATO Secretary General on 27 March 2006 for help in fortifying the ability of the African Union force to restrain armed groups and ensure the safety of civilians. Lacking the mandate from a UN Security Council Resolution and the willingness of its member states, all that the North Atlantic Council could do was to announce its readiness to continue NATO's current mission. The formal statement to this effect came on 13 April 2006 when the NAC announced its readiness to continue NATO's current mission until 30 September 2006 in full consultation, transparency and complementarity with the EU, the UN and all other donors concerned.

Despite the good intentions and successes all those involved knew that more was needed and hence on 30 May 2006 the UN Under-Secretary General for Humanitarian Affairs, Mr Jan Egeland visited NATO HQ to discuss Darfur and the role of the military in disaster relief. This was complemented on 2 June 2006 when the Chairperson of the African Union Commission, Mr Alpha Oumar Konaré, requested that NATO extend its airlift and training support. The NAC consulted the contributing NATO member states and decided to extend NATO's assistance to AMIS until the end of 2006.

This was affirmed on 8 June 2006 by NATO Defence Ministers who stated NATO's willingness to expand its training assistance to AMIS in the fields of Joint Operations Centres, pre-deployment certification and lessons learned. They also stated the Alliance's willingness to consider support to an anticipated follow-on UN mission to the AMIS mission. This follow-on AU-UN hybrid peacekeeping mission was at the time in the planning stage but was formally announced on

16 November 2006 in Addis Ababa and would later be officially created in UN Security Resolution 1706 (31 August 2006). It would come into being on 1 January 2008 as UNAMID when AMIS was disbanded. Egeland's efforts were successful to the extent that his initiatives were in time to be placed on the agenda of the NATO Riga summit held on 28–29 November 2006. At the Riga Summit, NATO reaffirmed its support to the African Union and its willingness to broaden this support. It also reiterated its commitment to coordinating with other international actors.

NATO documentation (2006) shows that some 18 months after the first lift NATO decided to extend its support mission for six additional months. This was after a meeting on 15 December 2006 between, the Secretary General of NATO, Jaap de Hoop Scheffer and US Ambassador Andrew Natsios, (US Special Envoy to Darfur). Ambassador Natsios, had just returned from an extensive mission in the region. They discussed the security and humanitarian situation in and around Darfur and concluded that any larger NATO commitment would be expensive, difficult due to the terrain, especially the lack of water, could not be set up in a hurry and would be met by strong resistance from the Government of Sudan who might view it as an act of war. Having concluded that a NATO Reaction Force intervention was not possible, other options for enhanced support were considered and on 15 January 2007 NATO documentation (2007) shows that NATO agreed to provide staff capacity-training at the AU Mission HQ in Khartoum capital of Sudan, in addition to training provided in the city of El Fasher in Darfur and in Addis Ababa Ethiopia.

Conclusion

Drawing a line under the chronology of NATO support to AMIS which concluded on 31 December 2007 when AMIS was disbanded and UNAMID was created, leaves this chapter to draw conclusions about the role of regional alliances (the AU and NATO), about regional alliances supporting other regional alliances (NATO supporting the AU), and specifically about NATO as a trans-regional actor.

Firstly, it is clear that regional alliances have an important role to play. States in Africa are perhaps the latest to recognise this and to create a continent-wide alliance with a mandate to intervene should circumstances permit. This is manifest in the creation of the African Union with a Constitutive Act permitting this. Previous experiences by ECOWAS/ECOMOG (Economic Community of West African States/Economic Community of West African States Monitoring Group), demonstrate that regional alliances in Africa can make a difference for the better. Peace operations by an Africa solution for an Africa problem justify the continuation and strengthening of the African Union (AU). African states have granted the AU the authority to intervene. African states are not reluctant to offer manpower to the AU and this is accepted in the African 'brotherly context' where intervention is not seen as a bellicose act. So the AU looks ready to become a major actor in Africa, as NATO has been in Europe.

Secondly, the AU has been pragmatic about its limited capabilities in many areas. This includes the lack of experience in being a regional alliance as well as tangible issues, such as limited airlift capability. In requesting help, the AU has shown that it is willing to recognise its deficiencies and to ameliorate them. The assistance that NATO provided the AU offers a unique basis to construct new theories and notions about trans-regionalism and to break the historical bad connotations of colonialism. Such activities highlight the evolving and dynamic world order and system that permits global humanitarian assistance across state boundaries. This overcomes the constraints of state sovereignty vested in the Westphalian system which implies the sanctity of state borders preventing any other states or organisation from intervening in the domestic affairs of an independent state. Such a Westphalian system proved especially painful to Africa where lines were drawn on maps during the colonial era and at independence to create states, often dividing traditional ties and sometimes imposing political systems that could not offer functional government. In a post-Westphalia era a regional organisation such as the African Union has the mandate from its member states to intervene to protect and assist individuals without regard to sovereign state boundaries should a government not be able to do so or should it be wanting in its actions against individuals.

Thirdly, the specific NATO-AMIS experience was positive to the extent that additional trans-regional assistance between NATO and the AU emerged. By March 2007, during a visit to NATO headquarters, the AU Commissioner for Peace and Security, Said Djinnit, evoked expansion of NATO-AU cooperation into new areas including possible long-term capacity-building support. In June 2007, NATO agreed in principle to provide support to the AU Mission in Somalia (AMISOM). On 5 September 2007, as part of NATO's capacity-building support to the AU, the North Atlantic Council agreed to provide assistance to the AU with a study on the assessment of the operational readiness of the Africa Standby Force (ASF) brigades. On 13 December 2007, consultations between AU and NATO staff were conducted to identify further specific areas for NATO assistance to the ASF. Only time will tell whether NATO-AU relations can and will evolve further to the stage of trans-regionalism with a unique secretariat for research, policy planning, preparation and coordination of meetings and implementation of decisions.

In the final analysis, regional alliances have an important role to play, regional alliances helping other regional alliances for peace-support operations seem likely to increase, with NATO firmly committed to the AU where such trans-regional activity bears no resemblance to colonial intervention, to hegemonic interference or to the detriment of sovereignty.

Bibliography

African Union (2000) *Constitutive Act of the Union*, Article 4, retrieved 23 August 2009, from http://www.africa-union.org/root/au/AboutAu/Constitutive_Act_en.htm.

AFP Editorial (2005) NATO Agrees on Darfur and Sets Aside Strains with the EU. *AFP.* 9 June.

Albright, M., Cook, R., Dini, L., Axworthy, L., Palacio, A., Derycke, E. and Pitsuwan, S. (2005) Statement by former Foreign Ministers. *International Herald Tribune*, 25 May 2005, retrieved 23 August 2009, from http://www.iht.com/articles/2005/05/25/opinion/edalbright.php.

De Hoop Scheffer, J. (2005) A Changing Alliance in a Changing World, speech at Bratislava, retrieved 23 August 2009, from http://www.nato.int/docu/speech/2005/s050630a.htm.

DFID Press Release (2006) released on 18 July 2006, retrieved 23 August 2009, from http://dfid.gov.uk/news/files/pressrelease/amis-brussels.asp.

Dombey, D. (2005) NATO-EU Spat Hits Airlift to Darfur. *Financial Times*, 8 June.

East Standard Editorial (2005) Darfur Mission on as Partners Deny Split. *The East Standard (Kenya)*, 11 June.

Feinstein, L. (2007) *Darfur and Beyond: What Is Needed to Prevent Mass Atrocities*. New York: Council on Foreign Relations.

Hauser, G. and Kernic, F. (2006) *European Security in Transition*. Aldershot: Ashgate.

Hendrickson, R.C. (2005) Public Diplomacy at NATO: An Assessment of Jaap De Hoop Scheffer's leadership of the Alliance. *Journal of Military and Strategic Studies*, 8(2), 2–28.

House of Commons Defence Committee (2008) *The Future of NATO and European Defence: Ninth Report of Session 2007–08*. London: The Stationery Office.

ISIS (2005) Support for the African Union in Darfur: A Test for EU-NATO Strategic Partnership. Europe European Security Review, 26. London: ISIS.

NATO (2005), Press conference by NATO Secretary General, Jaap de Hoop Scheffer after the Plenary Meeting of the EAPC Security Forum, June, retrieved 23 August 2009, from http://www.nato.int/docu/speech/2005/s050525j.htm.

NATO Documents (May 2005) NATO Secretary General pledges Darfur support, 26 May retrieved 23 August 2009, from http://www.nato.int/docu/update/2005/05-may/e0526a.htm.

NATO Documents (June 2005) Meeting of the North Atlantic Council in Defence Ministers Session, Brussels, 9 June, Final Communique, para. 9 NATO Press Release (2005)076.

NATO Documents (July 2005) NATO Starts Airlifting African Union Troops to Darfur, 1 July, retrieved 23 August 2009, from http://www.nato.int/docu/update/2005/07-july/e0701a.htm.

NATO Documents (2005) 1,300 African Union Peacekeepers Airlifted to Darfur, 3 August, retrieved 23 August 2009. from http://www.nato.int/docu/update/2005/08-august/e0803a.htm.

NATO Documents (2005) First NATO Airlift of Civilian Police into Darfur. 7 August, retrieved 23 August 2009. from http://www.nato.int/docu/update/2005/08-august/e0810b.htm.

NATO Documents (2006) *NATO News*, 12 December, retrieved 23 August 2009, from http://www.nato.int/docu/update/2006/12-december/e1215b.htm.

NATO Documents (2007) NATO's Assistance to the African Union for Darfur, 2 April, retrieved 23 August 2009, from http://www.nato.int/issues/darfur/practice.html.

NATO Documents (2007) African Union Looks to Long-term Cooperation with NATO, 3 March, retrieved 23 August 2009, from http://www.nato.int/docu/update/2007/03-march/e0302a.htm.

NATO Organisation Record (2008) Africa Development Information Service of January 2008, retrieved 23 August 2009, from http://www.afdevinfo.com/htmlreports/org/org_56574.html.

NATO Speeches (2005) The Transatlantic Alliance in the 21st Century. 11 July 2005. retrieved 23 August 2009. From http://www.nato.int/docu/speech/2005/s050711i.htm.

NATO Speeches (2006) Background Briefing by NATO Secretary General Jaap de Hoop Scheffer on the upcoming ministerial meeting in Sofia Bulgaria, 25 April, retrieved 23 August 2009, from http://www.nato.int/docu/speech/2006/s060425a.htm.

NATO STOPWATCH (2005) Debate 1: NATO, the African Union, the United Nations and Darfur Special interactive video forum series with Jamie Shea, 30 September, retrieved 23 August 2009, from http://www.nato.int/docu/speech/2005/s050930a.htm.

Raftopoulos, B. and Alexander, K. (eds) (2008) *Peace in the Balance: The Crisis in Sudan*. London: African Minds.

Reeves, E. and Brassard, M.A. (2007) *Long Day's Dying: Critical Moments in the Darfur Genocide*. London: Key Publishing House.

Richard, M. (2007) *The EU-NATO Relationship: A Legal and Political Perspective*. Aldershot: Ashgate.

Segell, G. (2008) 'The United Nations African Union Mission in Darfur - UNAMID', Strategic Insights, VII(1), February. retrieved 23 August 2009, from http://www.ccc.nps.navy.mil/si/2008/Feb/segellFeb08.pdf.

Rüland, J. (2005) Inter- and Transregionalism: Remarks on the State of the Art of a New Research Agenda, National Europe Centre Paper No. 35, retrieved 23 August 2009 http://www.anu.edu.au/NEC/Archive/ruland2.pdf.

UN Documents (2005) Document A/60/L.1 Sixtieth Session, 20 September. New York: United Nations Press.

Van Ardenne, A. Salih, M., Grono, N. and Mendez, J. (2006) *Explaining Darfur: Four Lectures on the Ongoing Genocide.* Amsterdam: Amsterdam University Press.

Van deHei, J. and Lynch, C. (2006) *Washington Post* Editorial, 17 February, retrieved 23 August 2009, from http://www.washingtonpost.com/wpdyn/content/article/2006/04/09/AR2006040900957.html.

Chapter 8

Between Shadows and Hopes:
Discursive Representations of Female
Suicide Bombings and the Global Order

Tanya Narozhna

Introduction

9 April 1985 marked the onset of a new phase in the modern history of political violence. On that day, a 16-year-old Lebanese woman named Sana'a Mehaidli drove an explosive-laden truck into an Israeli military post in South Lebanon, killing two soldiers and herself and injuring two other soldiers. Since then, nearly 300 women of diverse socio-cultural backgrounds followed in her footsteps. They challenged male monopoly on suicide bombings by embarking on the deadly missions in various geographic locations and delivering their violent messages to the front pages of major international newspapers. Female suicide perpetrators shattered societal taboos and contested entrenched stereotypical images of 'naturally' peaceful, maternal, and nurturing women. They killed and injured hundreds of people, intensified military conflicts, and changed the political destiny of several militant groups, both secular and religious.[1] The apparent novelty and shocking nature of their final acts granted female perpetrators an exceptional status in public discourse in their own communities and in the West. These acts of violence produced enormous publicity and attracted attention of millions worldwide, prompting intense discussions about women's violence, gender identity and roles.

Women have long participated in political violence. They performed various roles within militant groups, ranging from supportive, subservient tasks of caring for the wounded, collecting intelligence, providing safe houses, acting as messengers,

---

1 The militant groups that have employed female suicide bombers include Syrian Socialist National Party (SSNP), Lebanese Communist Party (LCP), Hezbollah, Liberation Tigers of Tamil Eelam (LTTE), Kurdistan Workers Party (PKK), various Chechen rebels, especially Salakhin Riadus Shahidi, Al Aqsa Martyrs Brigade, Hamas, Palestinian Islamic Jihad (PIJ), and various Al Qaeda-affiliated groups, including Al Qaeda group in Iraq, Malik Suicidal Brigades, and Moroccan Islamic Combatant Group. Secular groups were the first ones to employ female suicide perpetrators. Their 'success' in gaining popular support prompted some religious organizations to resort to the practice of martyrdom.

and smuggling ammunition, money and documents through the checkpoints to serving as active combatants, recruiters, ideologues and leaders. Many of their responsibilities within terrorist groups have been similar to the routine household duties women are traditionally expected to perform. Thus, despite women's involvement in the broad range of terrorist activities, they remained overshadowed by their male counterparts. Conventional gender stereotypes and the gendered nature of militant groups certainly worked against politically violent women, rendering them and their contributions virtually 'invisible'. In this respect, female suicide perpetrators are in a category of their own: they step out of the gendered shadow of the militant groups and garner disproportionately more attention than male suicide bombers. Still, their acts are more often than not perceived through the lens of their identity as women (Sjoberg and Gentry 2007). Consequently, while female suicide bombers attempt to bring into the spotlight collective grievances of their respective communities, their various audiences focus primarily on the sex and gender identity of the perpetrators.

Indeed, in the West, the problem of female suicide bombings is discussed primarily in gendered terms. This discussion reflects an overwhelming tendency among orthodox academics, journalists and policymakers to make sense of the phenomenon of female suicide bombings by means of established gender norms, while ostensibly presenting their views in neutral, objective terms. As a result, popular and largely impressionistic knowledge about female suicide bombings is saturated with gendered images, signs and narratives produced in the narrow space between mainstream academia, media and the state. This knowledge reduces female suicide perpetrators either to 'romantic dupes,' manipulated or coerced into becoming deadly 'throw-away weapons' by men (Zedalis 2008: 55), or to feminist rebels fighting for gender equality within oppressive patriarchal societies (Ness 2008: 3). Both images convey disproportionately inflated emphasis on victimhood and attribute the phenomenon of female suicide bombings to orientalized patriarchy. The latter refers to a system of social relations in the Orient based on gender inequality and male domination. The explanatory framework built around the notion of orientalized patriarchy not only helps mainstream researchers to draw a gendered line between their representations of female and male suicide perpetrators, but more importantly it helps them to construct mutually exclusive boundaries, within which 'our' identity and 'their' otherness are negotiated, naturalized and communicated. Prevalent narratives carry a powerful message that 'who "we" are or who "we" like or relate to … [is contingent upon] who "we" are not, who "we" fear or hate' (Spencer 2006: xiv).

This chapter draws on Robert Cox's (1996) classification of problem-solving and critical theories in order to expose the politics of difference that underlines mainstream scholarship on the phenomenon of female suicide bombings. I argue that this literature engages in the double othering of female suicide perpetrators and their societies in order to serve particular interests and power relations in today's global order. Mainstream scholarship (re)produces hierarchies of gendered/ sexualized/racialized difference within the existing global order, while obscuring the constructed nature of such hierarchies and the role of its own discourses in sustaining hierarchical ordering of the world. As a result, knowledge produced by mainstream problem-solving scholarship serves as a self-reinforcing foundation for the preservation of the global power-relational *status quo*. In other words, dominant academic discourses and modes of studying female suicide bombings in the West are complicit in sustaining and reproducing colonial-like relations of subordination and exploitation in a formally post-colonial world.

My first purpose is to scrutinize the discursive construction of ideologically charged and gendered representations of female suicide bombers in the dominant, problem-solving discourses in Western academia. My aim is to reveal troubling assumptions about the agency of female suicide bombers and to illuminate the complex and nuanced ways in which the popular notion of a female suicide bomber in the West is overloaded with stereotypical understandings of gender, sex, race, ethnicity, culture, and religion. The second goal is to trace the emergence of orientalist epistemology in recent debates on terrorism and political violence by examining prevalent Western academic accounts of female suicide bombers. Central to this type of epistemology is the ideological function of justifying and perpetuating asymmetric hierarchical power relations within the existing global order. Power in my analysis is understood in broad social relational terms and includes such multiple forms as material capabilities, differential structural capacities, as well as the ability to produce norms, rules and intersubjective meanings (Barnett and Duvall 2005). Thus, knowledge production is an integral part of power. And a concern with knowledge production, as Hurrell (2007: 36) astutely pointed out, 'leads ... to the problem of language', which 'is central to the attainment and stabilization of power' (37).

To achieve these purposes, I draw mainly on critical theoretical perspective, which emphasizes the salience of context and self-reflexivity. From a critical theoretical perspective, the phenomenon of female suicide bombings can be seen as a problem of the socio-political complex as a whole. Against the backdrop of unequal power relations within the existing world order, female suicide bombings represent a way of expressing collective views on the nature and legitimacy of current power relations, advancing distinct claims of justice, as well as defending competing values held by those in the shadows of the current world order. Critical theoretical perspective calls us to challenge commonly held assertions about female suicide bombings and to uncover the ideological assumptions and political interests behind Western academic representations of this socio-political phenomenon. This task entails the acknowledgement that our understanding of female suicide bombings is shaped by the tightly intertwined discourses of gender, sexuality, religion, culture, and colonialism. My approach is explicitly deconstructivist in that it seeks to reveal the ideological biases and political agendas in the prevalent academic narratives on female suicide bombings. I engage in deconstruction not in the spirit of presenting a 'true' or 'correct' essence of the phenomenon, but in order to demonstrate that this problem can only be analyzed and dealt with fruitfully if we recognize and expose the relative and constructed nature of the images of female suicide bombers and their societies produced by dominant academic discourses in the West.

My argument is structured in the following manner. First, I briefly outline the distinction between problem-solving and critical theoretical approaches. Second, I demonstrate that a large body of mainstream Western academic works on female suicide bombings falls into the problem-solving category and highlight some of the central assumptions in the problem-solving literature on female suicide bombings. Finally, I analyze mainstream academic representations of female suicide bombers from the critical theoretical perspective and bring to light some of the ways in which problem-solving discourses are complicit in the differentiating and hierarchizing (re)production of difference within the existing world order.

Theory and Context: Two Approaches

Robert Cox's (1996: 87) highly acclaimed statement that 'theory is always for someone and for some purpose' suggests that social scientific research is inevitably value-laden. Social theories, according to Cox, serve one of the two purposes: either to provide a guide for solving specific problems within a particular historical perspective, or to transcend the institutional and power relational parameters within which a particular theory originates by reflecting upon its initial perspective. Accordingly, all theories can be categorized as 'problem-solving' or 'critical'.

Generally conservative, static and ahistorical, problem-solving theories contain a clear set of assumptions and values shaped by the particular context of their origin. The context is viewed as timeless, objective, and of a universal condition so as to accentuate the assumptions of fixity, legitimacy and universality with regard to the prevailing socio-political order. Extant institutions, structures of power and the social relations that underpin them are treated as 'natural'. At the same time, the claims of objectivity conceal the contextualized nature of problem-solving theorizing, obscure its ideological leanings, and downplay its imbrications with the existing unequal social relations and structures of power. The objective of problem-solving theory and praxis is to ensure the longevity of the prevailing socio-political order by upholding and reproducing institutional, normative, and power relational *status quo*. This objective fundamentally affects problem-solving methodology. Such methodology fragments holistic social reality and compartmentalizes specific problems within specialized areas, thus allowing problem-solving theorists to treat the general socio-political order as unproblematic.

In contrast, critical theorists, while embracing an historically conditioned perspective as their point of departure, recognize the salience of self-reflexivity and context. That is, rather than treating their initial perspectives as 'natural', critical theorists attempt to reflect upon and transcend the normative frameworks and socio-historical contexts within which such perspectives originate. Admittedly, the multiplicity and diversity of critical theories make it difficult to group them within a single category. However, despite significant variations, all critical theories share a number of epistemological, methodological, ontological and normative commitments that enable one to think of them as a single family of theories (Price and Reus-Smit 1998: 261).

Recognizing their own relativity, historicity and constructedness allows critical theorists to open up room for the alternative, non-traditional perspectives that challenge existing power structures, question how these structures came about, and critique how these structures influence both the identification of specific problems and the knowledge about them. Crucially, an inherent normative concern with emancipation, understood as the freeing of people from repressive structural constraints (Booth 1991), enables critical theorists to contemplate the feasible venues for the potential transformation of the existing world order and to interrogate the discourses that legitimate and reproduce global power-relational *status quo*.

Problem-solving Approach to Female Suicide Bombings

A large body of Western scholarship on the subject of female suicide bombings has embraced an orthodox problem-solving approach (see Victor 2003; Bloom 2005; Skaine 2006; Zedalis 2008). The perspective in these mainstream analyses is conservative in that its ideological and conceptual underpinnings readily accept the prevailing global power relations and social structures as given and unproblematic. Instead of exploring the embeddedness of the instances of female suicide bombings within their relevant socio-historical contexts, problem-solving authors compartmentalize the issue by engaging in the production and popularization of a fairly consistent set of key inter-related assumptions. Minor differences in the narratives of individual authors notwithstanding, these assumptions can be summarized as follows. First, the source of the problem of female suicide bombings is ostensibly located in the personal lives of individual perpetrators. Women's participation in suicide bombings is explained through troubled relationships with men, inability to bear children, exposure or experience of abuse, all of which make female lives untenable under the conditions of orientalized patriarchy (Victor 2003; Bloom 2005; Von Knop 2007; Eager 2008). Second, female suicide bombers are framed as victims, rather than agents of violence. Instead of making their decisions as conscious purposeful agents, these women are said to have been manipulated or forced by men into participating in suicide missions. Finally, female suicide bombers are dismissed as expendable 'cannon fodder', used by male leaders to increase the strategic and tactical advantages of the militant (masculine) groups.

The cumulative implication of these assumptions is that the gender of the perpetrator renders the acts of female suicide bombings qualitatively different from male suicide bombings. The latter represent full dedication to a political cause, while the former are simply a 'solution' to personal problems. Problem-solving authors have notably little, if any, empirical evidence to substantiate gendered distinction between male and female suicide perpetrators. However, even though such a distinction rests merely on the simplistic, stereotypical understanding of gender identities and roles, it allows mainstream scholars to dichotomize male and female suicide bombers as agents and victims, deny the commitment and contribution of female suicide bombers and effectively exclude women as a group from the rights and benefits associated with bearing arms and being prepared to kill and die for collective causes.

The theme of victimization permeates problem-solving discourses of female suicide bombings. In line with the standard problem-solving account, Victor (2003), for example, engages in the retroactive (re)construction of the biographies of four Palestinian female suicide bombers to accentuate personal problems that allegedly drove these women on the violent path of martyrdom. She suggests that *all* women were 'seduced' or 'indoctrinated' by men, many of whom have been trusted family members or respected religious leaders (7). Her narrative carves a narrow niche for Palestinian women, who according to Victor, are not driven to their final acts by nationalist aspirations or religious motives. Rather, they embark on the path of martyrdom out of desperation, powerlessness, confusion, and/or oppression experienced by women in oriental patriarchal societies.

Admittedly, Victor's account may be reflective of the first and fourth Palestinian female suicide bombers, Wafa Idris[2] and Andaleeb Takafka,[3] although even in these two cases any direct causality between the personal problems experienced by these two women and their acts of martyrdom is not (and cannot be) proven. However, some evidence about the second Palestinian female suicide bomber, Dareen Abu Aisheh, makes her an uneasy fit within Victor's general explanatory framework centred on victimization. A 21-year-old English literature student at Al-Najah University in Nablus, Dareen Abu Aisheh, has been described by her relatives and friends as career-oriented and independent. Abu Aisheh was also reported to have suffered humiliation at an Israeli checkpoint, when she utilized

---

2   On 27 January 2002 Wafa Idris, a 28-year-old paramedic working for the Palestinian Red Crescent Society, blew herself up in a West Jerusalem shopping mall, killing one Israeli man and wounding 131. This act prompted a range of speculations – from the claims that her death was an accident and suggestions that she may have been clinically depressed after witnessing the carnage and suffering of Palestinian people to the assertions that her status of a divorced barren woman caused her to become a martyr. Interestingly, Wafa carried out her mission on the day when Yasser Arafat addressed a crowd of more than 1,000 Palestinian women in Ramallah stressing the equal role of men and women in the Intifada. 'You are my army of roses that will crush Israeli tanks,' he proclaimed. '*Shahida* all the way to Jerusalem,' he continued, 'coining on the spot the feminized version of the Arab word for martyr, *shahide*, which previously existed only in the masculine form' (Victor 2003: 19). The responsibility for the attack was claimed three days later by the nationalist al-Aqsa Martyrs Brigade – a military wing of Arafat's Fatah party that received its formal title following the outbreak of the second Intifada.

3   Andaleeb Takafka was allegedly compromised by her relationship with a Fatah activist, with whom she became pregnant.

her English skills to help a Palestinian woman with a sick baby to pass through the checkpoint to the hospital. Allegedly, Israeli soldiers told her to kiss her cousin as their condition for letting the woman with an infant through. As the cousins kissed, the baby stopped breathing. This humiliating episode is suggested to have made Abu Aisheh publicly disgraced and unmarriageable, leading her on the path of martyrdom (Eager 2008: 189). On 27 February 2002, she detonated the explosives at an Israeli checkpoint in the West Bank, near Maccabim settlement, acting on behalf of al-Aqsa Martyrs Brigade – a secular nationalist militant group. Allegedly, prior to getting in touch with al-Aqsa Martyrs operatives, Dareen Abu Aisheh approached Hamas and Palestinian Islamic Jihad (Brunner 2005: 32), but was rejected by both organizations as a potential martyr, because at the time Islamic leadership opposed women's participation in martyrdom operations, raising religious and social objections. Even if the personal experience of humiliation was a contributing factor in Abu Aisheh's decision to become a martyr, she does not fit the image of a victim, devoid of a sense of autonomy, direction, volition, self-discipline and commitment required by suicide perpetrators. It is difficult to deny that she acted as a self-conscious agent when she purposefully sought contact with a number of militant groups.

Recently, in a deliberate attempt to rationalize the phenomenon of female suicide bombings along the lines of cost-benefit analysis, some problem-solvers shifted their analytical focus towards strategic and tactical advantages of the organizations utilizing female suicide perpetrators. Importantly, even though their overall analyses represent a more sophisticated and rigorous analytical engagement with the problem of female suicide bombings than Victor's work, a stereotypical gendered focus on the personal motives remains intact. Mia Bloom (2005), one of the most illustrious and prolific authors on the subject of suicide terrorism, sees female suicide bombers driven by personal reasons. Potential motives, according to Bloom, include 'revenge for a personal loss, the desire to redeem the family name, to escape a life of sheltered monotony and achieve fame, and to level the patriarchal societies' (143). In contrast, male suicide bombers are alleged to be motivated by nationalism and/or religion. Having examined instances of female suicide bombings in the Middle East, Turkey, Chechnya, and Sri Lanka, Bloom (2005: 143) singles out a very specific motivation behind the acts of female suicide bombings, when she notes that 'so many of these women have been raped or sexually abused in the previous conflict either by the representatives of the state or by insurgents themselves'. In a similar manner, Eager (2008: 171–211) offers 'a standard set of reasons' for Kurdish, Palestinian and Chechen women's involvement in suicide missions. These reasons range from personal loss, severe trauma, and emotional response to loss and trauma to a failure to fulfil female roles, and easier control over women.

The emphasis on personal issues in problem-solving analyses is curiously in discord with the set of reasons identified by the female suicide bombers in their farewell messages. Certainly, the role of the organizations in producing these testimonials cannot be neglected, as cannot be the fact that all of the testimonials were intended for specific audiences. Still, these messages deserve consideration, as they often point to the deep politicization some of these women underwent prior to becoming suicide bombers. For example, in her videotaped final testament, Palestinian female suicide bomber Ayat al-Akhras reproached Arab leaders for 'doing nothing, while Palestinian women are fighting to end Israeli occupation' (Victor 2003: 209). Andaleeb Takafka, another Palestinian female martyr, pointed to the repressive politics of Israeli occupation, when she said: 'When you want to carry out such an attack, whether you are a man or a woman, you don't think about the explosive belt ... We are suffering. We are dying while we are still alive' (Eager 2008: 191). Reem al-Riyashi disclosed the complex web of her religious and nationalist commitments, stating: 'God gave me the ability to be a mother of two children who I love so. But my wish to meet God in paradise is greater, so I decided to be a martyr for the sake of my people' (Sjoberg and Gentry 2007: 121). Similarly, Hanadi Jaradat, a trainee attorney, pointed to the nationalist politics of her religiosity, declaring: 'By the will of God I decided to be the sixth martyr who makes her body full of splinters in order to enter every Zionist heart who occupied our country. We are not the only ones who will taste death from their occupation. As they sow so will they reap' (ibid., 123).

In other geo-political settings, female suicide bombers were reported to have explained their acts in terms of political motivations. Lebanese Sana'a Mehaidli, while mentioning her hope to go to paradise, expressed the importance of liberating her community from foreign invaders:

> I have witnessed the calamity of my people under occupation. With total calmness I shall carry out an attack of my choice hoping to kill the largest number of the Israeli army. I hope my soul will join the souls of the other martyrs ... I am now planted in the earth of the South irrigating and quenching her with my blood and my love for her. (Quoted in Pape 2005: 134)

Kurdish Zeynep Kinaci (Zilan), who became the first PKK female suicide bomber, allegedly wrote an open letter to the PKK's leader, Abdullah Öcalan, in which she stated the following:

> We are the children of a people that has had their country taken away and has been scattered to the four corners of the world. We want to live in freedom in our own land like human beings ... We do not want to cause war, to die or to kill. But there is no other way of gaining our freedom. (Özcan 2006: 176)

The first Chechen female suicide bomber, Hawa Barayeva, supposedly said that she was going to sacrifice herself 'in the name of Allah' and for 'the freedom of the people of Chechnya' (BBC News 2000). The first two female suicide bombers in Iraq also left videotaped messages. One of them, wearing red-checkered *keffieh*, self-identified as 'martyrdom-seeker Nour Qaddour Al-Shammari' and swore on the Qur'an 'to defend Iraq ... and take revenge from the enemies of the (Islamic) nation, Americans, imperialists, Zionists'. The second woman, Wadad Jamil Jassem, stated: 'I have devoted myself for Jihad for the sake of God and against American, British and Israeli infidels and to defend the soil of our precious and dear country' (Von Knop 2007: 402).

The final testimonials of individual female suicide bombers reveal a complex cluster of potential motivations ranging from personal problems, including humiliation and a desire for revenge, to deeply felt commitments to the political cause of national liberation, and, at times, strong beliefs in the religious calling. These public statements signal profound anxiety over the political destiny of their communities. The messages of female suicide perpetrators project a strong sense of collective identity and deep loyalty to their respective communities. They convey aspirations for justice on behalf of the groups that 'stand in ambiguous or highly conflictual relation to existing institutional and political structures' and whose 'many fundamental social choices [are] being made in the shadow of unequal and often coercively exercized power' (Hurrell 2007: 10). They seek (justifiably from their perspective) the right to collective self-governance and cultural autonomy within the institutional framework of their own states. Their violence is not private, but rather has clear political purposes. Their final acts are the acts of contestation of the subordinate status of their communities within the hierarchical world order based on unequal power structures. Yet, instead of acknowledging the plurality of potential causes driving individual women on the path of suicide bombings, problem-solving analyses reiterate a gendered adage that presents women as *always/already* victims of their culture and/or nature.

Frequent references to bodily metaphors betray the gendered nature of the problem-solving representations of female suicide perpetrators. Female suicide bombers are said to strap explosives to their 'wombs'. The framing of their acts of violence in terms of feminine corporeality blurs the physical and cultural aspects of the female body. Both naturally and symbolically, women's ideal-typical role is to be a giver of life. The act of bombing then becomes a symbolic dimension of natural motherhood (Cunningham 2003). Bloom's (2005: 143) much celebrated statement that the 'advent of women suicide bombers has transformed the revolutionary womb into an exploding one' encapsulates the gendered reasoning of problem-solving authors that uncritically reduces women to 'the single dimension of sex' (Meintjes et al. 2001: 13) and reiterates stereotypical understanding of women's roles presumably based on their immutable anatomical characteristics.

Closely related to such reasoning is the argument about the 'natural' female place within the private realm. Thus, even when committing public acts of suicide bombings, female suicide perpetrators are inevitably 'mediated through [their] sexuality and [their] bod[ies] – a discursive terrain carrying the prime sites of female identity and patriarchal control' (de Mel 2004: 80). Naturalization of gender roles within problem-solving accounts inevitably limits our understanding of the dynamics of gender relationships within specific social contexts and overlooks that female suicide bombers, even within a single cultural context, are not a homogenous category. Other than a generally young age, they share little commonality in terms of education, marital status, socio-economic background, religiosity, etc. In addition, individual female suicide bombers do not experience general social and cultural conditions uniformly. There are serious internal differences within their cohort, as mediating factors of class, age, ethnicity, culture, to name just a few, shape individual encounters with broader social and political realities. Downplaying these differences leads to an unfortunate bias of 'defining women as archetypal victims [which] freezes them into 'objects-who-defend-themselves,' men into 'subjects-who-perpetrate-violence,' and every society into powerless (read: women) and powerful (read: men) groups of people' (Mohanty 1991: 57). Violent women are simply invisible within this framework. Even when engaging in terrorist activities, females are predestined to live events and situations in 'the feminine way' (Neuburger and Valentini 1996: 81).

In contrast to these mainstream accounts, critical theoretical perspective emphasizes the importance of challenging a persistent refusal of problem-solving scholars to acknowledge a rich complexity of female suicide bombers' experiences and contexts. Critical theorists also ask whose political interests problem-solving analyses serve by perpetuating troubling and largely unsubstantiated assumptions about individual female perpetrators.

Critical Theoretical Approach to Female Suicide Bombings

Critical theoretical approach brings to light a number of problematic analytical and normative aspects of problem-solving analyses of female suicide bombings that I cannot address in detail here. But two major concerns should be pointed. First, problem-solving scholars advance two contradictory claims. They declare a commitment to positivist epistemology, which entails a belief in the possibility of separating subject and object, and of producing objective, neutral knowledge. Concurrently, problem-solvers also profess a politically motivated objective of their scholarship to rationalize and legitimize Western, and more specifically US, counter-terror policies. A second related concern is with a strong inclination of mainstream authors to bring to the foreground gendered insecurity and male structural violence against women outside of the Western world in order to essentialize female suicide bombers' societies in terms of orientalized patriarchy. The coalescent dynamics of these two issues reinforces ideological functions of the problem-solving research on female suicide bombings and serves Western power and domination within the existing global order.

First, a core set of problem-solving scholars insists on the objective nature of their research efforts and outputs, while demonstrating a strong, politically consequential bias towards Western and, more specifically US, counter-terror agenda. In an effort to understand the phenomenon of female suicide bombings, this scholarship claims to collect value-neutral empirical facts and formulates a number of general propositions about female suicide bombers, all of which are grounded allegedly in pure observation and logic. The fact that the selection and organization of collected data into general explanatory frameworks entails a considerable degree of interpretation, as well as a fair number of normative assumptions is either downplayed or ignored. Explicit concern with how Western states 'view, treat, and strategize against [female suicide bombers]' (Ness 2008: 1), as well as with the ways of improving these strategies (Zedalis 2008) is not perceived to be in tension with the claims to objectivity. Rosemarie Skaine (2006: 7), for example, openly states her concern with the US counter-terror concerns, when she cites Jennifer Hardwick, a senior director of the Terrorism Research Center Inc.: 'My most pressing concern is that the US is completely unprepared for suicide bombings, especially by a woman.' Indeed, the two commitments – to generate objective independent analysis and to serve American counter-terrorism – are accepted by problem-solvers as perfectly compatible. Moreover, support for the official Western/US counter-terror policies is presented as an ethical and political commitment to women's emancipation from oppressive patriarchal societies.

Even if we accept the understanding of female suicide bombings as acts of feminist rebellion against orientalized patriarchy, even if we accept that the driving force behind problem-solving analysis is preoccupation with gender inequality outside of the Western world, it remains unclear why female suicide bombings remained largely ignored by Western mainstream academia for nearly two decades and became a subject of serious inquiry only after Palestinian women began to blow themselves up in Israel. Ness (2008) observes that prior to 2002, when the first Palestinian woman, Wafa Idris, joined the ranks of the male martyrs, females committed acts of suicide bombings in places that were not centrally important to the West. Only after this practice migrated to the Palestinian-Israeli theatre of conflict and posed a direct challenge to Israel did Western nations take notice of it. As Ness (2008: 3) puts it, following 2002 female suicide attacks in Israel 'the idea that females were capable of inflicting unapologetic carnage, and subsequently, were of great strategic importance to terrorist operations across the globe, was indelibly lodged in the Western subconscious'. Other researchers also noted that earlier instances of female suicide bombings failed to attract scholarly interest for the simple reason that they were taking place in geo-political locations that were of little serious concern to the West. However, Israel's paradigmatic location within the West meant that Palestinian female suicide bombers presented a threat not only to Israel, but to the entire West (Brunner 2007). It is not surprising, then, that disproportionate attention in problem-solving scholarship has been given to the acts of female suicide bombings within the Israeli-Palestinian theatre of violence. In the majority of mainstream analyses, Palestinian female suicide bombers serve as a model around which generic explanations of female suicide bombings are constructed. Moreover, with the launching of the global war on terror, Palestinian female suicide bombings have also been seen as part of the globalization of terror, having major strategic impact on the US as the leader of the global war on terror (Zedalis 2008: 53).

Ideological bias towards the American counter-terror agenda in recent problem-solving literature on female suicide bombings persists either through the employment of biographical narratives to create an image of a depoliticized, essentialized, irrational woman who threatens the West/US (Davis 2003), or by framing the acts of female suicide bombings as a revolt against orientalized Third-world patriarchy (Bloom 2005). Within both frameworks, a decontextualized image of a female suicide bomber, often used in singular form, is implicitly linked with Islam, effectively locating the phenomenon of female suicide bombings within the 'new terrorism' thesis, elaborated at length by Bruce Hoffman (1998). It seems of little significance that the female suicide bombers in Tamil-Sri Lankan conflict were overwhelmingly Hindu; or that the PKK's female bombers in Turkey acted out of nationalist and Marxist motivations; or that two of the Lebanese female martyrs, Loula Abboud and Norma Abu Hassan, were of Christian background. Equally significant, the contentious link between female suicide bombers and Islam does not seem to be disturbed by the problem-solvers' acknowledgement that the practice of female suicide bombings was introduced as a 'tactical adaptation' (Bloom 2005: 144) by the secular nationalist groups and was at first criticized, even condemned, by Islamist organizations. For example, days after the first Palestinian woman blew herself up, Sheik Ahmad Yassin, the wheelchair-bound spiritual leader of Hamas, suggested that 'a woman martyr is problematic for Muslim society. A man who recruits a woman is breaking Islamic law. He is taking the girls or woman without the permission of her farther, brother, or husband, and therefore the family of the girl confronts an even greater problem since the man has the biggest power over her, choosing the day that she will give her life back to Allah' (Victor 2003: 30).

Having analyzed recent problem-solving literature on female suicide bombers, Claudia Brunner (2007: 968) concluded that counter-terror concerns frame 'every aspect of its epistemology, data collection, research methods … None acknowledges the impossibility of neatly separating a specific location in time and space from a larger geopolitical context. Thus all implicitly incorporate Western biases in general and US counter-terrorism concerns in particular into their frameworks and substantive analyses'. In other words, problem-solvers are preoccupied with understanding and explaining the instances of female suicide bombings within arbitrary ideological and normative boundaries. Viewed through the lens of the critical theoretical approach, problem-solvers' motives for pursuing research on female suicide bombings are inherently political (to serve Western counter-terrorism) and moral/normative (to liberate women in non-Western societies). Even though they are treated by problem-solvers as separate from their analyses, these motives profoundly affect research design, selection criteria and actual data collection, strategic objectives, conclusions, and importantly, practical implications of problem-solving analyses. Collectively, problem-solving scholars function as an exclusive 'epistemic community' (Haas 1992), generating authoritative 'common' knowledge about female suicide bombings and having major impact on how the individual perpetrators, the phenomenon in general, and the socio-historical contexts within which its instances occurred are understood. Considering the tight links between mainstream scholarship and policymaking circles, especially in the US, problem-solving research has far-reaching practical implications. This scholarship provides ideological underpinnings for and steers relevant, often coercive policies of Western states against groups and societies associated with female suicide bombers. Effectively, this scholarship shapes interactions between Western states and societies/communities whose political goals are perceived to run counter to Western interests and to undermine the existing world order. Problem-solving analyses, in other words, fulfill an important function of reinforcing *status quo* within existing global power structures and social relations.

The second closely related issue with the problem-solving literature on female suicide bombings is its tendency to frame female perpetrators as an inevitable attribute of the putatively oppressive, patriarchal societies. And as Brunner noticed, not 'any patriarchal society, but a very specific one becomes visible within these contours: Oriental, third-world, Muslim/Arab, far away and necessarily other' (2007: 964). Indeed, the essentialized image of a female suicide bomber allows the problem-solving authors to arrange a plurality of cultural differences within the existing global order into a recognizable register of dichotomies. In line with a long-standing tradition of Western exclusiveness, female suicide bombers' social and cultural contexts are cast as irrational, archaic, savage and violent Other of the rational, and morally, culturally, racially and sexually superior Western Self (Hurrell 2007; Brunner 2007; Spencer 2006; Coronil 1996). In both cases, a routine mode of gendered/sexualized/cultural/religious othering is employed, when an Oriental 'other' is contrasted with an emancipated, enlightened, rational Western 'self'. The principle of inclusion and exclusion differentiates the 'other' from 'self', and marginalizes the 'other' as alien, inferior and/or threatening (Cockburn 2007: 8). As a result, problem-solving discourses reproduce irreconcilable division between the West and the Orient – a division constitutive of the hegemonic dominant identity with its multiple and cross-cutting determinants. Mainstream scholarship positions women in non-Western societies as faceless, voiceless, helpless victims in need of Western intervention to liberate them from the clutches of oppressive orientalized patriarchy. Such discourse pits tradition against modernity and focuses on the conditions and rights of women in traditional societies in order to support Western coercive interventionism and militarized masculinity.

Paradoxically, problem-solvers' authoritative claims to knowledge function to reinforce the boundaries of orientalized patriarchy, at the same time as they assert their commitments to women's emancipation and gender equality outside of the Western world. Their analyses of female suicide bombings rest on Western-centric terms of comparison that contrast the achievements of Western liberal feminism with oppressive orientalized patriarchy. Bloom (2005) is illustrative in this context. She states that 'women's movement in the 1970s brought men and women in the first world to a level of relative parity in most areas of employment, status, and opportunities. However, in the rest of the world, the position of women remains seriously disadvantaged compared to that of men' (2005: 142). Analytical ambiguity and porous boundaries of orientalized patriarchy allow Bloom to stack together such culturally and historically distinct societies as Tamil, Sri Lankan, Chechen, Russian, Kurdish, Turkish and Palestinian. Bloom notes that even though the extent of women's participation varies from place to place, 'a patriarchal structure dominates all ... societies' outside of the Western world (147). Bloom's narrative is simultaneously differentiating and exclusive: it makes the other-ness of Oriental women an integral part of Western identity by turning them into essentially different exterior Other against whom identity of the Western Self is defined. For the sake of maintaining a clear sense of Self, the Other should remain excluded and distant.

Dichotomizing oppressive orientalized patriarchy and liberating Western feminism helps problem-solvers to create a very specific context of meaning for female suicide bombings and for the particular political struggles these acts represent. The political agency of female suicide bombers is diminished to a matter of sexualized orientalized patriarchy, which depoliticizes both women's causes for engaging in suicide bombings and the acts of bombings themselves (Brunner 2007: 962–3). Women's rights and gender equality represent the benchmarks against which similarities and differences are not only described, but also judged. Unsurprisingly, these benchmarks are associated with the West without being considered 'Western'. Rather, despite their origin and development in the West, problem-solvers present these benchmarks as universal. Conflating Western with the universal obscures the relative nature of Western values and standards. This, in turn, allows for the analytical rationalization of these particularistic values and standards as the general norm. At the same time, the particularity of the Others is devalued and denigrated as relative and backward. Problem-solving narrative thus registers cultural difference by way of a strong hierarchical ordering of the universal and the particular, disallowing the acceptance of the latter as anything other than marginalized and non-dominant. Secular, modern, egalitarian Western societies are represented as superior to Islamic, traditional, patriarchal Oriental ones. Within such framework of oppositional and hierarchical ordering, the lack of gender equality and women's rights are interpreted as an indication of general backwardness of culture and society. Such backwardness is then used to establish a temporal and social distance between Oriental and Western societies, relegating traditional Oriental societies to the past and eliminating culturally distinct ways of life as a source of critical reflection on the West.

Indeed, the temporalizing gesture in problem-solving works serves to elucidate irreconcilability of non-modern ways of life with Western models of progress and understandings of modernity. The categories of orientalized patriarchy and Western liberalism are deployed by problem-solvers to create an overall ideological message that privileges Western perspective and legitimizes its civilizing mission as a benevolent act of liberation – an act that frees Oriental women from oppressive indigenous patriarchy by offering them a chance to participate in Western universalism (Yeğenoğlu 1998: 102). Being Western effectively serves to reinforce 'our' legitimacy and power. Being Western suggests a responsibility, even a duty to universalize one's particular accomplishments, thus solidifying, or even exacerbating already significant inequalities of power within the existing world order.

As mentioned earlier, the notion of orientalized patriarchy is ambiguously intertwined with Islam. On the one hand, problem-solvers are careful to differentiate between religious and secular nationalist group contexts, within which suicide bombings are utilized. Bloom, for example, examines specific case studies of Palestinian-Israeli, Tamil-Sinhalese, and Kurdish-Turkish conflicts in order to capture and explain concrete conditions endogenous to each particular struggle. She notes that the role of religion in Tamil-Sinhalese conflict in Sri Lanka has been marginal. Therefore, the Sri-Lankan conflict 'has never contained the ideology of war of all against all, as it has in Palestine' (Bloom 2007: 46). On the other hand, when devising a general theory of suicide terrorism, Bloom points to the role of ethnic, linguistic and religious factors in organization's decisions to resort to suicide bombings. She cautions about the possibility of the potential negative rebound effects from targeting members of your own group. As empirical evidence, Bloom brings up 2003 Al Qaeda attacks in Riyadh and Istanbul and 2004 Beslan school hostage crisis. She concludes that these attacks resulted in 'significant Muslim casualties ... demonstrate[d] that such "collateral damage" is unacceptable to the larger Muslim community; and caused a self-examination and reconsideration of violence throughout the Muslim world' (80). Discussing in more detail the consequences of the attacks in Riyadh and Istanbul, Bloom quotes 'intelligence sources' to state that 'Al Qaeda loses the war of public opinion in the Islamic world by targeting Muslim women and children' (81). Against her own caution, Bloom conflates the heinous violence of suicide bombings with specific culture and religion. The combination of her choice of empirical examples and encoded rhetoric clearly alludes to the pernicious myth about religious terrorism being more deadly and lethal than ethno-separatist violence. This combination also reaffirms a popular link between suicide bombings, on the one hand, and Muslim culture and Islamic religion, on the other. Bloom's narrative is both misleading and deeply damaging: she focuses on the essentialized imagery of 'Muslim women' to epitomize uniformity of Islamic religion ('Islamic world') and homogeneity of Muslim culture ('Muslim world'). Not only does her one-sided account equate Muslim societies with Islam, ignoring their sizable Christian and other minorities, and essentializes Muslim women, societies and Islam, but equally important, she blends non-Muslim societies (for example, Tamil's mainly Hindu society) with the Muslim ones. This move allows Bloom to reiterate a stark self-other dichotomy based on sweeping generalizations and hasty conclusions.

A similar politics of othering that determines and affirms identities of the Western self and Oriental other can be traced in the works of other problem-solving authors. Seeking to explain female suicide bombings in comparative perspective, Skaine (2006) lays great emphasis on the Palestinian-Israeli case and underscores the role of Islam in inspiring the attackers. When discussing the terminology, she notes that the label 'suicide bomber' is a misnomer and agrees with Raphael Israeli, a former intelligence officer in the Israeli army and professor of Islamic and Middle Eastern history at Hebrew University in Jerusalem, that 'an Islamic frame of reference and diagnosis is necessary to comprehend this "unparalleled mode of self sacrifice"' (Skaine 2006: 11). Despite her observation that the female suicide bombers of the LTTE are not motivated by religion (14), Skaine proceeds with the discussion of the 'elements of the Islamikaze makeup' (15). This move helps Skaine to underplay the role of non-religious motivations and to add an additional weight to the imbrication between Islam and female suicide bombings. She then projects Islamic dimension of bombings onto society at large through the claim that '[r]eligion symbolically embodies society itself. It is power greater than individual people. It gives energy, asks for sacrifice and suppresses selfish tendency' (13). Hence, Skaine's comparative framework is narrowly construed to conflate female suicide bombings in various struggles with the Palestinian case and Islam. Along the same lines, Zedalis (2008:50) notes that 'religious terrorism is a particular potent form of violence' and stresses the role of religious sanctioning of female suicide bombings by Islamic clerics and the blurring between nationalism and Islam in the escalation of this practice. In a similar vein, Nivat (2008:130) states that Chechen women actively participate 'in the separatist-turned-jihadist struggle'. Cunningham (2008) specifically focuses on the evolution of women's violence from secular to Islamic religious settings, especially female involvement in the global jihadi movement.

From a critical theoretical perspective, it is crucial to recognize that the references to religion in problem-solving analyses represent important codes. These codes situate the practice of female suicide bombings within the framework of static, monolithic and oppressive Islam and imply a potential motivation for the actions of female suicide bombers. In line with the established Western tradition of pointing to the conditions of Muslim women to stress Western superiority, these works produce a flattened image of Muslim societies by drawing a direct link between women's precarious conditions and Islam. As a result, problem-solving literature backgrounds both the complexities of various discourses on women and gender issues within Islam, as well as the continuing process of reinvention of Islam through the confrontation between traditionalism and modernism. Mainstream analyses blur Islam as religion with the political use of Islam by and in the interests of particular militant groups (Salime 2008). And they fail to engage with the questions of how different interpretations of Islam developed within particular Muslim communities; how collective responses to these interpretations evolved over time; and what the challenges and opportunities of intra-Islamic dialogue are on matters of sex and gender.

Instead, problem-solving scholarship creates a perception of Islam as a fixed system of rules and practices, grounded in the beliefs that there are 'natural' differences between women's and men's capacities resulting in men having 'natural' superiority and authority over women (Salime 2008; Yaqoob 2008; Keddie 1999). Scholars embracing the critical theoretical perspective, notably Barbara Stowasser

(1994; 2001) and Kecia Ali (2006), have demonstrated the tensions surrounding issues of sex and gender in the interpretive tradition of Islamic revelatory sources and argued that much of the Qur'an has been interpreted against the meaning of its text. Their critical insights notwithstanding, problem-solving authors settle a string of deeply contentious and complex issues concerning gender, agency, religion, and ethics in a simplistic summary fashion, illuminating unquestionable exceptionality of the Western Self *vis-à-vis* Orientalized Other. Collectively, problem-solving literature on female suicide bombings conveys condemnation of orientalized patriarchy and Islam. And condemnation, as Butler (2005: 46) notes, is 'the way in which we establish the other as nonrecognizable or jettison some aspects of ourselves that we lodge in the other whom we then condemn'.

Discursive processes of cultural differentiation within problem-solving representations of female suicide bombings are intimately interlocked with the West's will to power and have profound practical implications. Mainstream scholarship capitalizes on its productive power to shape social reality and to justify (post-)colonial policies of violent engagement with and a cooptation of the threatening, unstable, unreliable 'other.' It deploys Orientalist discourses and functions as an instrument of Western political domination. For example, in her analysis of female terrorism in developing countries, Christine Sixta (2008) grounds her argument within the comparative framework, in which contemporary women terrorists in Colombia, Kurdistan, El Salvador, Sri Lanka, Chechnya and other 'developing societies' are judged against American 'new women' from the first wave of feminism. While asserting that today's women terrorists are the 'new women' of developing societies, Sixta notes an important distinction, i.e. that these women 'do not want to throw open the gate of Western modernity to their traditional societies' (263). She finds their position 'ironic', because 'Western imperialism would most likely bring Western democracy and Western capitalism to their countries' (283). This, in turn, would lessen patriarchal grip over the lives of women in developing societies. What is striking in Sixta's framework (and typical for problem-solving scholarship!) is the pronounced emphasis on Western modernity, which serves to reiterate the distinction between Western Self and non-Western Other, as well as the overt defence of Western imperial expansion. The emphasis on Western modernity is embedded in the Orientalist practices of representations.

Dichotomization of identities allows Sixta to introduce Western perspective as the only normatively acceptable and desirable option. The author cautions that 'for humanity's sake, we must find ways to stop the violence … While Western democracy is not appropriate everywhere, most western capitalist democracies have succeeded in reducing terrorism' (284). Critical theoretical perspective reveals the complicity of allegedly objective problem-solving analysis, such as Sixta's, in reproducing colonial subjugation of the Other in a formally post-colonial global order. The discursive and political realms of (post-)colonialism are inseparable. As Yeğenoğlu (1998: 16) notes, 'the production of the knowledge of the Orient and the process of its subjugation by colonial power do not stand in an external relation to each other'. Western power, understood in a Foucauldian sense, induces problem-solving discourse and knowledge. However, the contentious and politically biased process of knowledge production, as well as the very act of subjective representation are concealed behind the claims of objectivity and epistemological superiority. Assuming 'truth', authority and legitimacy, problem-solving authors exercise important productive power to construct meanings, including those of gender that reflect and reify Western interests and power. They '*create* not only *knowledge* but also the very reality they appear to describe' (Butler 1993: 94). The perspectives and interests of the women these authors purport to represent, if noted at all, are dismissed 'as false consciousness, the final effects of patriarchal colonization' (Hirschmann 2003: 171). A body of knowledge produced by problem-solving authors generates material effects when it is put in the service of (post-)colonial expansion and domination, as in the recent Global War on Terrorism, in which one of the justifications for invading Afghanistan was deplorable conditions of Afghan women.

A close reading of problem-solving works reveals the entanglement of the questions of colonialism, culture, religion, gender, and sex. Whether unwittingly or otherwise, problem-solving scholarship deploys representations of female suicide bombers to reduce religion to Islam, discredit Islam as a gender-oppressive ideology, and conflate Muslim culture with Islam. Their narratives are not only dichotomizing (as discussed above), but also hierarchizing in that they solidify a certain power dynamics that promotes inequality and domination (Chow 2006: 80) and points to the persistent legacy of colonialism in the formally post-colonial world.

Conclusion

Problem-solving research on the phenomenon of female suicide bombings brushes over remarkably the kaleidoscopic nature of various historical and geo-political contexts within which particular instances of female suicide bombings occur. Mainstream knowledge effectively obscures, downplays or simply ignores critical information about the political struggles these women engage in, insulates specific acts of female suicide bombings from the broader social struggles, brushes over the specificity of geo-political space, and dismisses both the agency of individual female suicide perpetrators and the collective grievances of the communities these women represent. De-contextualization thus works to explicitly emphasize the global dimension of this phenomenon and frame it as a threat to the West. Presumed or potential global expansion of the phenomenon of female suicide bombings, supported, financed and directed by a global network of Islamic Jihadi groups, becomes a centre stage preoccupation in the problem-solving literature (see, for example, Zedalis 2008). Individual conflicts are positioned at the global spatial scales, while their local and/or regional dimensions remain obscure. The struggles of stateless peoples of Palestine, Kurdistan, Chechnya and Tamil land, whose claims to national self-determination remain unrecognized for unique reasons of their colonial past, are all subsumed under the single category of global terrorism. A particular politics of difference that underscores problem-solving scholarship (re)produces exceptionality and superiority of the West and is directly complicit in sustaining global power asymmetry. At the same time, the immense popularity of problem-solving accounts of the phenomenon of female suicide bombings reflects a strong tendency in the West to perceive of the global order in terms of cultural/ civilizational inclusions and exclusions.

Critical scholars crystallize the sexual and cultural modes of differentiation that underwrite strong advocacy of (post)colonial domination and reveal multiple ways in which problem-solving discourses stabilize and sustain gendered/sexualized cultural hierarchy in today's global power relations. In many crucial respects, colonialism in the classic sense has perished, however it persists in various guises through intellectual, financial, economic and strategic control. Symbols, imagery, codes and representations in the problem-solving works on the phenomenon of female suicide bombings not only connote women's oppression outside Western world, but also signify the Orient as feminine, out of control, and threatening. Problem-solving discourse produces essential equality between the nature of the feminine and the nature of the Orient, 'creates a chain of equivalence in which woman is the Orient, the Orient is woman; woman like the Orient, the Orient like the woman, exists veiled' (Yeğenoğlu 1998: 56). At the same time, the binarism of the problem-solving representational model constitutes the identity of the Western subject in antithetic terms as masculine and imperialist, and marks the production of the 'other' as exterior threat. This threat, as well as fear and hostility associated with it, persist in the problem-solving inquiry into the female suicide bombings. In their endeavours to '*explain the unexplainable*' (Bloom 2007: 17, original emphasis) and by posing the questions, as Bloom (1) does, 'Are they scared, are they angry, do they fully understand what they are about to do?' and 'How bad must your life be if you think that it is better to be a sacrifice than to live?', problem-solvers betray their fear of and latent hostility toward cultural, religious and sexual difference.

Problem-solving rationalizations of the practice of female suicide bombings embody implicit notions of the world order based on Western moral, cultural, and sexual superiority. They intertwine discourses of sex, gender, culture, and religion in the differentiating and hierarchizing (re)production of difference. The notion of orientalized patriarchy occupies a central position within this process of othering. It marks the boundaries of difference and denotes a specific inscription of the relationship between West and East grounded in the persistent colonial legacies and power imbalance.

Bibliography

Ali, K. 2006. *Sexual Ethics and Islam: Feminist Reflections on Qur'an, Hadith, and Jurisprudence*. Oxford: Oneworld Publications.

Barnett, M. and Duvall, R. (eds). 2005. Power in Global Governance. Cambridge: Cambridge University Press.

BBC News. 2000. Suicide Bombers Strike in Chechnya, 8 June, found at http://news.bbc.co.uk/1/hi/world/europe/782079.stm, accessed on 23 May 2005.

Bloom, M. 2005. *Dying to Kill: The Allure of Suicide Terror*. New York: Columbia University Press.

Booth, K. 1991. Security and Emancipation. *Review of International Studies*, 17(4), 313–26.

Brunner, C. 2005. Female Suicide Bombers – Male Suicide Bombing? Looking for Gender in Reporting the Suicide Bombings of the Israeli-Palestinian Conflict. *Global Society*, 19(1), 29–48.

Brunner, C. 2007. Occidentalism Meets the Female Suicide Bomber: A Critical Reflection on Recent Terrorism Debates. A Review Essay. *Signs: Journal of Women in Culture and Society*, 32(4), 957–71.

Butler, J. 1993. *Bodies That Matter: On the Discursive Limits of Sex*. London and New York: Routledge.

Butler, J. 2005. *Giving an Account of Oneself*. New York: Fordham University Press.

Chow, R. 2006. *The Age of the World Target: Self-Referentiality in War, Theory, and Comparative Work*. Durham, NC and London: Duke University Press.

Cockburn, C. 2007. *From Where We Stand: War, Women's Activism and Feminist Analysis*. London and New York: Zed Books.

Coronil, F. 1996. Beyond Occidentalism: Toward Nonimperial Geohistorical Categories. *Cultural Anthropology*, 11(1), 51–87.

Cox, R. 1996. Social Forces, States and World Orders: Beyond International Relations Theory, in *Approaches to World Order*, Cox, R. with Sinclair, T. Cambridge: Cambridge University Press, 85–123.

Cunningham, K. 2003. Cross-Regional Trends in Female Terrorism. *Studies in Conflict and Terrorism*, 26, 171–95.

Cunningham, K. 2008. The Evolving Participation of Muslim Women in Palestine, Chechnya and the Global Jihadi Movement in *Female Terrorism and Militancy: Agency, Utility, and Organization*, edited by Ness, C. London and New York: Routledge, 84–99.

Davis, J. 2003. *Martyrs: Innocence, Vengeance and Despair in the Middle East*. New York: Palgrave Macmillan.

De Mel, N. 2004. Body Politics: (Re)Cognising the Female Suicide Bomber in Sri Lanka. *Indian Journal of Gender Studies*, 11(1), 75–92.

Eager, P.W. 2008. *From Freedom Fighters to Terrorists: Women and Political Violence*. Aldershot: Ashgate.

Haas, P. 1992. Introduction: Epistemic Communities and International Policy Coordination. *International Organization*, 46(1), 1–35.

Hirschmann, N. 2003. *The Subject of Liberty: Toward a Feminist Theory of Freedom*. Princeton, NJ and Oxford: Princeton University Press.

Hoffman, B. 1998. *Inside Terrorism*. New York: Columbia University Press.

Hurrell, A. 2007. *On Global Order: Power, Values, and the Constitution of International Society*. Oxford: Oxford University Press.

Keddie, N. 1999. The New Religious Politics and Women Worldwide: A Comparative Study. *Journal of Women's History*, 10(4), 11–34.

Meintjes, S., Turshen, M. and Pillay, A. 2001. *The Aftermath: Women in Post-Conflict Transformation*. London and New York: Zed.

Mohanty, C.T. 1991. Under Western Eyes: Feminist Scholarship and Colonial Discourses, in *Third World Women and the Politics of Feminism*, edited by Mohanty, C.T., et Al. Bloomington: Indiana University Press, 51–80.

Ness, C. 2008. Introduction, in *Female Terrorism and Militancy: Agency, Utility, and Organization*, edited by Ness, C. London and New York: Routledge, 1–10.

Neuburger, L. and Valentini, T. 1996. *Women and Terrorism*. New York: St Martin's Press.

Nivat, A. 2008. The Black Widows: Chechen Women Join the Fight for Independence – and Allah, in *Female Terrorism and Militancy: Agency, Utility, and Organization*, edited by Ness, C. London and New York: Routledge, 122–30.

Özcan, A.K. 2006. *Turkey's Kurds: A Theoretical Analysis of the PKK and Abdullah Öcalan*. New York: Routledge.

Pape, R. 2005. *Dying to Win: The Strategic Logic of Suicide Terrorism*. London: Random House.

Price, R. and Reus-Smit, C. 1998. Dangerous Liaisons? Critical International Theory and Constructivism. *European Journal of International Relations*, 4(3), 259–94.

Salime, Z. 2008. Mobilizing Muslim Women: Multiple Voices, the Sharia, and the State. *Comparative Studies of South Asia, Africa and the Middles East*, 28(1), 200–11.

Sixta, C. 2008. The Illusive Third Wave: Are Female Terrorists the New "New Women" in Developing Societies? *Journal of Women, Politics and Policy*, 29(2), 261–88.

Sjoberg, L. and Gentry, C. 2007. *Mothers, Monsters, Whores: Women's Violence in Global Politics*. London and New York: Zed Books.

Skaine, R. 2006. *Female Suicide Bombers*. Jefferson, NC and London: McFarland and Company, Inc.

Spencer, S. 2006. *Race and Ethnicity: Culture, Identity and Representation*. London and New York: Routledge.

Stowasser, B. 1994. *Women in the Qur'an: Traditions and Interpretation*. New York: Oxford University Press.

Stowasser, B. 2001. Old Shaykhs, Young Women, and the Internet: The Rewriting of Women's Political Rights in Islam. *The Muslim World*, 91(1/2), 99–119.

Talbot, R. 2000–2001. Myths in the Representation of Women Terrorists. *Éire-Ireland*, 35(3–4), 165–86.

Victor, B. 2003. *Army of Roses: Inside the World of Palestinian Women Suicide Bombers*. Emmaeus, PA: Rodale.

Von Knopp, K. 2007. The Female Jihad: Al Qaeda's Women. *Studies in Conflict and Terrorism*, 30(5), 397–414.

Yaqoob, S. 2008. Muslim Women and War on Terror. *Feminist Review*, 88, 150–61.

Yeğenoğlu, M. 1998. *Colonial Fantasies: Towards a Feminist Reading of Orientalism*. Cambridge: Cambridge University Press.

Zedalis, D. 2008. Beyond the Bombings: Analyzing Female Suicide Bombers, in *Female Terrorism and Militancy: Agency, Utility, and Organization*, edited by Ness, C. London and New York: Routledge, 49–68.

Chapter 9

Burying Sovereignty in its Birthplace: Back to the Middle Ages

Erdem Özlük and Murat Çemrek

Introduction: Westphalian (Dis)Order

The modern international system, with all its components, is an outgrowth of the Westphalian order. Although the Westphalian order, which dates back to 1648, experienced several challenges, the essential elements of the system survived intact. However it would not be incorrect to argue that the end of the Cold War, globalization, advancements in technology, the emergence of non-state actors and the rise of trans-national problems such as immigration, terrorism, environmental problems has led to some changes in the fundamental principles of the Westphalian order (Cusimano 2000). In the traditional Westphalian order, state sovereignty was considered to be one of the defining characteristics of the system. This view of the traditional Westphalian order is changing rather rapidly (Leonard 2001) and change, in general, means the attrition of established patterns, the lessening of order, and the faltering of governance (Rosenau 1992).

Today, a world composed of post-modern states contrasting with the Westphalian state (Caporaso 1996) is turning into a post-Westphalian, post-sovereign, territorially confused, culturally heterogeneous (Alker 2005) order. The distinction between domestic and international politics is blurred (Gourevitch 1999), and states are no longer the sole or even the most important actors in international relations. The notion that the state system came into existence in 1648 has been under constant attack (Caporaso 2000). The Westphalian order suggests 'a beguiling simplicity of form: all is neatly contained in a collection of sovereign states, each with the same defined and identifiable line of internal, exclusive authority' (Harding and Harding 2006). Now, we are moving back to a more complex, more fragmented form of the Westphalian order.

With the end of Westphalian order, the students of international relations face many difficulties in understanding the debate of order-disorder which is at the core of the burgeoning debate on the nature of international system after the Cold War (Roberts 1995). According to traditional understanding, sovereignty was not only the main characteristic of the Westphalian order but also the founding principle of international relations. This chapter contends that it is not possible to understand the debate of order-disorder in International Relations without touching upon the concept of sovereignty.

Any academic discipline is conceptualized by its own scholars and the scholar of other disciplines. There should be main assumptions and concepts as demarcation lines in order to formulate the borders that define the discipline. In this context, International Relations (IR) as a discipline has less differing concepts compared to other disciplines (Ferguson and Mansbach 1989). One of these concepts is sovereignty. Despite the fact that sovereignty is the main theme of international relations and the basis of discussions, it is difficult to define. Defining sovereignty is especially hard within the twilight zone that we are trespassing when the meanings are in the process of changing.

Although discussions/practices/discourses do not seem to be directly related to sovereignty in the post-1990s international relations studies, sovereignty lies within the focus of all discussions. The extensive discussions about sovereignty and the change of its domestic and external dimensions (especially in the post-Cold War era) have paved the path of the transformation of sovereignty into a narrative. The transformative experience of the European Union (EU) has essentially triggered the change of sovereignty as a 'reality' and the 'discourse/narrative'. The depth that the European integration process has reached has brought a new dimension to the discussions of sovereignty and this has led to a disruption of the myth adopted for the last four centuries (Özlük and Doğan 2009).

Through the new meanings gained within the European integration process, sovereignty has changed our perceptions about the roles and the actors of IR and the international system. Any analysis lacking the formulation of the process described above will be missing in any context. Therefore the main premise of this study is sovereignty.

First, we will try to answer the transformation of sovereignty as an extension of the Westphalian system while emphasizing how the historical evolution of sovereignty has shaped its meaning. We will prioritize the meaning of sovereignty within the disciplines of law, political science and IR and formulate a new definition within the IR terminology. We will also particularly focus on the EU which has been efficient in the transformation of sovereignty in the epistemological platform and in practice.

We will discuss the change in the perception of sovereignty related to the EU enlargement and especially deepening after 1992 while accepting the Maastricht Treaty as the breaking point. We ascertain the answer if Europe, the inventor of sovereignty – the founding principle of the modern international system- is ready to bury it 'into the land where it was born'. Europe,[1] as the birthplace of sovereignty, has been changing the meaning of sovereignty in the EU since the Maastricht Treaty. Sovereignty and its components empowering the modern state is exposed a great transformation through the EU's deepening process. The dissemination of deepening process via enlargement has changed the meaning of sovereignty within the European continent.

---

1 By Europe here we mean, specifically, the western part of the Europe.

In addition to the EU integration, globalization, non-state actors and their roles, global governance and global threats and opportunities have led to the erosion of sovereignty and nation-state, two fundamental principles of the Westphalian Order.[2] This erosion brings us to a kind of pre-Westphalian era. Today we witness a return to the Middle Ages, which lacked political and social importance of borders. This return brings a multiplicity of governing bodies and constituents of sovereignty, insufficiency of any single political form in providing legitimacy and loosening of local loyalties. Since sovereignty is the best tool to comprehend this return, we need to handle discussion related to sovereignty.

Defining Sovereignty: Understanding Transformation

Although sovereignty was initially used by Jean Bodin in 1576, it remains one of the most difficult concepts to define since everyone applies a different meaning. We could easily say that Bodin reflects his anticipations on sovereignty while defining it as perpetual, absolute, indivisible and inalienable. Sovereignty is the final political authority in the society according to F.H. Hinsley (1986), the most referred scholar on sovereignty. However, sovereignty is not only composed of political but also sociological and economic practices. That is why institutionalizing sovereignty as political authority is presented as a concrete structure.

As a contested concept, sovereignty has several dimensions and it is difficult to put a single analytical definition adopting these dimensions (Zaum 2007). It is difficult to define sovereignty since it doesn't make sense in and of itself. Sovereignty always needs an adjective to qualify itself. Since its first use, sovereignty has benefited from such adjectives as *absolute, relative, eternal, constitutional, divisible/indivisible, transitional, outmoded, postmodern,* and *post-statist*. These adjectives mean three things. The first determines who possesses sovereignty. Sovereignty is not within the monopoly of an individual *vis-à-vis* Bodin and Hobbes; it could be within a troika government, within a committee as in the hands of people coming together through 'general will' as Rousseau argued. The second meaning is related to the domestic and external dimension of sovereignty. Lastly, the third meaning is related to absoluteness of sovereignty (Philpott 1999).

The frequency of adjectives used to describe sovereignty results in some ambiguities. Initially, these ambiguities could come to surface as if the concept is definitive, descriptive, analytical, and discursive or if it is a guide for policy-makers. There are also normative ambiguities about the meanings and connotations of sovereignty (Camilleri 2008). These ambiguities with the legal/judicial, political and sociological dimensions of sovereignty deepen such conceptualization problems.

2　Krasner finds transformation of sovereignty by globalization to be an exaggerated and mythical discourse (Krasner 1999 and 2001).

Sovereignty should be dealt with parallel to the birth of the nation-state and international system in any form conceptualization. God is at the top of the feudal hierarchy composed of the Pope, the Monarch and the Feudal Lord as other constituents and representatives. However, sovereignty identified with God began to be defined with state institutions in line with the Monarch's divine authority after the Peace of Westphalia of 1648 (Hardt and Negri 2001). According to Gross (1948) 'Westphalia marks the end of an epoch and the opening of another and it represents the majestic portal which leads from the old into the new world'. This led sovereignty to be state-centric and territorial since the Peace of Westphalia. Such a perspective identifying sovereignty within the Monarch's personality has brought body politics an important seat within Western political thought. This 'sacred body' which is not exposed to natural deterioration could not be destroyed except by war. This definition of sovereignty is attributed to the state that has been consecrated (Agnew 2005).

Sovereignty as the extension of the Westphalian system is one of the founding principles of the modern nation-state as a political form (Behr 2008). Moreover, sovereignty has been conceptualized as the 'virginity' of the nation-state causing assaults against the nation-state to be evaluated as 'rape'. This discourse also determines the canonization of the borders framing the nation-state. Thus, the border is not just a simple demarcation line but it is one of the constituents of sovereignty informing them about the identity of society as well as indicating who will be part of the political society (Ham 2001). The change of perceptions related to sovereignty and borders have become the ever-reproducing practices of the state (Devetak 1995).

State and sovereignty are socially constructed and are redefined by different principles and practices. In short, state and sovereignty mutually constructed each other. The state defines the meaning of sovereignty through their engagement in practices of mutual recognition. State and sovereignty dually cover a territorial aspect because the Westphalian state has concrete borders and Westphalian sovereignty emphasizes the non-violation principle of these borders (Biersteker 2002, Inayatullah 1996). In sum, discourses of power, government and perpetuity are attributed to the state. Thus, sovereignty has always been identified in a state-centric form (Shapiro 1991).

Political science, in general, and international relations in particular, takes sovereignty as its main concept (Schmidt 1998: 44). However, this concept could not be solely explained as in the practices of Bodin and Max Weber. Sovereignty presented as a necessary tool to understand politics (Edkins and Pin-Fat 1999, Bickerton et al. 2007), is in fact a 'heroic narrative' (Elshtain 1996) empowered with its attachment to the state. The symbiotic link and the mutual interaction between the state and sovereignty is one of the main results of the Westphalian order. The modern state providing the security of the people attached to itself through citizenship bond (Agnew and Corbridge 1995) defines their rights and obligations. Thus, the state determines the 'space of movement' for its citizens despite whether it is binding or liberating them.

The space where the state exerts its sovereignty cannot be entirely defined by itself since it needs domestic and external units for comparison (Friedman et al. 2005). A state executes its power in a determined geography with concrete borders (Butler and Spivak 2007) in which 'domestic' becomes the sovereign and 'external' becomes the anarchical (Walker 1993). As a result, sovereignty is conceptualized as a reality, an ideal that brings order; while anarchy is evaluated as endangering this ideal. Sovereignty symbolized as a rational identity is depicted as homogenous, perpetual, and hierarchic (Ashley 1998). However, the discussion about the state's ability of control focuses on loosening the bonds among the state, sovereignty, anarchy, and power.

The rhetoric about the lessening efficiency of the state at both the domestic and external levels shows that Westphalian sovereignty has started to lose its central point. This process, evaluated as the evaporation of sovereignty, has two spurring factors; globalization and the EU's performance as a supranational organization (Saskia 1996). Interdependence and developments in the field of international law increasingly limit sovereignty (Jacobsen et al. 2008). Moreover, the state is paradoxically using more power to limit its own sovereignty (Jennings 2002).

Sovereignty has started to erode and, perhaps, it faces such an acute crisis for the first time in its history. This erosion is due to the claim that sovereignty is natural and constant while it is an artificial and historical concept (Jackson 1999). Today the discourse mounting sovereignty as omnipotent and almighty has lost its validity. The myth about the inviolable borders of the state and Weberian monopoly of the legal use of violence by the state has started to be questioned more (Ferguson and Mansbach 2007). The concept of sovereignty which evolved during the Cold War has especially started to lose its meaning since it is recognized that the state has started to lose its power on the flow of capital, information, goods and services (Philpott 2001). Through this crisis, starting with the mid-1970s, the Westphalian system has been under attack. Globalization has an important role in the demystification of the legends related to Westphalian sovereignty.

Most discussions centre on the idea that globalization has resulted in a new model of sovereignty; wherein the separation of national and economic sovereignties is apparent (McGowan 1999). It is also understood that we are in the age of post-sovereignty in which Westphalian conceptualization of sovereignty has started to lose its meaning (Sindjoun 2001, Jackson 1999). Despite all, if sovereignty has lost its traditional meaning it is still a useful rhetorical and political tool (Fowler and Bunck 1995). Today, insofar as sovereignty regains its new meaning in international organizations (Shinoda 2000) a new perception of sovereignty has also been constructed. While sovereignty is continuing its voyage where it began in the middle ages, the foundation, organization and result of integration of the EU could be seen as a new revolution (Philpott 1997). Because of all these, the EU needs to be discussed in a detailed way to comprehend the transformation of sovereignty.

New Meanings of Sovereignty and the European Union

'Less than a federation but more than a confederation' (Habermas 2001, n.p.) is perhaps one of the best mottos to define the EU while also depicting the integration the EU has achieved. Defining the EU as, 'not a state, though it acts like one' (Heartfield 2007) or underlining its supranational and *sui generis* integration is a referral to the new sovereignty of the EU. The constituents of sovereignty have varied and changed in this way. Sovereignty has begun to be shared at the local, national, regional and global levels within different international organizations (Jacobs 2007). Therefore, understanding the new meaning and constituents of sovereignty could be performed through an analysis of the EU.

The EU as a final result of European integration has led to a change of our perception of sovereignty in many dimensions (Waever 1995). Initially, the EU – when compared to other international organizations – has interfered with everything using power that no other international organization has done before. Second, the EU has the last word over its member states regarding issues of national security, defence, migration, and human rights which have been historically viewed as the bases of state sovereignty. Finally, the role of the European Court of Justice as an independent law maker coupled with the direct effect its decisions have on laws that an individual state creates (Werner and de Wilde 2001) are indicators of how the EU has transformed the discussion of sovereignty.

Today, the final point of European integration has reached a post-ontological stage. We are discussing the process and results of the EU rather than how we classify it. Briefly, this process has become more important than structure and institutions. The weak centre framed through multiple spatial alternative centres (Caporaso 1996) where the political power is shared, indicate that transformation of sovereignty is inevitable. As much as the EU eliminates the borders, empowers human rights and consolidates democratic governance, 'state sovereignty' gets deproblematized and sovereignty is no longer the source of legitimacy (Petersmann 2002). Today, we largely discuss 'governance without government' (Shore 2006: 709) and stress limited sovereignty accumulated in a pool of sovereignties' (Keohane 2002).

The EU is essentially trying to settle alternative governance logic rather than design a new definitional sovereignty. The multi-level governance defined through a perpetual negotiation system at the supranational, national and regional levels (Marks 1995) brings an erosion of a state's central role. It also eliminates the traditional separation of domestic and foreign politics like the end of the dichotomy of external anarchy and internal hierarchy of the Westphalian system. Moreover multi-level governance shows that integration is not a zero-sum game (Aalberts 2004). The EU, as a result of integration between the institutions and states, passes this two dimensional structure and settles a new perception of sovereignty (Walker 1998). Although this conceptualization has started since Maastricht we could see it even in the early days of integration.

The process, starting with the Paris Treaty (1951), has ripened with the Maastricht Treaty (1992) which ultimately led to the deepening of discussions on how the bases of relation between the EU and its member nation-states will be shaped (Çalış 2008). One side of this discussion argues that too much power has been delegated to Brussels and subsequently the sovereignty of the states should be protected *vis-à-vis* Brussels. The other side argues that sovereignty has become anachronistic and the Union should be further deepened (Newman 1996). The essence of this discussion relies on the fact that EU members have delegated their authorities in no other example of international organizations (Barents 2004).

Briefly understood, classical sovereignty implies that the state is the absolute, single and is the exclusive power on a land with determined borders. However, there is no such classical understanding of sovereignty practiced in any state. If sovereignty is taken as the state power -holistic and single- or it is the definer and executor of norms, the EU members no longer have exclusive authority anymore after their delegation of power to the EU. When the EU's relations with member states are analyzed through indivisible and absolute sovereignty, then we come up with a serious legitimacy problem. From this perspective, the definition of sovereignty does not see the state as the single sovereignty owner. Instead, this perspective focuses on both political and public organization as they bring common sovereignty and a better legitimization tool for the EU (Meehan 1999). Then, in order to understand the EU integration there is also a need for the internationalization of some authorities which were already specified with the nation-state (Göztepe 2008, Golub 2001).

Conclusion: Back to the Middle Ages

In the post-1990 era, sovereignty has been most discussed subject in the field of IR. This frequent discussion on sovereignty parallels the questioning of modernity (Onuf 1991) since sovereignty is the product of modernity and the child of Europe. Sovereignty as well as the nation-state are the founding factors of IR and are also European inventions (Gelber 1997).

The modern nation-state employing sovereignty as a discourse and a practice essentially organizes space as its main function. The modern nation-state and even modernity itself are inherently geographic constructs. Political power is defined through these geographic parameters and it rises above them (Camilleri and Falk 1992). Today, the reason why sovereignty is in crisis is because the 'sick man' (nation-state) has started to lose its ability to organize space.

Pre-modern political forms like feudalism, the Church and the Holy Roman Empire lack the territorial fixity and exclusivity (Spruyt 1996). On the other hand, globalization, EU integration, interdependency and global governance function as catalysts in the erosion of sovereignty coupled with the identification of the modern nation-state's function as territoriality. Interestingly, we do experience a return to the pre-1648 in the post-1990 era. As Friedrichs (2001) has indicated, multiple powers, multiple loyalties and two universal claims in competition are the main denominators of this return. Previously, the Holy Roman Empire and the Catholic Church had these universal claims in competition as today the nation-state system and transnational market economy and global society possess such universal claims.

As the Westphalian order responds to the transition period about three centuries of IR history perspectives have elapsed. We are currently experiencing 'system change'.[3] All the factors as constituents of the Westphalian order have lost their meanings. While modernity is in question, borders are evaporating, sovereignty is eroding, and the nation-state is no longer the unitary and single actor in the international system. The hierarchy of sovereignty starting with the God and ending in the monarch and feudal unit has convened in the monopoly of the nation-state within the Westphalian order. However, today the nation-state is exposed to several problems of power, sovereignty and legitimacy. When someone analyzes the meaning of sovereignty and its place in the IR historically, Europe as the inventor and exporter of sovereignty is at the end of a road that begins with Westphalia. Last but not least, we are all witnessing the establishment of a new conceptualization of IR as a discipline and many new 'international relations'.

Bibliography

Aalberts, T.E. 2004. The Future of Sovereignty in Multilevel Governance Europe: A Constructivist Reading. *Journal of Common Market Studies*, 42(1), 23–46.

Agnew, J. 2005. Sovereignty Regimes: Territoriality and State Authority in Contemporary World Politics. *Annals of the Association of American Geography*, 95(2), 437–61.

Agnew, J. and Corbridge S. 1995. *Mastering Space: Hegemony, Territory and International Political Economy*. New York: Routledge.

Alker, H. 2005. Order and Disorder in Global Affairs, available at http://college. usc.edu/sir/pdf/382.pdf.

Ashley, R.K. 1998. Untying the Sovereign State: A Double Reading of the Anarchy Problematique. *Millennium: Journal of International Studies*, 17(2), 227–62.

Barents, R. 2004. *The Autonomy of Community Law.* New York: Kluwer Law International.

Behr, H. 2008. Deterritorialisation and the Transformation of Statehood: The Paradox of Globalization. *Geopolitics*, 13(2), 359–82.

---

3   In his seminal work on change in world politics, Gilpin (1983) distinguishes three broad types of change characteristic of international systems. These are systems change, systemic change, and interaction change. Systems change is a change in the nature of the actors or diverse entities that compose an international system.

Bickerton, C.J. et al. 2007. Introduction: The Unholy Alliance Against Sovereignty, in *Politics without Sovereignty: A Critique of Contemporary International Relations*, edited by C.J. Bickerton et al. New York: UCL Press.

Biersteker, T.J. 2002. State, Sovereignty and Territory, in *Handbook of International Relations*, edited by W. Carlsnaes et al. London: Sage.

Butler, J. and Spivak, G.C. 2007. *Who Sings the Nation-State? Language, Politics, Belonging*. Oxford: Seagull Books.

Çalýþ, Þ.H. 2008. *Türkiye-Avrupa Birliði Ýliþkileri: Kimlik Arayýþý, Politik Aktörler ve Deðiþim*. Ankara: Nobel.

Camilleri, J. 2008. Sovereignty Discourse and Practice: Past and Future, in *Re-envisioning Sovereignty: The End of Westphalia?*, edited by T. Jacobsen et al. Aldershot: Ashgate.

Camilleri, J. and Falk, J. 1992. *The End of Sovereignty the Politics of a Shrinking and Fragmenting World*. Aldershot: Edward Elgar.

Caporaso, J.A. 1996. The European Union and Forms of State: Westphalian, Regulatory or Post-Modern? *Journal of Common Market Studies*, 34(1), 29–52.

Caporaso, J.A. 2000. Changes in the Westphalian Order: Territory, Public Authority, and Sovereignty, in *Continuity and Change in the Westphalian Order*, edited by, J.A. Caporaso. Oxford: Blackwell.

Cusimano Maryann K. 2000. Beyond Sovereignty: The Rise of Transsovereign Problems, in *Beyond Sovereignty: Issues for a Global Agenda*, edited by Maryann K. Cusimano. New York: Bedford/St Martin's.

Devetak, R. 1995. Incomplete States: Theories and Practices of Statecraft, in *Boundaries in Question: New Directions in International Relations*, edited by J. MacMillan and A. Linklater. London: Pinter.

Edkins, J. and Pin-Fat, V. 1999. The Subject of the Political, in *Sovereignty and Subjectivity*, edited by Jenny Edkins et al. Boulder, CO: Lynne Rienner.

Elshtain, J.B. 1996. Rethinking Sovereignty, in *Post-Realism: The Rhetorical Turn in International Relations*, edited by F.A. Beer and R. Hariman. New York: Michigan State University Press.

Ferguson, Y.H. and Mansbach, R.M. 1989. *The State, Conceptual Chaos, and the Future of International Relations Theory*. Boulder, CO: Lynne Rienner.

Ferguson, Y.H. and Mansbach, R.M. 2007. The Myths of State Sovereignty. *The Bologna Center Journal of International Affairs*, 10, 9–20.

Fowler, M. and Bunck J.M. 1995. *Law, Power, and the Sovereign State: The Evolution and Application of the Concept of Sovereignty*. Pennsylvania: Pennsylvania State University Press.

Friedman, E.J. et al. 2005. *Sovereignty, Democracy, and Global Civil Society: State-Society Relations at UN World Conferences*. New York: SUNY Press.

Friedrichs, J. 2001. The Meaning of New Medievalism. *European Journal of International Relations*, 7(4), 475–501.

Gelber H.G. 1997. *Sovereignty through Interdependence*. London: Kluwer Law International.

Gilpin, R.G. 1984. The Richness of the Tradition of Political Realism. *International Organization*, 38(2), 287–304.

Golub, J. 2001. Globalization, Sovereignty and Policy-Making: Insights from European Integration, in *Global Democracy: Key Debates*, edited by B. Holden. London: Routledge.

Goodhart, M. 2001. Sovereignty: Reckoning What Is Real, review essay. *Polity*, 34(2), 241–57.

Gross, L. 1948. The Peace of Westphalia, 1648–1948. *American Journal of International Law*, 42(1), 20–41.

Gourevitch, P.A. 1999. The Governance Problem in International Relations, in *Strategic Choice and International Relations*, edited by D.A. Lake and R. Powell, Princeton, NJ: Princeton University Press.

Göztepe, E. 2008. *Avrupa Birliði'nin Siyasal Bütünleşmesi ve Egemenlik Yetkisinin Paylaþýlmasý Sorunu*. Ankara: Seçkin Yayýncýlýk.

Habermas, J. 2001. Why Europe Needs a Constitution. *New Left Review*, 11, http://newleftreview.org/?page=article&view=2343.

Ham, P.V. 2001. *European Integration and the Postmodern Condition: Governance, Democracy, Identity*. London: Routledge.

Harding, C. and Harding, N. 2006. Who Designed the Westphalian System? Probing the Epistemology of the Westphalian Debates: 'Moses was but a Juggler and King James the New Solomon'. *Law, Culture and the Humanities*, 2, 39–419.

Hardt, M. and Negri, A. 2001. *Ýmparatorluk*, trans. A. Yýlmaz. Ýstanbul: Ayrýntý Yayýnlarý.

Heartfield, J. 2007. European Union: A Process Without Subject, in *Politics Without Sovereignty: A Critique of Contemporary International Relations*, edited by C.J. Bickerton et al. New York: UCL Press.

Hinsley, F.H. 1986. *Sovereignty*. Cambridge: Cambridge University Press.

Inayatullah, N. 1996. Beyond the Sovereignty Dilemma: Quasi-States as Social Construct, in *State Sovereignty as Social Construct*, edited by T.J. Biersteker and C. Weber. Cambridge: Cambridge University Press.

Jackson, R. 1999. Introduction: Sovereignty at the Millennium, in *Sovereignty at the Millennium*, edited by R. Jackson. London: Blackwell.

Jacobs, F.G. 2007. *The Sovereignty of Law: The European Way*. Cambridge: Cambridge University Press.

Jacobsen, T. et al. 2008. Introduction, in *Re-envisioning Sovereignty: The End of Westphalia?*, edited by T. Jacobsen et al. Aldershot: Ashgate.

Jennings, R. 2002. Sovereignty and International Law, in *State, Sovereignty, and International Governance*, edited by G. Kreijen. Oxford: Oxford University Press.

Keohane, R.O. 1993. Sovereignty, Interdependence, and International Institutions, in *Ideas and Ideals: Essays in Honor of Stanley Hoffman*, edited by L.B. Miller and M.J. Smith. Boulder, CO: Westview.

Keohane, R.O. 2002. Ironies of Sovereignty: the European Union and the United States. *Journal of Common Market Studies*, 40(4), 743–65.

Krasner, S.D. 1999. Globalization and Sovereignty, in *State and Sovereignty in the Global Economy*, edited by D.J. Solinger. London: Routledge.

Krasner, S.D. 2001. Abiding Sovereignty, *International Political Science Review*, 22(3), 229–51.

Leonard, E.K. 2001. Seeking Sovereignty: Gaining Understanding Through Critical Analysis, *New Political Science*, 23(3), 407–28.

Marks, G. 1995. European Integration and the State. *EUI Working Paper*, RSC No. 95/7. Florence.

McGowan, F. 1999. Globalisation, Regional Integration and the State, in *Politics and Globalisation: Knowledge, Ethics and Agency*, edited by M. Shaw. London: Routledge.

Meehan, E. 1999. Member States and the European Union, in *The State: Historical and Political Dimensions*, edited by R. English and C. Townshend. London: Routledge.

Newman, M. 1996. *Democracy, Sovereignty and the European Union*. London: C. Hurst and Co.

Onuf, N.G. 1991. Sovereignty: Outline of a Conceptual History, *Alternatives: Local, Global, Political*, 16(4), 425–46

Özlük, E. and Doğan F. 2009. *Türkiye-Avrupa Birliği ilişkilerini egemenlik devri tartýþmalarý üzerinden okumak*. Türkiye-AB Ýlişkilerinde 50 Yýl (Ankara Üniversitesi, ATAUM).

Petersmann, E.U. 2002. International Activities of the European Union and Sovereignty of Member States, in *The European Union as an Actor in International Relations*, edited by E. Cannizzaro. The Hague: Kluwer.

Philpott, D. 1997. Ideas and Evolution of Sovereignty, in *State Sovereignty: Change and Persistence in International Relations*, edited by S.H. Hashmi. Pennsylvania: Penn State Press.

Philpott, D. 1999. Westphalia, Authority and International Society, *Political Studies*, 47(3), 457–73.

Philpott, D. 2001. Usurping the Sovereignty of Sovereignty. *World Politics*, 53(2), 297–324.

Roberts, B. 1995. *Order and Disorder after the Cold War*, Cambridge: MIT Press.

Rosenau, J.N. 1992. Governance, Order, and Change in World Politics, in *Governance without Government: Order and Change in World Politics*, edited by J.N. Rosenau and E.O. Czempiel. Cambridge: Cambridge University Press.

Saskia, S. 1996. *Losing Control: Sovereignty in an Age of Globalization*. New York: Columbia University Press.

Schmidt, B.C. 1998. *The Political Discourse of Anarchy: A Disciplinary History of International Relations*. New York, State University of New York Press.

Shapiro, M.J. 1991. Sovereignty and Exchange in the Orders of Modernity, *Alternatives*, 16(4), 447–77.

Shinoda, H. 2000. *Re-Examining Sovereignty: From Classical Theory to the Global Age*. New York: Palgrave.

Shore, C. 2006. Government Without Statehood? Anthropological Perspectives on governance and Sovereignty in the European Union. *European Law Journal*, 12(6), 709–24.

Sindjoun, L. 2001. Transformation of International Relations – Between Change and Continuity: Introduction, *International Political Science Review*, 22(3), 219–28.

Spruyt, H. 1996. *The Sovereign State and Its Competitors: An Analysis of Systems Change*. Princeton: Princeton University Press.

Staden, A.V. and Vollaard, H. 2002. The Erosion of the State Sovereignty: Towards a Post-Territorial World, in *State, Sovereignty, and International Governance*, edited by G. Kreijen. Oxford: Oxford University Press.

Waever, O. 1995. Identity, Integration and Security: Solving the Sovereignty Puzzle in EU studies, *Journal of International Affairs*, 48(2), 389–431.

Walker, N. 1998. Sovereignty and Differentiated Integration in the European Union, *European Law Journal*, 4(4), 355–88.

Walker, R.B.J. 1993. *Inside/Outside: International Relations as Political Theory*. Cambridge: Cambridge University Press.

Werner, W.G. and de Wilde J.H. 2001. The Endurance of Sovereignty, *European Journal of International Relations*, 7(3), 283–313.

Zaum, D. 2007. *The Sovereignty Paradox: The Norms and Politics of International Statebuilding*. Oxford: Oxford University Press.

Epilogue

The contemporary era constitutes a historical breakpoint in the development of the international system. Consequently, we are increasingly challenged to re-examine the forces that define and shape the world order. These forces are increasingly complex, synergistic, and dynamic. They underlie relations between states and determine the power configurations that characterize the international system. In addition, the components of the international order are subject to modification by forces that empower non-traditional actors and operate within a realm of asymmetric tensions. The ability to discern goals and predict behaviour is complicated by these forces. Moreover, attempts to identify order and disorder are obscured by the reality that both may exist simultaneously. Disorder is often a manifestation of change rather than instability and order is less descriptive of entrenched patterns than of a realization that management is a solution to potential threats and conflict. In short, existing conceptual and methodological premises are often insufficient to adequately comprehend the intricate strands of the interconnected world. While efforts have been invested in developing new analytic instruments, a fundamental problem that persists involves the absence of conceptual terminology. A conspicuous deficit of the postmodern world has been the inability to adjust our imagination to the spatial dimensions of the interconnected world. The new perspective requires an expanded vision to comprehend the place of community, security, and environment within the wider canvas of humanity. While this need for a broad view was initially impelled by emerging concerns surrounding the development of nuclear, radiological, chemical, and other technologies that would impact humankind, it is now being equally driven by cyber technology.

A major challenge has been to understand the impact of new technologies on one of the key foundational components of international relations – the principle of sovereignty. Broadly defined as referring to the autonomy and authority of the state in ordering its internal affairs and in its policies towards other states, sovereignty has traditionally been accepted as the predominant organizing principle of the international system. New technologies have, however, given rise to a series of developments that make it difficult for the state to maintain its traditional role. In the first place, the global system of the twenty-first century has a number of new actors empowered by the information revolution and easy access to weapons development. The significance and enduring impact of the diffusion of power from the state to non-state actors and groups is something that has yet to be fully assessed. The suicide bomber and the terrorist group represent one strand in the growing significance of non-state actors. International bodies, such as Human Rights Watch, Amnesty International, and other powerful NGOs have a profound impact on public opinion, as well as serve to provide guidelines for governments in their policy making process. Secondly, the new trans-border networks are increasingly reliant on cooperation in setting technological standards and controls, requiring the intervention of international institutions in the process of network governance. As states attempt to confront the challenge of developing common security policies in response to global challenges it becomes obvious that multilateral consultation is increasingly compelling. Thirdly, the relative anonymity conferred by the communications networks makes it increasingly difficult to identify the actors involved in efforts to destabilize the current global order. Fourthly, the widespread acceptance of freedom of expression increasingly limits the ability of the state to impose controls on communications and to monitor individuals and groups that may be seen as subversive. Modern communications technology undermines closed societies and, as such, constitutes a profound change unique to the contemporary global order. It is possible to predict that the structure of the international system and its power configurations will continue to be influenced by technological change. The present exponential rates of change and invention suggest that mankind has entered an era of development corresponding in cultural importance to that of the industrial revolution. Just as the industrial revolution was based on the substitution of complex machines for physical labour, computers have begun to take the place of brain functions. There is every reason to anticipate that this change may be a revolutionary development for society and culture. In conjunction with major discoveries in human biology and chemistry this is likely to transform many previously held conceptions about the possession and exercise of international power. Indeed, the asymmetric threats which might ensue from breakthroughs in the understanding and control of memory, learning, and genetics present unprecedented challenges for the global community. It is increasingly clear that the future changes in international relations associated with scientific and technological developments will prove at least as consequential as those of the past.

The crucial difference from previous eras is that the contemporary international system is less state-centric than it was a century ago. Existing cultural patterns and institutional structures confront a global tide of influences impacting all humanity. Environmental degradation, security threats, human rights violations, and other issues have an impact on more than the individual nation-state or region. Global issues require global solutions which necessitate the involvement of a diverse, collective, global community. The global collectivist approach transcends previous regional alliances that sought to formulate cooperative policy. As interconnectedness generates issues with global consequences and globalization continues to bring about a convergence of interests, the direction of national policy will increasingly have to move towards international cooperation. A further break from traditional policy formulation is the inclusion of a broad range of individuals, nation-states, NGOs, institutions, and organizations in the collective effort involving in many instances a private/public coalition.

The contributions in this volume share a common awareness that the international system is undergoing a metamorphosis and that, in order to understand that transformation, analysts will increasingly be required to adopt innovative methodological approaches. The methodological and conceptual diversity represented in this collection is a preview of the direction of future research seeking this sort of understanding. The exploration of the forces contributing to instability reveals that both systemic and individual factors play an important role. There is a great opportunity for scholarly examination to enter a realm of investigation that has not previously been encountered in the study of the international system.

Index

Printed in Great Britain
by Amazon

85702259R00120